DAVE TRIPPIN

TRAVEL STORIES

BY DAVE LAVENDER

PHOTOGRAPHY BY TORIL LAVENDER

ISBN - 978-0-9801766-0-5

Printed in the United States of America
Published by Lavender Publishing
Cover photograph, design and text design by Toril Lavender
All photography by Toril Lavender except photos on pages 62,64, 67, 89, 211, 217 by Dave Lavender, page 12 by Jacob Lavender, page 63 by Skip Clegg, page 245 by Katie Lewis, page 79 and 80 courtesy of Mountain Stage, page 111 and 145 unknown.
Dave Trippin caricature by Thom A. Marsh

Dedication

Dave Trippin' is dedicated to our parents Roger and Sheri Lavender and Tom and Randi Starmer, who always found enough change in their polyester pants, enough room in their Volkswagen Beetles and enough time in their busy schedules to take their kids trippin' all over the place.

Also, to our kids, Will and Jacob Lavender, who have made travel and day trips more fun than a barrel of monkeys.

Contents

Kentucky

Ohio

Introduction

A week after our first child Jacob was born in 2000, I grabbed up the little fellow, tucked him into the papoose-like Snugli on my chest, and the new Lavender family headed out for a day hike in the Tennessee woods.

In doing so, we were probably breaking about 17 rules of "What to Expect When Expecting," but we couldn't contain the joy of sharing this sweet old world with a new child and celebrating the fact that in spite of dire predictions - by doomsday opportunists - Y2K had not ended life as we know it.

By mid-March, and thanks to Jeff Henson, I was sitting for an interview with *Herald-Dispatch* editor Bob Gabordi at Bobby Pruett's Steakhouse. Coach Pruett strolled over to the table, shook my hand and said it would be great if I came back home and joined *The Herald-Dispatch* "team."

Since that team included such journalism heroes as Ernie Salvatore, Tim Massey, Bob Withers, Jim Casto and Dave Peyton, it didn't take much convincing as long as the H-D team didn't make reporters run windsprints .

By April 2000, I was back home in the Tri-State with my new family and wanted to give them the grand tour of the place - from my hometown of Franklin Furnace, Ohio, still one of the only places I know where you exit on the left - to beloved childhood haunts such as Camden Park, Lake Hope, Dreamland Pool, Greenbo Lake and The Scioto Breeze Drive-In.

A couple years after joining the H-D, I convinced our features editor that with gas prices higher than the smoke rolling out of Willie Nelson's tour bus, it was prime time to start up a Sunday day-tripping travel series to explore what was in our own proverbial backyard.

And since I was born and raised in Southern Ohio, got my education in Kentucky (University of Kentucky), now lived in West Virginia, and had lived or worked in many nearby cities such as Lexington, Georgetown, Cincinnati, Chillicothe, Portsmouth, Waverly and Parkersburg, I was just the homegrown hobo journalist for the job.

We would load up our little Saturn station wagon with fishing rods, wife, kids and sleeping bags and head out like Chevy Chase on "Family Vacation" to treat the Tri-State like a tourist and, if we survived the chaos, share the dispatches with our dear readers.

We did our first trip for *The Herald-Dispatch* in 2003 when our second son Will was three months old.

In the past five years, we've done a little bit of everything from wild caving, skiing, fishing and whitewater rafting with kids to searching for the Mothman, grooving to Mountain Stage, staying all night with the Hare Krishnas, defying gravity in the Mystery Hole and looking and then looking some more for the Moonbow.

Although sometimes embarrassed, sometimes lost as a ball in high weeds, and sometimes covered in spilt chocolate milk, we've lived to laugh and tell about it.

Since we're always being asked where to go Trippin' we decided to put down the Gameboys and get back behind the wordplow.

With the blessing of the H-D leadership (Pat Frantz and Ed Dawson), we've compiled and freshened up the best of these Sunday travel pieces that includes about 10 stories each from Ohio, Kentucky and West Virginia as well as "If You Go" pages at the end of each story. Those are packed with specific info about traveling to those special places.

We also list directions and miles tripped. Those are both calculated from our home near downtown Huntington.

We've also included three stories about new ways to explore our own backyard such as the new high-tech treasure hunt called Geocaching, Kentucky State Park's Family Adventure Quest and info about visiting the sites where "We Are Marshall" was filmed in Huntington, as well as other cool film locations in the region.

We hope that, like the Sunday travel series, the book will inspire you and your crew to load up and go trippin,' leaving a trail of muddy bootprints and happy tracks all over our region.

West Virginia

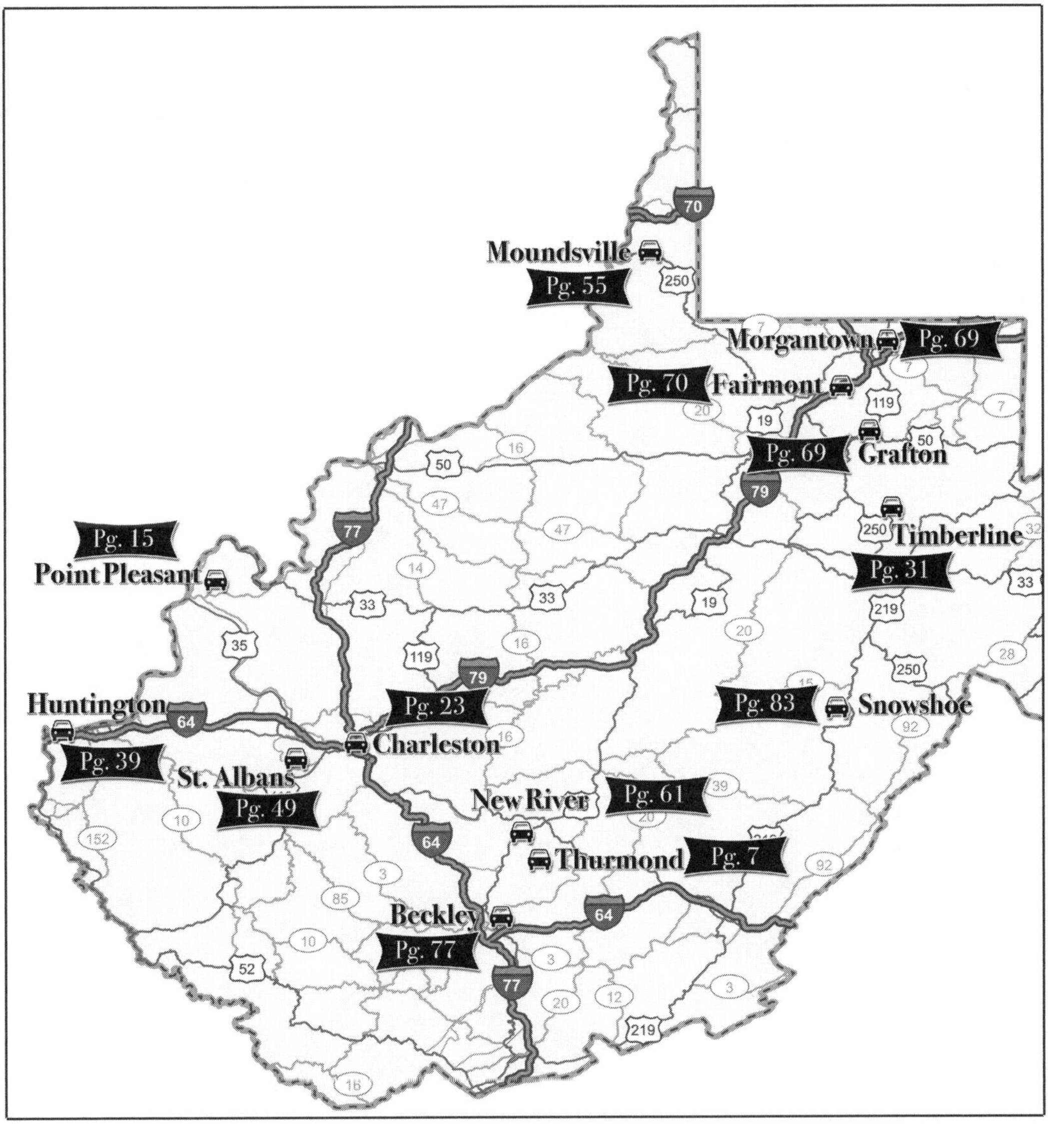

Thurmond
West Virginia

As someone raised in a town where there's no stoplights, I've always loved a good, small town.

The late, great Greenup County, Ky., author Jesse Stuart called these special places "somewhere for some and nowhere for many."

Miles:
122

Original Trip
June
2004

Not that I haven't soaked up every minute of the rare chance to visit great cities such as Paris, London and New York City, but often the heart and soul longs for a little place that sprouted way up some creek or holler where nature envelopes and nobody knows your name.

We travel to the heart of the New River Gorge to bicycle and hike back in time to the historic railroad town of Thurmond, the smallest city not only in West Virginia but also in the States.

Inspired by reading Brad Herzog's just-released travel book, "Small World: A Microcosmic Journey," in which he road-tripped across the United States stopping in some of its quirkiest and oddly named small towns such as Calcutta, W.Va., and Baghdad, Ariz., we thought we'd load up the Dave Trippin' station wagon (and, boy, did we load it) and head out for one of West Virginia's smallest towns.

With a population of seven (depending on how many of Jon Dragan's kin are gone for the weekend), Thurmond is a town that, while it may be short on people, is long on history, gorgeous nature and an abundance of good times in the outdoors.

Located in the heart of the **New River Gorge** (and they still have the weathered sign to prove it), Thurmond is a great day-trip for folks already heading down the Gorge to do some whitewater rafting, rock climbing, biking, hiking, visiting Tamarack or catching an outdoor theater show at nearby Grandview.

Located off U.S. 19 at **Glen Jean** (between **Oak Hill** and **Beckley**), Thurmond is seven windy miles down WV 25, which follows **Dunloup Creek**, a mountain stream that cascades down several waterfalls and is rimmed by rhododendron.

If you've ever gone whitewater rafting, you've been ferried down this snaky road in a colorful school bus at speeds that probably made you ring those prayer bells of heaven.

Already cooled by the canopy of trees, we pulled off 25 and into the Thurmond-Minden Trailhead parking lot, where we were greeted by only four cars and a colorful array of butterflies.

The 3.2-mile **Thurmond-Minden trail** is just one of three hiking/biking trails near Thurmond. There's also the 6-mile Brooklyn-Southside Junction Trail and the 2.7-mile Stone Cliff Trail, which is accessed across the river at the Dunglen Day Use Area.

For fans of Celebrity Poker Showdown, here's some useless but absolutely mind-blowing card-playing trivia. **The Day Use Area** is named for the former sin-city of Dunglen (across the river from Thurmond) which housed the Dunglen Hotel, home to plenty of liquor, prostitutes and a 14-year poker game that made it into Ripley's Believe it or Not.

Back on the trail, we found the "mostly level" trail was mostly climbing up the side of a hill.

After a bit of much-needed huffing and puffing, we arrived at an overlook that made it all worth it.

Through a window of sassafras and maple branches, we saw a clear view of the little town of Thurmond, which was used as the town of Matewan in John Sayles' 1987 movie, "Matewan."

Then we heard the sounds that still keep Thurmond, inaccessible by car for 35 years, on the map.

First from way below came a rising chorus of joyous amusement-park-like shrills as whitewater rafters, who had just put into the New River, were already grooving on the rollercoaster-like river rapids.

Then, our 1 1/2-year-old son Will called the second sound right away, "Oh, Oh, Oh, choo, choo, choo" with a finger-pointing, happy dance that again made the sweat and muffled swearing worth it.

Though we could barely see it, the train clanged its bell echoing up the Gorge, tooted its whistle and muscled through Thurmond with that clickety-clack rail beat that sounded like a marching band rumbling through an empty town.

After lunch, we made our way across the railroad trestles, up a bunch of steps and nearly into Minden before we were stopped by a large tree over the trail.

We turned around, coasted all the way back down the hill (boy, did we love the trail now) and made our way into what was once Captain William Thurmond's big city, hoping to get for our red-headed, knee-high rail-nuts an up-close view of the trains that still come rolling through.

Restored in 1995 by the National Park Service, the **Thurmond Depot** serves as one of four visitor centers in the New River Gorge and a quiet place to try to wrap your mind around the history of what has come and gone in these railroad and coal towns.

It's not easy to imagine in these tree-covered silent mountains that in 1916, Thurmond Depot moved through 3.5 million tons of freight (mostly coal) and 97,740 passengers.

In 1910, the C&O operation at Thurmond was first in freight tonnage, producing more than Cincinnati and Richmond, Va., combined.

Today, three Amtrak passenger trains roll through each week.

Past the depot, the NPS has restored or is stabilizing what is left of the once-thriving business district that included two hotels, two banks, restaurants, clothing stores, a jewelry store, movie theater, several dry-good stores and many business offices in a town of 500 people.

A brochure tells the tales of the remaining buildings and what was in this row of buildings just feet from the railroad line in a town that didn't have a Main Street.

We loved the stories and the photos. Mrs. J.W. McClure, who ran a restaurant in the 1930s and 1940s, gave free meals to the trains of troops coming through going to war.

She put up their photos around her restaurant so people would not forget the boys; they sent her salt and pepper shakers.

Seventy-some odd years later, war again going on and on, the thought of that kindness filled the ghost town.

We didn't figure on meeting anyone, but we did, and we're glad for it.

Adrienne Jenkins of Oak Hill, W.Va., got her sociology degree from Marshall University, then came back home to work for the National Park Service.

Usually working at the extremely busy Canyon Rim Visitors Centers, the park employees take turns coming to the usual quiet of Thurmond.

Jenkins loves Thurmond and its almost-unbelievable tale.

"It's a piece of history," Jenkins said of Thurmond and the Depot. "It's like living history, but it's all gone. But you meet so many people who lived here, and they can tell you exactly how it was. You feel like you were there."

If You Go: Thurmond

DIRECTIONS: Take I-64/I-77 to Beckley (that's about 1 1/2-to-2-hours). Take U.S. 19 to the Glen Jean exit, north of Beckley. Follow the signs to Thurmond, seven miles down West Virginia 25. This route is winding and not recommended for RVs and trailers. There are no automotive services available in Thurmond. As you're driving Route 25 if it's in the morning, you will most likely encounter plenty of school buses that are filled with whitewater rafters. Be cautious.
BY TRAIN: Three of Amtrak's Cardinal line trains (running from Chicago to Washington, D.C., through Huntington) stop in Thurmond. The trains come through three days a week. Call 1-800-USA-RAIL or go online at www.amtrak.com.
BY RAFT: A great way to see the town, most of the full-day, Lower New River commercial whitewater rafting trips put in at the river access across from Thurmond. For more info, call 1-800-CALL-WVA or 1-800-344-RAFT or go online at the West Virginia Division of Tourism site, www.callwva.com.

BY TRAIL: The Thurmond-Minden Trail is a 6.4 mile round-trip journey, though you can choose a shorter 2.5 mile round-trip to the main overlook and back.
HOURS: The Thurmond Depot is open 10 a.m. to 5 p.m. Memorial Day through Labor Day.
WHAT TO DO: In Thurmond, there is a restored depot (with interactive museum and bathrooms), three hiking and mountain biking trails, two hiking-only trails, river access and picnic facilities across the river from Thurmond.
ON THE WEB: For more information about Thurmond, the other three National Park Service Visitor Centers (Grandview, Canyon Rim and Hinton) and the 70,000-acre New River Gorge National River area, go online at www.nps.gov/neri. CALL: (304) 465-0508.
MORE INFO: Stop by the New River Country Visitors Center, 310 Oyler Ave., Oak Hill, W.Va. Call (800) 927-0263 or go online at www.newriver cvb.com. Also, check out the Southern West Virginia Convention and Visitors Bureau, 221 George St., Beckley. Call (800)-VISIT-WV. Online at www.visitwv.com.

More Bike Paths

IN THE GORGE: In addition to the popular Thurmond-Minden Trail, the National Park Service also allows bicycles on these trails: Brooklyn to Southside Junction, Cunard to Kaymoor Trail and Stonecliff Trail. Go online at www.nps.gov/neri

BLUESTONE TRAIL: Bikes are allowed on the 10.5-mile Bluestone Turnpike Trail that follows the path of an old riverbank road and that connects Bluestone State Park and Pipestem Resort State Park in W.Va. Go online at www.nps.gov/blue

GREENBRIER RIVER TRAIL: The trail runs 79 miles through the spectacular scenery of the Greenbrier River Valley in Pocahontas and Greenbrier Counties in West Virginia. Directly adjacent to the beautiful Greenbrier River, the packed gravel trail passes through the Monongahela National Forest, Cass, Watoga, and Droop Mountain State Parks and Greenbrier and Seneca State Forests.
Go online at www.greenbrierrivertrail.com.

NORTH BEND TRAIL: A multi-use recreational trail operated by West Virginia State Parks. Formerly an abandoned spur of the CSX system, the trail goes 72 miles from I-77 near Parkersburg in Wood County to Wolf Summit in Harrison County; this scenic trail passes through 13 tunnels and crosses 36 bridges. Call (304) 643-2931

HOCKHOCKING-ADENA BIKE PATH: The 18-mile rail trail extends from the east end of Athens, Ohio, to Hocking College near Nelsonville. Rolls around the Ohio University campus and along the Hocking River. Go online at www.athenscyclepath.com.

TRI-COUNTY TRIANGLE BIKE TRAIL: There's 18.5 miles of rail trail bike paths from Chillicothe, Ohio, west to Frankfort, Ohio. Call (740) 773-8794.

Point Pleasant
West Virginia

Miles: 46

Original Trip December 2005

We venture up the river to see two of the region's best Christmas light displays as well as two new downtown museums, the Point Pleasant River Museum and the Mothman Museum.

It always happens just about this time of year.

The Lavender boys' eyes glow red, and like the Mothman himself, we take wings and fly about as fast as we can.

All jacked up on the coffee and cocoa, we have those 3-D glasses on (the better to see the Christmas lights with) and we're on the hunt, looking for great Christmas lights, with as much fervor as the Marshall University football team looking for wins.

When we found out that Point Pleasant's lake-side Krodel Park had flipped the switch on its fifth annual Christmas Fantasy Light Show, and that the Mothman Research Center and Museum had just become a permanent part of downtown Point Pleasant, we were on the road.

Located just about an hour from Huntington, along W.Va. 2, the fellow Ohio River city of Point Pleasant is having a nice little revival, and you're invited.

Point Pleasant boasts a big enough collection of museums, antique malls, local restaurants and Christmas lights to make a great day trip that's not heavy on the wallet or the gas tank.

With a late Sunday morning coming on, we decided to roll up the river and nose around.

Arriving a bit before the city's museums and businesses chug to life at about 1 p.m., our official Mothman and Santa Claus Search

Team member, 5-year-old Jacob, left some heavy breath of anticipation on the Mothman Museum store front window before we moseyed down Main Street to **Melinda's Restaurant, 509 Main St**.

Main Street has a variety of restaurant choices from the upscale **Iron Gate Fine Dining, 625 Main St**., and Carolyn Harris' cozy diner, **Harris Steak House, 324 Main St**., to the new bar and grill, **The Red Parrot, 4th Street and Main Street**, adjacent to the hotel and a haven for weekend-made live music from such popular regional acts as Steve Free.

Filled with a hearty breakfast (served all day at Melinda's) and the lingering echo of Johnny Paycheck's "Take This Job and Shove it," which emitted from the kitchen, we headed out onto the street, promising Jacob we would take a picture if we happened upon the Mothman or his footprints.

We crossed the street over to **The Mason Jar**, a 15,000-square-foot Antique and Craft Mall, **408 Main St., (304-675-4477)**, and in spite of the warning of hidden cameras, found the Mothman. Well, at least the Mothman doll, coffee mugs, ornaments and my favorite, the Mothman candle cozy.

Featuring a nice collection of antiques as well as the work of 100 area artisans and crafts (including a Marshall University booth), The Mason Jar is a good shopping spot if you're headed that way.

On heightened alert for Mothman info, we resisted the urge to buy another Johnny Cash 45 and hopped Main Street again, where Ohio University film student Todd Wiseman was opening the doors to **The Mothman Museum and Research Center**.

Suspended from the ceiling, Tim and John Frick's 10-foot-long Mothman sculpture – and chunks from faux concrete from the set of "The Mothman Prophecies" – greet you as you enter the small museum that has already drawn people from Idaho, Iowa and Wisconsin.

Filled with lots of props from the major motion picture that starred Richard Gere and Laura Linney, and tons of newspaper clips and photo books, the museum is the place to dig into the many layers of the Mothman legacy from the

sightings, to the Men In Black and UFO sightings, as well as the Silver Bridge collapse.

Formed up in part by Jeff Wamsley, who has written two books about the Mothman, the museum runs a documentary about the bizarre occurrences back in the 1960s that freakishly hit a crescendo before the collapse of the Silver Bridge at 4:55 p.m. on Dec. 15, 1967.

Wanting to know more about Point Pleasant history and the Silver Bridge collapse, which killed 46 people, we went a little further down Main Street to **Point Pleasant River Museum, 28 Main St. (304-674-0144)**.

Before stepping inside, we couldn't help but soak up the history and panoramic views at the scenic **Tu-Endie-Wei State Park (304-675-0869)**, where the Kanawha River flows into the Ohio River.

It is also where on Oct. 10, 1774, Shawnee chief Cornstalk and 1,000 or so Native Americans battled 1,100 Virginia militiamen in what many consider to be the first battle of the American Revolution.

Mesmerized as always by the driving skills of the towboat pilots on the Ohio, we watched one navigate a turn that most of us could probably barely manage with a houseboat. We then crossed Main Street again to duck inside the River Museum.

Painted fire engine red on the outside, it is just as inviting through the doors, where this museum whittles away at life on the river from just about every angle from shantyboats and the dams to showboats and the families who operate the towboats.

It's a river rat's paradise. You can lay hands on working steamboat whistles from the *Steamboat Huntsville*, play the *P.A. Denny*'s old Calliope, and even get behind the wheel of the historic towboat pilothouse *The Jean Ann*, where you can pretend to steer a towboat through the string of Ohio River islands up river at St. Marys.

On the second floor of the museum past the pilothouse and near a quite remarkable riverboat painting done entirely with pasta, the museum has a model of the Silver Bridge and runs a short documentary about the tragedy.

It doesn't take too many moments to be enveloped by the weight and the sadness of the tragedy. It happened in December, without warning, as Christmas shoppers and workers rushed home to their families.

With night coming on and with the River Museum workers ears more than filled with our pitiful steam boat whistling, we decided we best roll over on West Virginia 62/2 South to the fifth annual **Christmas Fantasy Light Show at Krodel Park (304-675-3844)**.

At the park, you can drive around the small lake and get a better look at the 250,000 lights and more than 150 displays including a pink hippo, a windmill, a 20-foot Santa and the red-eyed, green-light-winged Mothman peering through the lighted pines.

Since it was unseasonably warm, we walked around the lake. I'm glad we did. Light reflections shimmered off the wa-

ter and those 3-D glasses made every set of car lights look like the Star of David.

Even Fort Randolph, built in 1776 and rebuilt in 1976, is outlined in lights, making the Fantasy Light Show definitely worth the drive.

It's not St. Albans Festival of Lights, but definitely on par with Ashland's Winter Wonderland of Lights (800,000 lights and more than 50 displays).

That hour-long drive is more than worth it because the well-known Christmas lights at the West Virginia State Farm Museum, located just north of Point Pleasant off of WV 62 , also run for a couple weeks in December.

With our now sleepy eyes glazed over by gazing at the abundance of Christmas lights on the ground, and the real stars starting to show themselves in the night sky, we turned back onto the Ohio River Road, W.Va. 2, and headed back to Huntington with at least one member of the Mothman and Santa Claus Search Team still on heightened alert.

"Daddy," Jacob said in an anxious whisper. "You look out your window for Mothman. I'll look out my window for Santa Claus."

If You Go: Point Pleasant

DIRECTIONS: From Huntington, take West Virginia 2 northeast and follow the Ohio River Road for just under an hour to Point Pleasant.

MOTHMAN MUSEUM: Noon to 6 p.m. seven days a week. Admission is $3 and $1 for children under 10. Read more about the museum, the Mothman Festival (which happens in mid September) and about Mothman at the Web site www.mothmanlives.com.

RIVER MUSEUM: 10 a.m. to 3 p.m. Tuesday through Friday; 11 a.m. to 4 p.m. Saturday and 1 to 5 p.m. Sunday. $3 and $1 for children. Call (304) 674-0144.

THE LIGHTS: Krodel Park's Christmas Fantasy Light Show runs 5:30 to 11 p.m. daily late November through Dec. 31. Call (304) 675-3844.

WEST VIRGINIA FARM MUSEUM: in Point Pleasant presents a Christmas lights show 6 to 9 p.m. early December through Christmas. Donations accepted Call (304) 675-6788 to see when they've got live music and a live nativity. Museum is also open April through November and features General, which was the world's third largest horse.

STAY ALL NIGHT: The historic Lowe Hotel, built in 1901, is located at 4th and Main streets., a block from the Ohio River. The hotel has a wide range of rooms from Jacuzzi Suites to small rooms. Call (304) 675-2260.

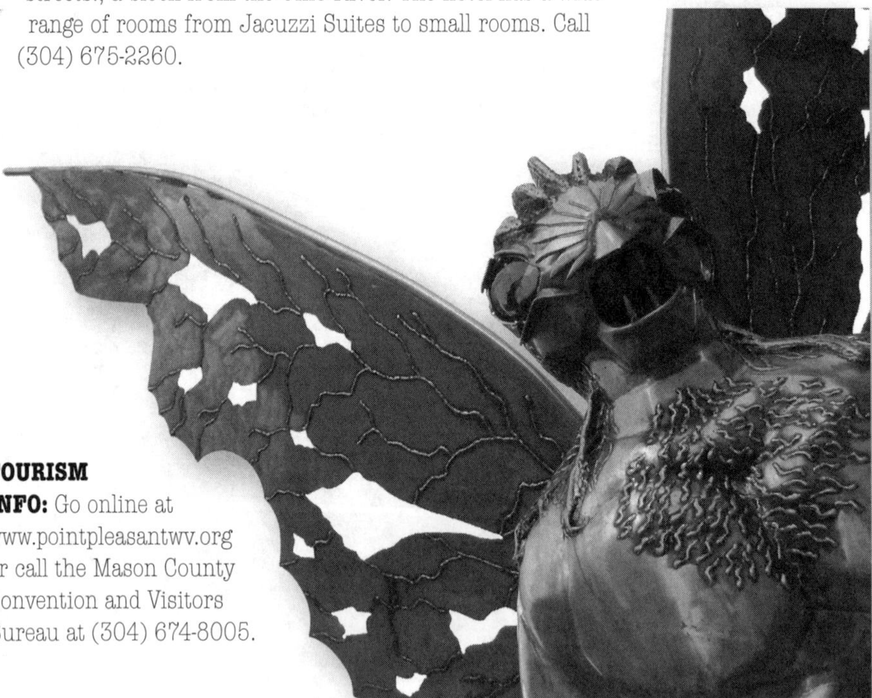

TOURISM INFO: Go online at www.pointpleasantwv.org or call the Mason County Convention and Visitors Bureau at (304) 674-8005.

More Wonderfully Odd Places

MYSTERY HOLE: A classic road-side attraction where the laws of gravity are defied. Open April through October, the Mystery Hole is located a mile west of Hawks Nest State Resort Park in Ansted, W.Va., on U.S. 60. Check out Hawks Nest, too, for a great tram ride down to the New River. Call The Mystery Hole at (304) 658–9101 or go online at www.mysteryhole.com.

PUMPKIN HOUSE: Kenova's mayor Ric Griffith and his army of Halloween elves carve up more than 3,000 pumpkins at Griffith's historic home on Beech Street in Kenova (just west of Huntington). The nightly display goes up a week before Halloween and continues a few days past Halloween. Featured on national TV, the show features light displays synchronized to music. Habitat for Humanity uses the pumpkins to make pumpkin butter as well.

KENTUCKY DOWN UNDER: Meet some kangaroos, play a digiridoo and feed a lorikeet. And do that without a 9,500-mile trip to Australia as Horse Cave, Ky. is home to Kentucky Down Under. Call (270) 786-2634 or go online at www.kdu.com.

HILLBILLY HOTDOGS: Now with several locations around the region, the original Hillbilly Hotdogs, at 6591 Ohio River Road, Lesage (between Huntington and Point Pleasant on WV 2) has original hot-dog-stand-grub including the Homewrecker (a 15-inch loaded dog). The downtown Huntington location is known nationally for The Doublewide (10 pound burger) and a Singlewide (5 pound burger). At Lesage, eat on the school buses and enjoy your favorite 8-tracks. Be sure to pet Simon the Goat (after you eat, of course). Call (304) 762-2458 in Lesage or (304) 522-0044 in Huntington.

PHILIPPI MUMMIES: The Barbour County Historic Museum, located next to the old depot in Philippi, W.Va., has Civil War artifacts, info on the nearby covered bridge, and oh, yeah, the famous Philippi Mummies. The museum is open May to Oct. Call (304) 457-3700 for information.

Charleston
West Virginia

As much as I love Huntington – and I do – sometimes you need to pack up the family unit and head over to see its big sister city of Charleston.

Like typical sisters, the two similar-sized-and-situated cities have their share of hair-pulling, name-calling spats over whose city is five people bigger or who had what idea first, and the probably-never-to-be-decided donnybrook – to build or not to build a regional airport.

That said, entertainment-wise the two cities seem strangely compatible and complimentary – rarely butting heads with competing festivals or big shows.

When it comes to saying adios to summer, it's hard to find a city in the region that does it with more style than Charleston with its **Charleston Sternwheel Regatta**, founded in 1970 by then-12-year-old Nelson Jones.

With the Regatta rolling down the river at us, we thought we'd explore just a few of the many tourist treasures tucked downtown just off of the Kanawha River.

Confessing that most trips to Charleston since my family moved back to the Tri-State have been to see a "**Mountain Stage**" show, we have to give a shout out to West Virginia's coolest export – great music heard 'round the world weekly now on both radio and TV.

Celebrating more than 20 years on radio, "Mountain Stage" is a godsend for young parents who can quickly lose any trace of coolness when they get tag-teamed with daily singing dinosaur doses of Barney and now

Miles: 51

Original Trip December 2005

Huntington's big sister of a city, Charleston, is a great place to go ramble around with the kids. We visit The Clay Center and love such downtown treasures as the Capitol Market and Taylor Books.

Dorothy via The Wiggles. "Mountain Stage" shows are inexpensive, they get you inside the state's Cultural Center and its theater – and after taking our critters to see everyone from Norah Jones to Leon Redbone – it seems OK to bring small children.

Just a bit upriver from the heart of downtown, we landed the station wagon loaded with picnic supplies beneath the towering, giant sycamores lining the banks of the Kanawha at **Daniel Boone Park (304-348-6860)**.

While I always thought Daniel Boone was as Kentucky as Col. Harlan Sanders' original recipe fried chicken, I found out at the park that not only did he chill in Charleston from 1788 to 1795, but he also represented Kanawha County in the General Assembly in 1791.

Since a trip to Charleston is not a trip to Charleston without a visit to what Will calls "The Play Center," actually referred to by people who don't wet their pants frequently as **"The Clay Center," 300 Leon Sullivan Way (304-561-3575)**, we packed the peanut-butter-faced critters back in for an afternoon of exploring. With our knee-high "Finding Nemo" fans in tow, we first nabbed tickets for the large format film, "The Living Sea," that swallows nearly two-thirds of the Electric Sky Theater's 61-foot dome.

Although the films are shown as many as four times a day Wednesday through Saturday, they're shown only twice Sunday, so get tickets as soon as you get in the door to the 175-seat theater.

We spent two hours before the show exploring the center's **Avampato Discovery Museum** and its KidsSpace, Health Royale and Milton Gardner's Earth City. In the sliver of time left after "The Living Sea" and before the museum closed, we rushed downstairs to the Gizmo Factory and the WSAZ Newschannel 3 First Warning Weather Station.

Parents' mistake. Like riding with Hunter S. Thompson, we'd been so nervous about a full public freak-out by our sometimes wailing critters we hadn't allotted enough time. At closing time, we looked longingly at the 9,000 feet of art wrapped around a three-story atrium as we made our way to the maw of the August heat.

However, "The Living Sea" alone was worth the trip. It was full film immersion as we visually swam along with schools of fish and through coral reefs while Meryl Streep's sultry voice and Sting's soft pop whispered how fragile we are. Of course, the clownfish-loving kids were snoring before it was over, but not before our 3-year-old made his family proud by correctly identifying in drill-sergeant volume – The Cuttlefish.

Although I'm usually at a mall about as often as Madonna attends Amish barn-raisings, I reluctantly agreed to check out **The Charleston Town Center (304-345-9525)**, one of the country's largest downtown malls with more than 130 shops and stores.

A team of draft horses couldn't get me into most mall-over-America chain stores, but dinner-time hunger pains led us inward into the always dangerous-to-the-wallet and a man's sanity – 1 million square feet of stores. Somehow we made it out unscathed and thankfully without my sitting listlessly defeated with the other men, staring into space, rocking back and forth and talking out loud to myself on a bench. After some searching I saw the neon and knew the rep - we scurried over to hit Tidewater Grill.

Located at the mall's edge, **Tidewater, (304-345-2622)** which has a nice patio dining area, can be accessed from the street or from folks coming from inside the mall.

We went and found that the mostly seafood restaurant is a refreshing lunch stop.

It was a nice treat for us, and certainly not your big brother's mall-based food-stop. This ain't Sbarro, not that there's anything wrong with that.

Dinner was reasonable ($30, including tip, for two adults and the one child eating "real food"). The Maryland crab meat balls were excellent, and folks there were more than accommodating for our stroller-pushing posse. The kids' menu was good – crayons included. We all got a good laugh at one of the

menu items: the hopefully misprinted "Kid Fingers" that we're sure tasted like chicken.

With the afternoon and our energy speeding downward, my wife and I pushed forth desperately seeking coffee downtown, landing at one of the area's few mom-and-pop book shops, **Taylor Books, 226 Capitol St. (304-342-1461)**.

English native Ann Saville started Taylor Books in 1995, and it has blossomed into quite the quaint, yet spacious, epicenter of activity in the heart of downtown. It's surrounded by a good lot of cool places to check out – from **Ellen's Homemade Ice Cream (304-343-6488)** and **Steve Payne's photo gallery (304-343-7254)** across Capitol Street to a wide number of restaurants, including **Mykonos Café, 218 Capitol St., (304-347-9220)**, a nice and reasonably-priced family-run Greek restaurant just down the street.

We thoroughly enjoyed Taylor's – reading children's books in a corner rocking chair, watching the fish in the aquarium, browsing and buying good books and thanking the good Lord that the sculpture our 3-year-old had pawed was one of Mark Blumenstein's playful and probably indestructible welded metal sculptures.

Taylor's has free live music every Friday and Saturday night, more than 20,000 books, an espresso and wine bar with homemade baked goods, an art annex, wonderful, requisite squeaky wood floors and a nice bathroom surprise – a changing station for the diapered crowd.

Carrying our kicking 3-year-old Jake out into the hot August afternoon, we realized we needed to wrap up this rascal and get these critters (Jake and his little brother Will) back to the ranch for much-needed naps.

But we had one more quick stop for some fresh food to take home.

So with a promise of possible chocolate for choir-boy-esque behavior we pulled into **Capitol Market, 800 Smith St. (304-344-1905)**, a great and efficient stop to fresh grocery shop in downtown Charleston.

Located in the old train depot, the market that was started in 1997 is open seven days a week year-round. It is filled with more than a dozen outside fresh produce vendors; and on the inside, there is a bit of everything. There's another dozen or so shops including fine dining at **Soho's** restaurant. There is also for your home-grown shopping pleasure **TerraSalis Flower and Garden, The Fresh Seafood Company, Johnnie's Fresh Meat, Cranberry Faire Bakery, Capitol Roasters, The Wine and Cheese Shop, The Purple Onion, Frog Creek Books** and the so-good-it-should-be-illegal, **Holl's Swiss Chocolates**.

With that sweet taste lingering on our tongues, we swore to ourselves that - like after a great visit with family - it had been way too long, and that we'd be right back soon to visit our big sister city.

If You Go: Charleston

ALONG THE WAY: There's a lot of cool stops in the valley. One real gem for dining is Thai House Dunbar, at 2059 Roxalana Road. It's closed Sundays and open weekdays for lunch and dinner only (4:30 to 9 p.m. Saturdays). Call (304) 720-3228. Online at www.thaihousedunbar.com.

A GOOD TIME TO GO: The Charleston Art Walk is held on the third Thursday of each month. It starts at 5 p.m. downtown. Charleston is also chock full of national-act concerts, as well as festivals such as Multi-Fest that takes place each August. Not to miss too is the now nine-day FestivALL Charleston, a city-wide arts festival in mid June. Go online at www.festivallcharleston.com.

TAKE A HIKE: Charleston is blessed with really cool local places to hike such as the nearby Kanawha State Forest and the Dunbar Wine Cellar park. Another close-by great space for mountain biking, hiking and even soapbox derby action is Little Creek Park, in South Charleston. It's open for hiking April through October, and the hiking trails take you to a number of neat rock formations including the infamous Devil's Tea Table. Go online at www.southcharlestonwv.org.

KID-FRIENDLY GRUB: Bluegrass Kitchen, 1600 Washington St., East, Charleston, is an eclectic, art-filled, kid-friendly restaurant that makes great, fresh, herb-infused fare. There often is live music, too, in the evenings. Call (304) 346-2871.

FUN AND FREE: Vandalia Gathering is the state's annual celebration of the traditional arts, music, dance, crafts and food of West Virginia. Like a family reunion meets a state fair, Vandalia Gathering has been happening since 1966 on the Capitol grounds. Go online at www.wvculture.org.

PLAY BALL: The West Virginia Power play April through August at Appalachian Power Park in downtown Charleston. There are lots of discounts and fun, wacky promotions as well as live music. There's also free fireworks on Friday home games. Go online at www.wvpower.com.

Other Kid-Friendly Museums

HIGHLANDS MUSEUM AND DISCOVERY CENTER: Located at 1620 Winchester Ave., Ashland, Ky., the Discovery Center has a treasure trove of exhibits for kids including Discovery Cavern and the River Expedition that features Lil' Joe, a pilothouse from a towboat. There's also a flight simulator and front porch with old-time games. Open 10 a.m. to 5 p.m. Tuesday through Saturday. Call (606) 329-8888. Go online at www.highlandsmuseum.com.

COSI: The hands-on science center in Columbus, at 333 W. Broad St., COSI is packed with interactive exhibits. There's a 7-story Extreme Screen theater and exhibits that explore space, life, oceans, progress and gadgets. The museum is open 10 a.m. to 5 p.m. Wednesday through Saturday and noon to 6 p.m. Sunday. Family Friday Nights are the last Friday of each month with reduced admission and late hours. Call (614) 228-COSI. Go online at www.cosi.org.

HUNTINGTON MUSEUM OF ART: Located at 2033 McCoy Road, the Huntington Museum of Art is built for art lovers of all ages - even those that prefer the Crayola medium. Saturday KidsArt is a free program especially for K-5 that takes place 1 to 3 p.m. Saturdays. Also, in addition to the art exhibits, kids always love the C. Fred Edwards Tropical Conservatory that is full of colorful orchids, giant palms, fish and quirky plants like the Venus Fly-Trap. There's also a short hiking trail (easy for kids, too) just over the hill. The Tulip Tree Trail is also graced with the stone-carved artwork of Glenwood, W.Va. artist Earl Gray. Call (304) 529-2701. Go online at www.hmoa.org.

CINCINNATI MUSEUM CENTER: Located at the historic Union Terminal, 1301 Western Ave., Cincinnati, the Museum Center is packed with the Omnimax Theater, the Duke Energy Children's Museum and the Museum of Natural History and Science (can you say dinosaurs?). 10 a.m. to 5 p.m. Monday through Saturday and 11 a.m. to 6 p.m. Sunday. Call (800) 733-2077. Go online at cincymuseum.org.

EAST KENTUCKY SCIENCE CENTER: Located in Prestonsburg, Ky., at 7 Bert Combs Dr., the East Kentucky Science Center, is a new museum whose centerpiece is the Planetarium that is equipped with the GOTO Chronos Star Projector that can transform the dome with 8,500 optically projected stars depicting the night sky anywhere on Earth. The planetarium also has monthly star parties and rock music laser light shows as well. Call (606) 889-0303.

HERITAGE FARM: Located at 3300 Harvey Road, Huntington, The Heritage Farm Museum and Village has 20 buildings, and 20,000 square feet of interactive Appalachian history displays on progress and transportation. See model railroad layout, crawl through a coal mine, and enjoy a petting zoo as well. Don't miss Spring open house in early May. Call (304) 522-1244.

Timberline

Davis, West Virginia

One of the most pitiful sights of this global warming hasn't just been all of those penguins trapped in large melting crevasses, although I certainly mourn the loss of our fine-feathered friends – those great little movie dancers that starred in "Happy Feet."

No, it was coming home from work and seeing my two munchkins had freed the plastic sleds from the garage and were careening down our grass-covered hill in 50 degrees temps.

With another disgusting mix of rain and sleet needling down on us, the captain of the Dave Trippin' crew said enough was enough.

The station wagon was loaded with more wool than a sheep farm and at least a couple pairs of matching mittens to head over to "real snow country" where they frolic in the white stuff every winter like it's '77-'78 here in Huntington.

Drawing in skiers from around the south and east since the 1950s, **Canaan Valley**, located 31/2 to 4 hours east of Huntington, gets dumped with about 160 inches of snow every year.

In 1995-96 the valley got hit with a record 245 inches of snow.

So when the flakes fall, these folks know what to do with it – gear up, get outside and let the games begin.

Not that anybody's counting, but between **Canaan Valley Resort**, and **Timberline Four Seasons Resort**, the valley

Miles: 235

Original Trip January 2007

In the midst of winter, we trip to real snow country, over to Canaan Valley, the highest valley east of the Mississippi River. We bum around Timberline Four Seasons Resort, one of the biggest and the last family-owned ski resorts in the East, and discover quite a friendly Salamander along the way.

has 74 slopes and trails, seven lifts, terrain parks, a snowtubing park, and a packed plate of events both at the resorts and in the great little mountain towns of Davis and Thomas.

With the critters in tow, we decided to head over to Timberline that was opened in 1983 by the Herz family and has grown into one of the largest family-owned-and-operated ski resorts in the East.

Since we didn't get even one good snowfall the prior winter, the Lavender posse started getting pumped when we started hitting the hills on the drive over, desperately seeking anything remotely looking like snow in the air.

Just outside of metropolitan **Big Otter** along I-79, the flurries began and clouds of white wisps ghost danced across the road.

"It's snowing," said our chorus of boys.

"That's flurries," said my wife Toril, who grew up in Syracuse, N.Y., which averages 200 inches of snow annually. "I'll tell you when it starts snowing."

By the time we got to **Elkins**, though, it was game on and indeed the valley would rack up more than a foot of snow.

Like many ski and snowboard beginners, we were drawn to Timberline to be one with the Salamander – the rightfully famous and most scenic two-mile long trail that takes you up to 4,238 feet and then slides you down easy, meandering through the pines giving you long drinks of the mountains sitting several miles away on the other side of this three-to-five-mile-wide valley.

Before we even grabbed our skis, though, it was first things first. Jacob headed over to a snow pile outside the Ski Patrol hut, planted a snow angel and started cranking snowballs while the snow fell from God's window up above and from the snowguns all around.

"It's winter here every day," Jacob said.

Yes, it is.

While Jacob, 6, and Will, 4, both did lots of time on the Timberline bunny hill, it was here in these snow piles in front of the hut that we would return to play often over the weekend, watching the hundreds of families of all ages and sizes smiling and skiing down the slopes.

With sweet, slope-side deals for youth groups, Boy and Girl Scout troops at Timberline, we met lots of kids and parents soaking in the best of winter together at the resort, which has children's programs for ages 4 to 7 and 8 to 12, as well as a licensed child care center for wee tots.

A card-carrying hillbilly music-loving nut, I also grooved on the sweet acoustic stream of Jimmy Buffett, John Denver and Cox Family songs coming out of the speakers outside the lodge as we sat making our snowman village including a Red Bull-fueled attempt at making the world's smallest snowman.

Hey, people making tiny snow creations with mittens need wings, OK.

That music only got better on the inside of Timberline's multi-story lodge that has a three-floor-high wall of windows facing the slopes.

Inside, the lodge has lots of good eats at the **Timberhaus Cafeteria**, and upstairs at the **Timbers Pub and Fireside Grill**.

And every ski weekend, there is live music from 4 p.m. to 2 a.m. at the Grill and the Pub.

Since 9 p.m. is the new midnight for young parents, getting to enjoy a 4 p.m. start time to the tunes was a real treat especially when the music is not accompanied with dancing bears.

Since we couldn't locate the "indoor ski lift," we clopped like a team of Clydesdales up the stairs in ski boots, sitting above the Fireside Grill for a couple nights listening to 32-year-old Elkins-based musician J.B. Tenney, playing guitar while his father Pete played old-time and Celtic music on mandolin, fiddle, banjo and a Concertino squeezebox.

Glad that Timberline's "Celtic Festival" served up a BBQ rib special (Hey, who really wants Haggis and cold taters?), we sat back and watched darkness fall, letting the stream of music from the old country provide a surreal

soundtrack as we watched out the window at the night skiing that's offered from 4:30 to 9 p.m. during the regular season.

With Sunday sun pouring in windows, we contemplated another Salamander run since **Canaan Valley Baptist Church** holds a unique mountaintop church service at 12:30 p.m. each Sunday at Timberline.

But with the big flakes falling, we figured we lowlanders might better get on the highway and roll.

Before we left the valley, though, we had one more mission, heading over to Canaan Valley Resort, which celebrated its 35th Anniversary in 2007.

Although we were wiped out and didn't have the time and energy to take in the Eurobungy, sledding, snowboarding, ice skating, paint-balling and the 78 other things offered at the state park, our little pirates had juice for one short treasure hunt.

With out last burst of energy, we fired up the hand-held GPS, parked the wagon and rambled down a trail (that shall remain nameless) to do some Geocaching at Canaan, one of the first state parks in the country to promote this new outdoor sport that is like a high-tech treasure hunt using GPS coordinates to hide little treasures in an ammo box or Tupperware container out in the woods.

We stashed our Jeep travel bug into the ammo box cache called "Easy Does It," and with flakes the size of silver dollars falling, we stumbled back to the car to slip slide our way back to the hills of Huntington where green stalks of daffodils greeted us, wondering where have all the winters gone.

If You Go: Timberline

PLACES TO STAY: Accommodations of all levels available at Timberline from group bunkhouses to family chalets and cabins. Call Timberline Four Seasons Reality at (866) 438-7259 for ski and stay packages.

BRINGING THE GANG: Timberline has special deals for 20 or more, whether it's scouts or a church or college group. Prices start at about $79 for skiing, lodging, meals, rentals, lift ticket, and lesson. Call (800) 392-0152 or e-mail biggroups@timberlineresort.com.

A GOOD PLACE TO EAT: You can eat fireside at Timberline's multi-level lodge that has Timbers Pub and Fireside Grill that has great rib specials and live music. There's also Timberhaus Cafeteria on premise.

FIDDLING AROUND: Although Timberline has live music every weekend, you may want to venture into Thomas, home to the well-known Purple Fiddle Coffeehouse and Mountain Market, 21 East Ave., that draws in regional and national act bands Fridays through Sundays. Located in the old DePollo General Store, this funky and homey joint is a great place to hang and hear great Americana music, The Fiddlers Roost Guest House is next door. Call (304) 463-4040 or go online at www.purplefiddle.com.

IN THE LONG RUN: Did you know Timberline, one of the largest family-owned resorts in the East, also boasts the longest ski run in the South. The Salamander is 2 miles long and a great trail for beginners. Salamander is just one of 37 slopes and trails at Timberline.

GOOD TIMES TO GO: Since Canaan Valley gets an average of about 180 to 200 inches of snow a year, you can hit the resort early and often and up through even April when you can ski in shorts if the spirit moves you.

SKI THE VALLEY: Timberline Four Seasons Resort and Canaan Valley Resort, which is located just down the road from Timberline, offer a two-day lift ticket and can be purchased at the lift ticket windows of both ski areas. Go online at www.SkiTheValley.com.

DID YOU KNOW?: Davis, W.Va has been named on the Top Ten Coolest Mountain Towns by *Men's Journal* Magazine. Also, in a *USA Today* article titled "Where do men like to ski", Davis, W.Va was given the title of "Best Kept Secret."

More Ways to Frosty Play

AIRBOARDING: Added at Canaan Valley Resort in the 2005/2006 ski season, Airboarding is like sledding on inflated "air rockets" that are more controllable than snow tubes. Canaan was the first ski area in the country to offer an Airboard terrain park. Go online at www.canaanresort.com.

SNOW TUBING: Four of West Virginia's downhill resorts have snow tubing. Winterplace, south of Beckley, has the largest. Kids must be 44 inches tall. When you buy a lift ticket, add on snowtubing for only $11.50. Go online at www.winterplace.com.

SNOWSHOEING: Located in Canaan Valley, White Grass has been offering Cross-country skiing, snowshoeing, ice skating and much more since 1979. The low-key, family-friendly skiing center is open 9 a.m. -to Dark-Thirty, seven days a week December-March. Go online at www.whitegrass.com.

ICE SKATING: Ashland's Central Park is the hot-spot for ice skating as the city of Ashland maintains an ice rink from December through March. Go online at www.ashlandky.org.

SNOWMOBILING: You can get out there on a snowmobile daily during season at Snowshoe Mountain in Snowshoe, W.Va. These evening and night-time tours are unforgettable. Cost is about $125 weekends and $45 for ages 6 to 15. Go online at www.snowshoemtn.com.

WINTER HIKE: The annual 6-mile winter hike goes from Old Man's Cave to Ash Cave in Hocking Hills, Ohio each January. Go online at www.hockinghills.com. Call (740) 385-6165.

Camden Park

Huntington, West Virginia

With Jefferson Starship's 1975 dream-weaving hit "Miracles" wafting through the hot, humid afternoon air above Camden Park's ice cream shop, a look around at the carousel, the Haunted House, the Big Dipper and the Tilt-A-Whirl makes you forget what decade you're in.

Miles:
5
Original Trip
June
2003

Any moment you expect the late John P. "J.P." Boylin, who owned the park from 1946 until 1980, to come barreling down the Midway to check on things and scoop up his grandkids to enjoy the 26 mostly vintage rides. But that was then.

Now, it is one of those grandkids, Jack Boylin, who in these days of corporate-owned, mega amusement parks, is guiding this nostalgic, 26-acre family-run park into the future.

A visit to West Virginia's only amusement park, Camden Park on its 100th birthday.

In 2003, the country's 18th oldest amusement park and West Virginia's only amusement park, celebrated 100 years on West Virginia Day with a dinner for invited guests, the swing band Blue Max out on the Midway, fireworks and giant historical photographs of the park.

Jack Boylin, who manages the park with front office help from his mother Jane, said the park's existence is owed to the Tri-State's continued support and respect for its history.

"Huntington is interesting that way," Jack Boylin said. "There are a lot of things here that you don't find other places like the Frostop. They don't have that anymore - anywhere else.

There is a lot of history here that other places have replaced with something else."

Built as a picnic spot along Camden Interstate Railway's street car line between Huntington and Ashland, Camden Park was named for its original owner Sen. Johnson Newlon Camden of Parkersburg.

In the 100 years since, Camden Park, which has survived everything from the Great Depression to two World Wars, has ridden a rollercoaster of Tri-State history's highs and lows.

When Huntington furniture salesman John P. Boylin bought the park in 1946 along with partners Harry Nudd and H.J. Malloy (Bob Burley would later join that group), the park had only nine rides and many of the buildings were still damaged by the historic 1937 flood.

The park also has ridden the rails of social changes as well.

Huntington native Jackie Jackson, 49, remembers when her mother would not let her go to Camden Park as a child.

In the 1950s during segregation, blacks were only allowed to go one day a year.

Jackson's mother said if they weren't welcome the rest of the year, they wouldn't go at all.

By the time Jackson was a mother, times had thankfully changed.

Jackson, who took her four children and now her seven grandchildren to Camden Park, remembers the sweet feeling of acceptance for people of color.

In the 1970s, on an outing with Barnett Child Care Center, one of her three daughters got lost.

When Jackson heard about a lost child over a loudspeaker, she went to check and found her daughter with a face full of ice cream and cotton candy.

"Here she was, this little black child, the center of attention," Jackson said laughing. "Several workers were being so attentive and sweet, filling her with all the goodies she could possibly hold."

Judy Cornett, vice-president of operations for Clear Channel Communications, remembers Camden Park itself being the center of attention in country music in the early 1990s when Cornett , then running WTCR, booked 32 country acts at the park.

The park has had music throughout its history from the dance bands of the Cabaret Room to classic country stars such as Porter Waggoner and Leroy Van Dyke.

But Cornett, who grew up attending those classic country shows, turned it up a notch - a big notch.

Garth Brooks played Camden Park twice, and once after a rain, directed traffic in the parking lot, trying to get folks out so he could get equipment loaded in his white Volkswagen van. Brooks then mentioned the park in one of the first cuts off of his album, "Fresh Horses."

Vince Gill, hot off of his first solo No. 1 single, "When I Call Your Name," received his first standing ovation at Camden Park, answered the park's phones and then wrote about the experience in his book.

Calling from a cell phone headed to Nashville, Cornett said the memories come flowing back warm of shows with Emmylou Harris, Diamond Rio, Mark Chestnut, the late, legendary Roy Orbison, Brooks and Dunn, Shenandoah, Pirates of the Mississippi, and Mary Chapin Carpenter, whose dressing room was the roller rink girls' bathroom.

And, of course, Marty Stuart, who loved visiting the park so much he used one of his many photographs of Camden Park on the inside of a CD cover.

Cornett also booked one of the first local country stars to play the park, a long-haired Flatwoods, Ky., singer named Billy Ray Cyrus, who tried out a new song on the crowd called "Achy Breaky Heart," before it was recorded.

Although Camden Park still gets some national acts - mostly on holidays - and well-respected regional acts of all musical flavors, Cornett said the flood of soon-to-be-stars that played the stage which no longer exists was a special place in time.

"Camden Park has a great legacy and the music has always been a big part of it," Cornett said. "We used to kid around that if you play this stage, you will be big time. There was a kind of magic on that stage."

While the early 1990s were the heyday of the park's country music heritage, they were the beginning of the end for a group of Virginia investors who had bought and operated it since 1980.

In 1992, the excursion boat the *Camden Queen* left, then the rare, wooden horses from the 1907-era carousel were auctioned off.

In 1993, more than 50 people were injured on a ride called The Enterprise, in one of the few accidents in the park's history.

In 1994, suits piled up high against the former owners, Bill and Bev Roberts, who owed more than $2 million to a long list of creditors including the Boylin family which still owned the property, according to *The Herald-Dispatch* articles.

In the spring of 1995, the Boylins, John, his wife Jane, and their son, Jack, who had just finished art school, stepped in to save the family park, where attendance was in a free fall after peaking at about 400,000 in the 1970s.

While the park was still operational and still passing inspection, Jack and Jane said many things had fallen into disrepair.

A 1996 fire that caused $1 million in damage didn't help matters. It took out the park's office, the Skeeball area and the skating rink.

"They had put in two new rides and they put them in nicely, but that was it," Jack Boylin said. "It was as if nothing had been painted for 15 years and nothing landscaped in 15 years. And the hidden things that nobody takes into account - like the pavement and the roofs, and plumbing and electricity - none of that had been taken care of."

That has changed in a dramatic way; just ask thirtysomething South Point, Ohio, resident Shawn Wellman.

He started working at Camden Park when he was 16 as a dishwasher in the cafeteria and hasn't left the park in summers.

Now a math teacher at Rock Hill High School and ride supervisor at Camden Park for the past five years, Wellman wouldn't think of giving up the best summer job he's ever had.

"When I first started here it was under the old ownership and it was really in bad shape," Wellman said. "I like being a part of seeing the park growing and making it look better every year. They are really spending a lot of time, money and effort. It makes you feel good to be a part of that."

Parks Becker, a cousin of the Boylins who moved back from Florida to work year-round at the park, looked out from the gift shop window at the roses getting ready to bloom by the Tilt-A-Whirl and at the new menu at the West Virginia Grille and smiled.

"Have you eaten yet?" said Becker, one of 20 year-round employees. "The snapper's as good as anything I ate in Florida,"

Camden Park's full-service cafeteria has morphed into the West Virginia Grille serving up everything from giant burgers and Cuban chicken wraps to fresh fruit, salads and blackened snapper.

"That you can now get anything from the park famous corn dog, the Pronto

Pup, to smoked brisket is a good sign," Becker said.

"We're really getting there," Becker said.

Getting there has meant many things. It has meant a new family ride each year as well as maintaining the park's treasure trove of rare, antique amusement rides which includes the park favorite, Big Dipper, a wooden roller coaster built in 1958.

The 73-foot Skydiver was added in 2001; Swan Lake, a lake filled with pedal boats, was added in 2002 and to celebrate its 100th-year anniversary, the public voted and picked the new family-style ride, the Kite Flyer, that sends 24 people flying around high in the air while lying down.

Getting there has meant reaching out.

The park has added a Halloween-themed "Spooktacular" during off-season October weekends. In the spring before the regular season even begins they have added School Days, a day of fun and education with interactive programs lessons in history, music, science and other subjects.

School Days draws in more than 20,000 school kids from three states.

Through the West Virginia Education Alliance, the park gave 75 books to each school that came for its library, as well as hosting a grant-writing workshop for teachers.

Getting there has meant saying thanks and giving back.

For the first time the park, which had seen attendance rebound by 2002 to more than 100,000 people from 39 states, has given free days for mothers and fathers, on their respective holidays.

They have also linked up with many local media outlets and companies for ticket giveaways.

Matt Turner, spokesman for the West Virginia Division of Tourism, said the park's turnaround can be seen in everything from the quality of marketing, which has been given a boost by the division's tourism grants program to the new attractions and landscaping.

"A park can't remain stagnant," Turner said. "Even the classic parks have to do things to keep the guests coming back, to maintain the history and the original appeal while also building on new attractions... They recognize that. It has taken some work. We are really glad to see Camden Park is alive again and going to do great things for the community. It is the only place like it in the state. We don't have anything else like it in West Virginia."

If You Go: Camden Park

WHERE: Located five miles west of Huntington along U.S. 60. Turn at the sign of the Happy Clown.

ADMISSION: General admission is $20.99; children (48 inches and under) and seniors (55 and older) $14.99. Discount (Starlight) prices are after 5 p.m.

WHAT'S THERE: Kiddieland has nine rides including a carousel, kiddie boats and the handcars. For bigger kids and adults, there's about a dozen more rides including wooden rollercoaster, The Big Dipper and The Little Dipper, the new Kite Flyer, Swan Boats, Dodge 'Em Cars, the log flume, and the historic dark ride, The Haunted House.

GOOD TIMES TO GO: Dads get in for a $1 on Fathers Day and moms get in for a $1 on Mothers Day. Also, Children's Festival is every June with added attractions such as live puppet shows and petting zoos. The Hot Summer Nights Concert Series takes place weekends in August. Also, holiday celebrations for Memorial Day, July 4th and Labor Day with live music and more.

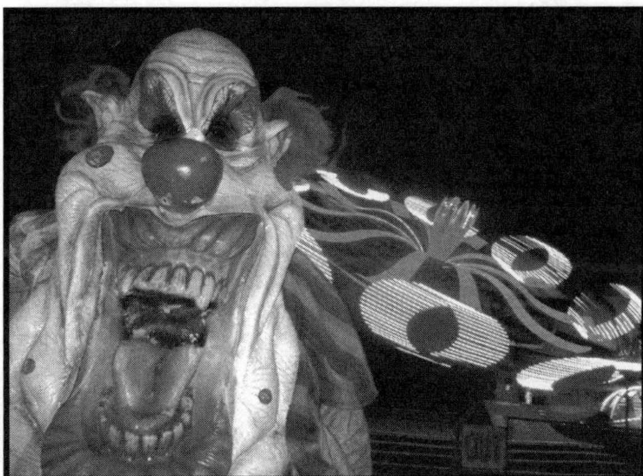

HALLOWEEN: Camden Park is open weekends in late September through Halloween with its seasonally-themed Spooktacular that has the region's only haunted train ride, the historic haunted house, haunted mazes, and other spooky, but family-friendly fun.

DID YOU KNOW?: Camden Park is home to an Adena burial mound that is located behind the Flying Scooters. It is located near the mouth of Twelvepole Creek, on the floodplain above the Ohio River and is the largest mound in the Huntington area, and is third in size in West Virginia. It has not been excavated; and was probably built by the Adena people between 1000 B.C. and A.D. 1.

IN THE DARK: Did you know that Camden Park's Haunted House is one of the last dark rides of its kind in the country? Check out more info about dark rides online at www.laffinthedark.com.

FOR MORE INFO: Call (304) 429-4321 Go online at www.camdenpark.com

Other Old-School Cool

Here's some other cool places still kicking it old-school in and around Huntington

BLENKO GLASS COMPANY: See the ancient art of glass-making at this factory that has been in Milton, W.Va. since 1921. You can view glassmaking during weekdays and see the Visitor Center and Museum seven days a week. Call (304) 743-9081. Go online at www.blenkoglass.com.

HERITAGE FARM MUSEUM & VILLAGE: Step back in time at this farm museum and village which preserves and recreates our Appalachian heritage and culture. There's a dozen buildings including four restored log cabins. The village portrays community life with its display of antique cars, blacksmith shop, meeting house, steam engine and much more. Guided tours from 10 a.m. to 3 p.m. Monday through Saturday. Located in a country setting, less than three miles from I-64, Exit 8, 3300 Harvey Rd. (304) 522-1244.

HERITAGE VILLAGE: Located in downtown Huntington's former B & O Railway Station, at 11th Street and Veterans Memorial Boulevard, this complex contains the Boston Beanery, authentic locomotive, a renovated Pullman Car, and is the site of the City's first bank once robbed by the James Gang Call. (304) 696-5954.

FROSTOP DRIVE-IN: Located at 1449 Hal Greer Blvd., under the giant rotating root beer mug, drive in for some of the area's best root beer (served in frosty mugs), chocolate malts, burgers and hotdogs. Call (304) 523-6851.

HUNTINGTON MUSEUM OF ART: Nationally acclaimed Museum features 19th & 20th century American and European art, American and European glass, Georgian silver, British portraits and antique firearms. The complex includes 10 exhibition galleries, research library, sculpture garden, nature trails and a tropical conservatory. Call (304) 529-2701.

CHARLIE'S HARLEY-DAVIDSON: Check out the history of Harley-Davidson from 1909 through the present at the Charlie's Harley-Davidson dealership, 408 4th St., Huntington. The 10,000-square-foot museum has an Evel Knievel motorcycle and memorabilia as well. There's also a '50s-style diner. Call (304) 523-1340. Go online at www.charlieshd.com.

JENKINS PLANTATION: Historic home of Brigadier General Albert Gallatin Jenkins, C.S.A. Built about 1835 and listed on the National Register of Historic Places. The grounds adjacent to the Greenbottom Wildlife Management Area are also open to the public. Call (304) 762-1059.

MUSEUM OF RADIO & TECHNOLOGY: One of the largest radio museums in the Eastern United States. See hundreds of old radios from the 1920's to the 1950's, telegraph items, early televisions, and the complete recreation of a 1920's radio shop, library and gift shop at this museum in the former Harveytown School. Call (304) 525-8890.

OLD CENTRAL CITY: West Huntington, a collection of more than a dozen antique shops, a farmer's market, specialty shops, museums and florists. Old Central City is home to Heiner's Bakery, one of the region's oldest and largest bakeries. Heiner's is open for guided tours a couple days a week. Also, Old Central City is home to the Taylor Auto Museum. Call (304) 525-1500.

STEWARTS HOT DOGS: 2445 Fifth Ave., Huntington. Around since 1932, this outdoor drive-in hot dog stand is the first of what now is many Stewarts locations in the area. Call (304) 529-DOGS.

ROLLER SKATING RINKS: You can party like it's 1979, when you take a spin or three around the wooden-floored roller rinks under the swirl of the disco ball and the thumping dance music. Go ahead and shoot the duck and limbo if you can. Roll-A-Rama: (137 7th Ave.), is one of the area's oldest indoor roller skating rinks and one of two still left in Huntington. Skateland is located in the Altizer neighborhood of Huntington. Skate sessions at both rinks are Wednesdays and weekends. Call Roll-A-Rama at (304) 529-0909. Call Skateland at (304) 525-1933.

JIM'S STEAK AND SPAGHETTI: 920 5th Ave. A Huntington classic for 70 years. Not much has changed since JFK ate here, and that's a good thing. Don't leave without checking out the photos of all the celebs that have eaten here, such as Muhammad Ali. And don't leave without ordering a piece of homemade pie. (304) 696-9788.

Festival of Lights

St. Albans, West Virginia

I have always loved the innocence and simplicity of Christmas traditions – especially if someone has wrapped that simplicity without ceasing in big, chunky colorful lights.

I love my dad's thirtysomething-year-old tradition of building a near full-sized manger in front of the old home place whose windows and gutters glow like mid-town Manhattan.

And of course, I still relish those yearly December pilgrimages to Blue Creek, Ohio, in Adams County, where Carl Rudd and his Rudd's Christmas Farm bathed the whole holler in Christmas lights, and everyone in two counties got to bask in his heartfelt Christmas glow.

So, on a December day when 70-degree weather and gale-force winds blew in and the Christmas spirit seemed lean, we loaded up the Dave Trippin' mobile with the kids and the wagon of misfit Burger King toys and set off to see if we could find a little Christmas peace and joy in the valley.

We were enticed onto I-64 after hearing rumblings of St. Albans penchant for savoring the simplicity of Christmas.

Just the weekend before, the Cunningham Memorial Park had put out a mere, 16,000 luminaries and the town also took its Christmas down to the Kanawha River, where they hosted a Christmas boat parade.

With whispers of a magically lit land of fiery dragons, sharks and even Spongebob Square

Miles:
42

Original Trip
December
2004

Folks living in the valley between Huntington and Charleston don't need any instruction on how to deck the halls. The Dave Trippin' wagon finds St. Albans Festival of Lights to be merry, bright and one of the region's best light displays.

Pants to be found in the hills above the river at the St. Albans Festival of Lights, we sped down east on I-64 with dreams of Christmas dragons dancing in our heads.

With a little bit of daylight left, we decided also to take in some of the local holiday color to be found along the way in downtown Hurricane along Main Street, which is filled with small boutiques and shops including a couple of note right downtown, **Dale Morton Studio Mascots (304-562-7503) at 2730 2nd. St.**, and **The Root Cellar, (304-562-4139) at 2739 2nd St.**

Although closed when we were rambling through at day's end, the **Caboose Museum (304-562-5896)** has railroad memorabilia as well as a bit of pre-history Hurricane, a 77" Indian Petroglyph which bears the image of the ancient "Water Monster's Daughter."

After admiring the lighted caboose, the adjacent fire station mural and the gazebo decked in lights, we loaded the car to hit a little lights appetizer, "Yuletide in the Park" at **Valley Park in Hurricane (304-562-5896).**

This was the fifth year for the lights at the park, which is known for its Wave Pool and the Museum in the Community.

Although no Ashland or St. Albans when it comes to Christmas light wattage, the Valley Park is still worth the drive-by if you're also hitting other lights.

After getting into an ooey-gooey great mess making peanut-butter and bird-seed-slathered pine cone treats for our birding friends at the Parks and Visitors Bureau, we enjoyed the lights display, which included a lighted Santa landing a bass out of the Wave Pool.

And the Wave Pool front office is filled to the brim with animated characters, thanks to Warren and Mary Hodges.

If you continue down West Virginia 34 toward St. Albans, you'll find it hard not to make a detour through the Teays Valley Meadows subdivision, which is lit to the nines.

With our 2-year-old Will gnawing on his Clifford book, we figured we better quit looking and start eating.

We pulled into the **Pizzerio Uno Chicago Grill, 4170 Route 34, Hurricane (304-757-2290)**, where we were greeted by festive door men, The Cat and the Hat and the Grinch, who further put us in the holiday spirit.

With bellies full of good food and rain starting to fall, we knew we'd better bust a move to St. Albans before this crew goes to dreamland.

After twisting and winding our way up into the hills above St. Albans, we followed the plain brown signs that said "City Park" through neighborhoods that also have caught the Christmas lighting bug.

Away from the light pollution of the city below and in an almost dream-like state, we ran into a true magic land of lights.

With only parking lights on, the black of night popped alive with hills filled with critters from the whole Spongebob gang to a 52-foot-long sternwheeler, various sharks, porpoises, seahorses, football helmets and other refreshingly odd Christmas creations.

We were all now fully awake and in true amazement of this wonderland that was built (except for the legions of Christmas-light trees) throughout the year by the guys in the St. Albans Park and Recreation Department.

We were so transfixed that after winding our way to the top of the hill and through a 40-foot castle and tunnel that the kids wanted to skip a Santa Claus visit (free hot cocoa and cookies if you do) and wanted to get back down the hill as fast as we could to do this one-way magically lit kingdom again.

Who could argue?

We went for seconds of lit Christmas cheer and were not alone. The folks at the front gate, who take donations and pass out programs, said they've had people go through as many as four times in one night and have had a record crowd of 1,344 cars go through in one night.

For good reason.

We spent less than $10 and were rewarded with two 10-mile-an-hour crawls up this winding Christmas mountain, which joyously restored our spirits and filled us to our light-flashing rooftops with the innocence and simplicity of the season.

If You Go: St. Albans/Hurricane

THE ST. ALBANS FESTIVAL OF LIGHTS: is up at City Park 6 to 9 p.m. nightly from late November past Christmas. There is hot cocoa and cookies. The lights are usually closed Dec. 24 and 25 and reopen Dec. 26. Call (304) 722-4625. Go online at www.salights.com.

DIRECTIONS: Take the I-64 east to the St. Albans exit. Right on Route 35 to Route 60. Left on Route 60 to Walnut Street. Right on Walnut Street to Kanawha Terrace. Right on Kanawha Terrace (one block) to Vine Street. Left on Vine Street (at the giant lighted arrow) and then follow the signs.

WHAT ELSE: If you get up to St. Albans early enough, check out one of the area's coolest music shops. Joe Dobbs, fiddler with The 1937 Flood, owns and operates Fret 'n' Fiddle at 809 Pennsylvania Ave., in St. Albans. They've got lots of new and vintage instruments, as well as a digital recording studio. Go online at www.fretnfiddle.com. Call (304) 722-5212.

YULETIDE IN THE PARK: Located at #1 Valley Park Drive in Hurricane. Runs 6 to 9 p.m. nightly in Valley Park late November past Christmas. Animated displays along a lighted trail. An animated toyland is on display in the Wave Pool Bathhouse. Free, but donations accepted. Call (304) 562-0518.

DIRECTIONS: Take I-64 east to the Hurricane Exit 34. Turn right onto Hurricane Creek Road to Route 34 where you take a left at the traffic light. Go two miles, turn left into Valley Park.

MUSEUM IN THE PARK: Check out the unique Museum in the Community, located in Valley Park in Hurricane. Call (304) 562-0484.

OTHER NIGHT-TIME ATTRACTIONS: One of the area's newest movie theaters is Teays Valley Cinemas, 170 Erskine Lane, Scott Depot. There's 10 screens and the theater also hosts birthday parties an hour before or after a movie in its party room. Call (304) 201-7469.

More Holiday Lights

WINTER WONDERLAND OF LIGHTS: Winter Wonderland of Lights Festival in Central Park in Ashland, Ky., with more than 50 light displays and 800,000 lights. Special events on weekends including Santa at the log cabin and Winter Wonderland Express train. Ice skating as well. Also, nearby is the Festival of Trees at the Paramount Arts Center. That runs for two weekends around Thanksgiving. Call (800) 377-6249. Go online at www.winterwonderlandoflights.com.

CHRISTMAS LIGHT SHOW AND DRIVE THRU: Point Pleasant. More than 3 million Christmas lights illuminate the West Virginia State Farm Museum. Every building, tree, shrub, fence and antique equipment are in lights. Admission is free but donations accepted. Hours are 6 p.m. to 9 p.m. Call the West Virginia Farm Museum at (304) 675-5737.

HOLIDAY IN THE PARK: Parkersburg, W.Va. Local businesses and individuals present this array of animated and still holiday light displays depicting Christmas. Hours are 6 p.m. to 11 p.m. Admission is free, but donations are accepted. Call (304) 424-8558.

THE WINTER FESTIVAL OF LIGHTS: Oglebay Resort and Conference Center, Wheeling. The nationally-known festival is viewable from dusk to 11 p.m. A per-car donation is requested. Trolley tours are also available throughout the evening. Call (800) 624-6988 or visit www.oglebay-resort.com.

WILDLIGHTS: Columbus Zoo, Powell, Ohio. More than 2 million twinkling lights illuminate your path at the Zoo. There's also an ice rink, Kwanzaa celebration and Ohio's largest ice festival. Go online at www.columbuszoo.org.

PNC FESTIVAL OF LIGHTS: Cincinnati Zoo and Botanical Gardens. More than 2.5 million twinkling lights and more than 50 light sculptures. Visit the ice-skating rink, holiday-themed shows and, of course, your favorite animal residents. Stop by and see Santa and his reindeer, grab a snack at Mrs. Claus' Cookie Kitchen and go on a virtual sleigh ride in the Zoo's wild motion theater. Go online at www.cincyzoo.org.

SOUTHERN LIGHTS STROLL: Kentucky Horse Park, 4089 Iron Works Parkway, just north of Lexington, Ky., has three miles of lights from Thanksgiving through the holidays. Call (800) 678-8813. Go online at kyhorsepark.com,

MOUNTAIN TOP LIGHTS: A spectacular display in a spectacular place, Breaks Interstate Park, in Elkhorn City, Ky., hosts Mountain Top Lights 6 to 10 p.m. nightly through the holidays. Call (800) 982-5122 or go online at www.breakspark.com.

BELPRE HOLIDAY LIGHTS DISPLAY: Belpre Parks and Business District, nearly 100 beautiful displays of lights during the holiday season and light on the bridges over the Ohio River at Belpre, Ohio, across from Parkersburg.

CHRISTMAS IN THE PARK: Thanksgiving through Jan. 1, a Christmas light display at dark until 10 p.m. nightly at Chief Logan State Park in Logan, W.Va. Call (304) 792-7125.

The Palace of Gold
Moundsville, West Virginia

As a couple that spent part of their honeymoon aboard the *Alexander Henry*, a retired ice cutter in Kingston, Ontario, it's safe to say the Lavender crew always has an eye out for someplace besides Motel 6 that will leave the light on for us.

Not that there's anything wrong with Motel 6, as Seinfeld would have said.

When a recent road trip caught us panhandling (rolling through one of those crazy chicken finger-like land masses attached to West Virginia's mid-section), we just couldn't pass up a chance to stay all night on the grounds of **Prabhupada's Palace of Gold**.

We heard about the Palace of Gold about five years ago when my wife, Toril, picked up a copy of Jeanne Mozier's must-have "Way Out in West Virginia" travel book at the Cathedral Cafe in Fayetteville.

Tossed on our "to-see" list of places in West Virginia that includes America's smallest chapel and largest teapot, the Palace of Gold is a true transcendental experience and the cheapest Indian vacation you'll ever enjoy. It's located about 12 winding miles south of I-70 near Wheeling.

Formed in 1968, this community called New Vrindaban was one of the largest of the Hare Krishna farm communities in the world. Though not in its heyday, the community is still standing. It had some serious trouble in the late 1980s and early 1990s that saw the community expelled from the international organization. Its leader, Bhaktipada, re-

Miles: 206

Original Trip June 2005

Filed "under you gotta see this," The Palace of Gold is a mouth-dropping place to see and a unique place to spend the night. We also check out Cabela's, an outdoors store rumored to be bigger than Pluto.

ceived a federal sentence for racketeering, and his henchmen were convicted of murder.

Today, there are still a few hundred devotees living on the premise and nearby. The community, recovering from bankruptcy, is open for folks to stop by and spend the night at the lodge (in hostel style settings) or to stay in one of the guest cabins that overlook the ponds.

After about seven hours on the road, an hour-long traffic jam around Pittsburgh and having come to the end of our sanity, we found the lush mountain-top retreat.

Shoving some fast-food bags under the front seat (this is an all-vegetarian community), we breathed a "finally-off-the-road" sigh of relief as we entered what truly is a world away.

We dropped our bags at our lodge room and set about to roam these exotic grounds echoing with the wild calls of peacocks that freely walk about the Hare Krishna community.

After the kids played on the playground, we walked to and admired the giant pink elephant and cow statues and strolled to the ponds rimmed by redwood cabins (also available for overnight rental) and to the boathouse, where the ritual swan boat rests between festivals.

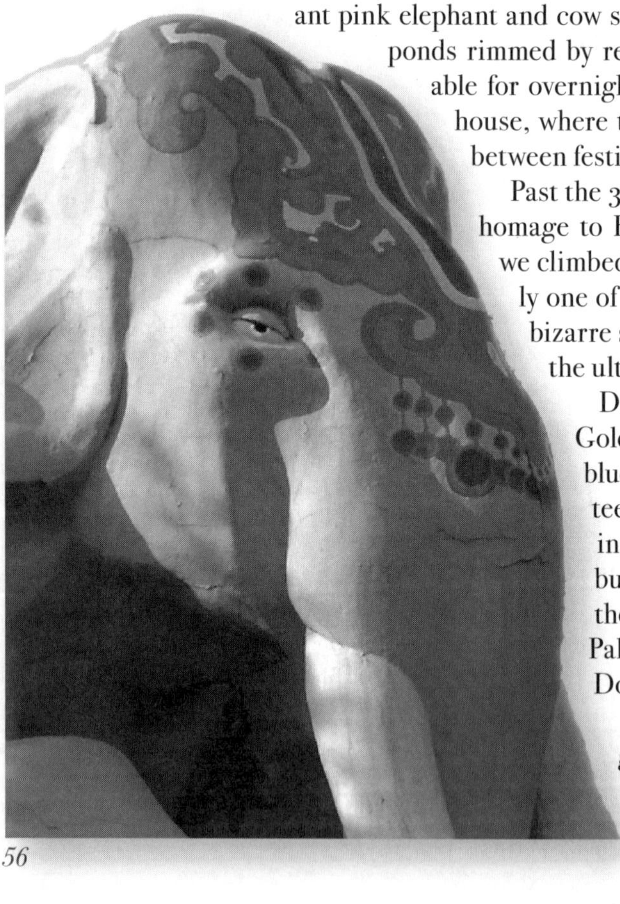

Past the 30-foot-tall statues paying homage to Hindu aspects of divinity, we climbed up the hill to what is truly one of the most spectacular and bizarre sites in West Virginia and the ultimate DIY project.

Described in the Palace of Gold book as "built without blueprints by young devotees reading DIY books and inspired by their desire to build a 'modest' home for their spiritual master," the Palace of Gold is modest like Donald Trump is humble.

The palace and its grounds are set high on a hilltop with a panoramic view of these beautiful layers of hills. It's easy to stay outside in the palace terraces and gardens that include great flower beds, including one of America's largest collections of miniature roses.

That said, it's also hard not to race for the doors of the palace.

Wearing covered slippers for our shoes and with a humble, humor-filled tour guide, we shuffled along, producing a constant surround sound of "whoas" and "wows" as we walked past the opulent splendor of the palace that has 35,000 feet of marble work with 50 varieties of marble, 18 murals in its dome depicting Krishna's pastimes (such as dancing with cowherd girls), a throne with a dome filled with more than 4,000 pieces of crystal, and lots and lots of gold.

With our eyes still in shock from seeing something akin to the Taj Mahal in West Virginia, we listened to the bullfrogs bring on the night before heading back down to the lodge, where we were treated to home-cooked vegetarian Indian dishes that included - for the boys - TVP burgers and fries.

With no TV, we read books and watched a wicked thunderstorm light up the night and send torrential rains.

In the morning, we rose recharged. The lodge manager apologized for the power outage and any inconvenience, and we thanked him for a wonderful visit to this beautiful and peaceful place.

With the power still off from the storm, we decided to visit one of the other wild places near Wheeling, the outdoors planet of Cabela's, located only about 15 miles and a world away from here.

If You Go: The Palace of Gold

GETTING THERE: From Wheeling, Take Exit #2, Bethlehem off of I-470. Turn left at the end of the exit ramp. Go 1/4 mile, and at Jays' Pharmacy and Sisson Motors, turn Right on 88 South. Go 9 miles until 88 dead ends at Route 250. Turn Left on 250 South. Go 1.5 miles. Look for sign on left that reads "Palace of Gold" Turn Left at that sign Go 5 miles, following the signs for the Palace of Gold.

GUIDED TOURS: You can tour the Palace of Gold year-round. Hours are 10 a.m. to 8 p.m. April through August and then 10 a.m. to 5 p.m. September through March. Cost is $6 and $3 for children 6 to 18. The tour is about 35 minutes long.

STAY THE NIGHT: Stay in a European style hostel (modest, clean and a shared bathroom) at this Hare Krishna community in the hills near Moundsville, W.Va. Stay in the Guest Lodge, and the Temple Lodge. Cost was $58 for a family of four to stay. There's also large and small cottages that rent nightly. They go for $100 and up. Call (304) 843-1600, ext. 102-107 or go online at www.palaceofgold.com.

OTHER COOL THINGS TO SEE NEARBY:

OGLEBAY: The more than 100-year-old Oglebay Resort and Conference Center has a little of everything from golf and tennis to even skiing and snowboarding in season. There's also The Good Zoo there as well. Call (800) 624-6988.

TOYS AND TRAINS: Kruger Street Toy and Train Museum, 144 Kruger St., is no secret as it has been featured on CNN and in *USA Today*. The museum is located in a restored Victorian school house. Call (304) 242-8133.

CABELA'S: This 175,000-square-foot retail store, located right off of I-70, is so much more with museum-quality animal displays, large aquariums, a full-service restaurant and educational, outdoors seminars on everything from deep-frying turkeys to tying flies. Call (304) 238-0120.

More Funky Places To Stay

OVERNIGHT GHOST HUNT: OK, you might not get much sleep, but there's some of you out there who would totally groove on an Overnight Ghost Hunt at the famous Ohio State Reformatory in Mansfield, Ohio. Cost is $50 and includes a late night dinner of pizza and soft drinks. Must be 21 and older to stay. The former prison has been in such films as "Shawshank Redemption." Call (800) 642-8282.

MOUNTAIN CREEK LODGE: Take a 3,600-foot aerial tram into the Bluestone Gorge at Pipestem Resort State Park in Pipestem, W.Va. The lodge has 30 rooms and is open May 1 through Oct. 31. Take your fishing rod and hiking boots; the lodge is right on the Bluestone River. There's also a nice dining hall and peace and quiet. Cost is about $77. Call (304) 466-1800 or go online at www.pipestemresort.com.

IN A CABOOSE: They don't take scrip, but you can stay overnight in a caboose, a company house or a wilderness cabin at Cass Scenic Railroad State Park in Cass, W.Va. Cass has three historic cabooses (from the 1920s and from the 1940s). Prices are $149 for the first night, plus train fare. Additional nights are $35. The train will uncouple the caboose then come back and get you the next day. Call (304) 456-4300 or go online at www.cassrailroad.com.

RAVENWOOD CASTLE AND MEDIEVAL VILLAGE: Ravenwood Castle near Hocking Hills in New Plymouth, Ohio, gives you the choices of everything from a gypsy wagon to the King Henry VIII Suite (which sleeps six) at the ivy-covered castle in the hills of Southern Ohio. Prices range from $45 to $220 for overnights. Go online at www.ravenwoodcastle.com or call (800) 477-1541.

THE YURT AT SALT CREEK: The Yurt at Salt Creek is a secluded, round canvas-cabin of sorts that is about a 15-minute drive from the heart of Hocking Hills. Cost is $50 per night on weekdays and $65 per night on weekends. Solar shower and two-night stay minimum. Call (614) 397-3422 or go online at www.1800hocking.com.

CCC CABINS: Several of the area state parks and forests have those vintage CCC-built rustic cabins. One of the closest places is Cabwaylingo State Forest. There are 13 standard cabins that start at $58 a night on weekends for two people. Call (304) 385-4255 or go online at www.cabwaylingo.com.

BOB EVANS FARM: Down on the Farm in Rio Grande, Ohio, Bob Evans does camping right. It's $4 a night for tents, and no burnt, bland eggs at the campsite? It's a short walk over to a Bob Evans Restaurant for breakfast. The 1,000-acre farm also has hiking trails, a craft barn, an 1800s village and a museum that tells the story of how Evans grew a tiny 12-seat diner into a restaurant chain. Call (800) 994-FARM or go online at www.bobevans.com.

HERITAGE FARM AND MUSEUM: Heritage Farm and Museum, 3300 Harvey Road, Huntington, has four log cabin homes that are bed and breakfast inns. Cost is $200 for weekend stays. Call (304) 522-1244.

New River Gorge
West Virginia

Enveloped by steep, green canopies of trees, clouds and the soothing surround sound of rippling water, Columbus resident Skip Clegg was overcome by the beauty of a summer Saturday in the New River Gorge.

"Look at the trees and the mountains," Clegg said to his 6-year-old daughter Morgan who was sitting in front of his two-person kayak on the Upper New River.

"Uh, I think I hear a waterfall," said a wide-eyed Morgan, wondering what adventures were to come.

Yes, Morgan there is a "waterfall."

It's called Surprise. More about that later.

With her 15 and 17-year-old sisters and the rest of the family tackling the famous raucous rapids of the Lower New, Morgan and her dad are part of a growing number of folks hopping in small rafts and inflatable kayaks (playfully called "duckies") and grabbing a great slice of summer splashing on the milder section of the New.

The back of Songer Whitewater's dust-covered school bus that takes you down to the river reads "Family Splashes to Big Water Bashes."

And indeed, the vast majority of the 200,000 commercial rafters are doing the latter – shooting the world-famous Class V rapids of the Gauley and New Rivers.

While back in the day, kids Morgan's age would have been left with grandma for a week-

Miles:

112

Original Trip

August

2006

The New River is one of the world's oldest rivers and one of the longest that's flowing south to north. Known for its wild whitewater on the Lower portion, we climb aboard a ducky (inflatable kayak) on the mild portion, the Upper, for a float that even 6-year-olds can do.

end of watching "Golden Girls" re-runs, grandma and adventurous kids like Morgan are now hitting the river, too.

The mild Upper New trips comprise about 15 percent of the business for the family-owned rafting company, Songer Whitewater, one of about 18 rafting companies.

Len Hanger, owner of Songer Whitewater, said that taking a wide range of folks on the milder portions of the whitewater rivers has grown nicely in the past 15 years.

"A neat thing that has been developing is we are seeing a lot more families and not just mom, dad and kids but they're bringing aunts, uncles and grandparents and it's really a way for them to spend the day together on the river," Hanger said.

In the spring when the New is rolling with a lot of water, the outfitters put in at McCreery and run the river down to Thurmond, where the National Park Service has a take-out and a seasonal visitor's center in the depot of the historic town that was used as Matewan in the John Salyes' film, "Matewan."

In the summer with lower water levels, outfitters put in at Thurmond (across the New from where the infamous 14-year poker game took place at the Dun Glen Hotel), and roll the river down to Cunard where you take out after hitting the only named rapid, the class III rapid, called Surprise.

With Toril and our littlest mancub, Will, (who was 4), doing a day-trip of play at nearby Summersville Lake and then a tram ride at Hawk's Nest State Park, I took Jake, 6, for his first whitewater experience.

A good swimmer and good little outdoorsman, I figured he was old enough to enjoy and soak in the "Almost Heaven" float from Thurmond on down the New.

Though it looks untouched now by human hands, the now federally protected New River Gorge had thousands of people living in the carved-out coal camps such as Brooklyn and Stone Cliff, mining towns that flourished from the 1870's into the 1960's.

Hanger, whose great-grandfather was a surveyor for the C&O Railroad in the Gorge in 1900, said for many of the older people who want to float the Upper New it is sometimes an emotional homecoming to float past the places their roots know.

"There are a lot of people whose families grew up in those coal mining communities in the Gorge and it is a part of our history in West Virginia," Hanger said. "I think it's something for people to say I went down and rafted from Prince and we went by Stone Cliff and Brooklyn and some of those communities where they or their families grew up."

With plenty of pools, or calm water, in between the spurts of small rapids, it is hard to stay "grown up."

The kid in everyone comes out as there is plenty of swimming and playing "king of the raft" (flipping over duckies and jumping on and trying to stay on longer than someone else). And, of course, there's always a stop to climb and then hop off "jump rock" into the water below.

"It's been a nice addition to our business and at the same time it is really offering families who have rafted the big water trips a way to share something with their families," Hanger said.

Although kindergarten age children can go on these Upper New trips, Hanger said they have never had to bring a child out that was scared or just throwing a fit, unhappy.

"I think for a 6-year-old they're ready if they can swim and if they are comfortable around the water and if they are a little adventuresome in hiking or on their bike," Hanger said. "They can go in a raft and get a feel for it and if they enjoy it then get the duckies on the next trip. Mostly we've found the children are more open than the parent is."

For the Lavender crew it ranks up there as one of our top adventures even if, like all the other duckies, we got slightly whitewater mauled; our boat flipped like a Waffle House pair of eggs, over easy, sunny side up.

"Let's do that again," Jake said when he got over the shock and got his breath.

"Oh, no," I said. "And you're toast if you tell Grandi or Mammaw about Surprise."

Even with a good flipping, it was priceless getting to share with Jake a trip on the whitewater, something I've been doing since my sister Jen actually found a college class in whitewater back in the '80's.

And Jake, he's now smart enough to ask if there will be any "Surprises" before we start any trip on water or land.

An insurance agent, Clegg said that even though his older teen daughters were tackling the rapids of the Lower New, he was apprehensive about taking Morgan, even though she's an adventurous spirit and a swim team member.

"As a dad sometimes you're scared to death because kids are going to get hurt," Clegg said. "But everything this place did made you feel safe and made it feel right. It was unbelievable. You have a hard time believing that God created something so beautiful."

If You Go: New River Gorge

DIRECTIONS: From Huntington, take I-64 east to Charleston and then I-77 south to Beckley. Go North up U.S. 19. You can also take U.S. 60 or The Midland Trail east out of Charleston. It's winding, but scenic and a wonderful drive along the Kanawha River and then up into the New River Gorge past such towns as Gauley Bridge and Ansted.

WHERE TO STAY: The New River Gorge is full of cabins and whitewater outfitters you can camp and stay with if you are taking a trip on the Upper or the Lower New River. Go online at www.wvriversports.com and click onto outfitters to get hooked up with one of West Virginia's professional whitewater outfitters and a place to stay. Also, Fayette County has six B&Bs and dozens of motels and hotels. Go online at www.visitwv.com for more info.

KID-FRIENDLY CAMPING: There's nearly two dozen different whitewater resorts but some have better kid-friendly camping set up. Songer Whitewater has "Family Camping" areas (with reasonable quiet hours) and has the region's only 18-hole disc golf course, which is free to play. Also, ACE Adventure Center in Oak Hill has a small lake, beach and lots of cool places for kids to play.

WHERE TO EAT: Pies and Pints Pizzeria, 103 1/2 Keller Ave., Fayetteville. Great pizza and Saranac root beer on draft. Call (304) 574-2200. Tamarack, the arts and craft Mecca located right off of I-77 in Beckley, also has a nice cafeteria-style dinner with such entrees as pan-seared trout. Call (304) 256-6843. Dirty Ernie's Rib Pit, 310 Keller Ave., Fayetteville. Good ribs and grub in a relaxing setting. Call (304) 574-4822. Cathedral Cafe, 134 S. Court St., Fayetteville. A local favorite for good reason. Located in a 100-year-old church. Call (304) 574-0202.

WHAT ELSE: Tons of great hiking, biking, fishing and outdoor recreation in the New River Gorge National River area. Be sure to check out the National Park Service sites at Canyon Rim (by the Gorge bridge) and Grandview for some spectacular views , great hiking and educational programs. Go online at www.nps.gov/neri for more info. Call (304) 456-0508.

PARK IT: lots of state parks in the region and in the surrounding mountains of Southern West Virginia. The closest to the Gorge is Babcock State Park in Clifftop, W.Va. Call (304) 438-3004. They've got hiking, swimming, horseback riding, and one of the most photographed sites in West Virginia – The Glade Creek Grist Mill.

DID YOU KNOW?: Fayetteville, W.Va. was named the "coolest small town in America" in 2006 by *Budget Travel*.

GOOD TIMES TO GO: New River Birding and Nature Festival in late April and early May; Daniel Vineyards Annual Wine Festival in mid June, John Henry Days Festival in mid July, Appalachian String Band Music Festival at Clifftop, W.Va., Bridge Day on the third Saturday in October and Hinton Railroad Days in mid October.

ON THE WEB: Go online at www.visitwv.com. Call (800) VISIT-WV.

Rolling on the Rivers

VALLEY GEM STERNWHEELER: Based out of Marietta, Ohio, this paddlewheel boat is docked in the 600 block of Front Street. Take a cruise on the Ohio River or one of the cruises up and down the Muskingum River. Special cruises include fall foliage, a fireworks dinner cruise and a tropical dinner cruise. Sternwheel Regatta is held each September. Call (740) 373-7862. Go online at www.valleygemsternwheeler.com.

GAULEY RIVER: One of the best two-day whitewater trips in the States, the fall release on the Upper and Lower sections of the Gauley River provides more than 100 rapids. Must be 16 or older and previous experience whitewater rafting is recommended, especially for the world-class Upper Gauley. There are nearly 20 outfitters in West Virginia that run the river. Go online at www.wvriversports.com.

COAL RIVER: The nationally recognized conservation group, The Coal River Group is literally "bringing life back to the Coal River." They've got a big group float each summer and have marked more than 30 public access sites in Boone, Lincoln and Kanawha Counties for day and overnight canoe trips on your own. Go online at www.coalrivergroup.com to see the maps of the Walhonde Water Trail.

HOCKING RIVER: A couple canoe liveries including the Hocking Valley Canoe Livery operate on the Hocking River near Logan, Ohio, and the Hocking Hills region, located northeast of Athens, Ohio. Check out special floats including full moon floats. Call (800) 686-0386.

NEW RIVER JETBOATS: Tickets sold at Hawks Nest State Park in Ansted, W.Va. The New River Jetboats give folks a ride on the "Miss M. Rocks," a 21-foot covered jetboat that roars back up the New for six miles (about 30 minutes) to the New River Gorge Bridge. Cost is about $18 for adults and $7 for children (5 to 16). Call (800) CALL-WVA and ask for Hawks Nest.

STERNWHEEL REGATTAS: The region is flush with summertime sternwheel regattas that take place in Charleston and Point Pleasant, W.Va., as well as Pomeroy and Marietta, Ohio. All are good for catching a sternwheel ride. If you're brave enough you can do the "Anything That Floats" race at the Charleston Sternwheel Regatta. Go online at www.sternwheelregatta.com.

Morgantown
West Virginia

Two days before I was born, my folks bought a brand new eggshell blue Volkswagen Beetle to bring their new son home in.

It seems I have been on the road ever since, so you think I would have this day trippin' thing down to a science.

Tell that to my pants.

Not a half hour into our latest trip (and while vigorously taking a screwdriver to a malfunctioning kid's toy on my lap), I had forgotten about my coffee. It fell over, forming the newest lake in West Virginia on me and my seat.

Although cussing came to mind, what this highly embarrassed and wet adult really needed that Mother's Day weekend was a hug. Yes, and dry pants.

With my mom too far away at that point, we opted for the next best thing, a side trip on our road to Morgantown to Grafton, home to the International Mother's Day Shrine and the beautiful 1,740-acre **Tygart Lake State Park (304-265-6144)**.

It was here in Grafton that Anna Reeves Jarvis paid respect to her mama (a Sunday School teacher for 20 years) by handing out 500 white carnations at the first official Mother's Day service at Andrews Methodist Church on May 10, 1908.

Miles: 227

Original Trip May 2005

Motown (Morgantown) is a great college town to explore when the bulk of the students are away. We roll along the river, at the conservancy, and, of course, ride Motown's super cool PRT.

Two years later, Mother's Day became official in West Virginia, and in 1914 the holiday went nationwide.

On a quiet Friday afternoon with a panoramic view of Tygart Lake from the lodge, we found the spirit of Jarvis very much alive. Some of the best homemade chicken noodle soup I have ever tasted was on the menu and was gobbled up by all of the Lavender crew.

Filled with this warm shot of chicken soup for the soul, the sun shining and the radio dialed up to the local K-Love station pumping contemporary Christian tunes, we hit 310N to stop by **Valley Falls State Park (304-367-2719)** located about seven miles south of Fairmont.

There's 18 miles of trails here, a popular whitewater run for hard boaters, a playground and great picnic spots at this quiet, off-the-beaten path, day-use park that is filled with cascades.

Since these are a bit off the path, travelers to Morgantown wanting a quicker picnic stop are blessed with a string of Mountain Lake choices right off of I-79 including Sutton, Burnsville and Stonewall Jackson lakes.

Back to the mission at hand, the Lavender crew - with a Marshall University and West Virginia University football series ready to roll in 2006 - were in Motown Mother's Day weekend to scout around and bring the love from H-town.

Hooking up with one of Toril's good buddies from the MOMS Club, Chris Knapp and her crew (husband Pete and sons Petey and John), we got the grand tour of a great college town.

With the campus being evacuated for the summer, this is prime time for day trippers to check out such great (but normally clogged) college towns in the region, such as Morgantown and Athens, Ohio (home to Ohio University).

Filled with funky shops, cheap eats, tons of trails and lots of art and entertainment, these towns are ripe for the picking this time of year.

Like H-town, Morgantown has a river running through it. **The Mon River Trails Conservancy (www.montrails.org)** shows the love with 46 miles of rail trails that include the Mon River/Caperton and the Deckers Creek Rail Trail.

You can bring a bike, rent one on the path downtown or just take an evening stroll on the eight miles of paved trail between Motown and Star City along the Monongahela River.

After a stroll, we jumped into one of half a dozen wing joints in town, Wings Ole, where a mere $35 fed a crew of four adults and four little guys.

If you're hanging with the SpongeBob-watching crowd, it takes all of five seconds in Motown to discover the Personal Rapid Transit System, which was the first totally automated computer-operated transportation system in the world.

For 50 cents, these electric mini-cars which seat eight people (and more standing) shuttle you from downtown to several stops on campus (including the stadium) on elevated tracks.

Built as a joint project of the U.S. Department of Transportation and WVU's Engineering School in the late 1970's, the PRT is a great way to buzz across campus and is a cheap "tourist railroad" of sorts for kids.

We got off the PRT at the Engineering College at the Evansdale Campus, gave a swoop of the pirate hats to the innovative young engineers of yesteryear and tromped down the hill, admiring the sculptures outside the Creative Arts Center, before crossing the street and stepping into another campus treasure.

Core Arboretum (304-293-5201), established in 1948, is a 91-acre wooded wonderland tucked between the river and Monongahela Boulevard (one of the main drags through campus).

Used for research and study, the Arboretum has three miles of trails that are a good distance for families and that are filled with hundreds of species of West Virginia native plants, trees and wildlife.

Back to the wildlife in downtown, Morgantown offers some unique tastes,

including the West Virginia Brewing Company, the Glasshouse Grille, the original Boston Beanery and the Mountain People's Kitchen and Co-op (for the vegetarian in the crew).

We gave two (very sticky) thumbs up to the sinful delights inside **Cold Stone Creamery, 256 High St. (304-292-2653)**, where you can get just about any legal - and sweet - items (such as M&Ms and graham cracker pie crust) pounded into your already creamy and good ice cream on the "cold stone." Cold Stone Creamery also can be found in Huntington at Pullman Square.

The sizes are "like it," "love it" and "gotta have it." The prices start at $1.99 for kids' creations and go on up. We didn't dare ask about the calorie

count (which would probably mean a trek all the way back to H-town to walk it off).

With the sticky sweetness of Cold Stone as a fond remembrance, we savored our May visit to Motown, which was voted as the No. 3 Best Small Town in America in 2004 by *Men's Journal.*

Like a bigger and older brother to Marshall, this fine college town housing WVU has got some cool things figured out, like lots of bike and walkways and information kiosks around town telling visitors what downtown offers.

To use a little Cold Stone reference, it would be great to see progressive ideas like these scooped up and worked into Huntington's already sweet offerings.

If You Go: Morgantown

GOOD TIMES TO GO: Obviously any MU-WVU game will be a great time to hit Motown, but there are also a few festivals and events worth making the trip: the Old Morgantown Glass Show each June; the West Virginia Public Theatre Season that runs June and July; The Sunshine Daydreams music festivals that run some weekends June through August; WV Mountainfest Motorcycle Rally, each July; and the Arts and River Festival on the Mon, each August.

IN THE AREA: There are some great outdoors destinations to check out in the area, not the least of which is West Virginia's largest state forest, Cooper's Rock at Bruceton Mills, W.Va. Go online at www.coopersrockstateforest.com. It's located just a few minutes east of the city on I-68 East, is right off the interstate and is a must-see. Also, the Cheat River is nearby for whitewater enthusiasts. Call Cheat River Outfitters at (888) 99-RIVER or go online at www.cheatriveroutfitters.com.

PARKING: Morgantown is serious with a capital T for Towing and Tickets. They even charge a $7.50 fine for backing into a parking spot and for going over the yellow line. Park smart and try to find a garage downtown to tie up your ride.

COOL DINING: The Glass House Grille, 7056 Beechurst Ave., is located in the restored Seneca Glass Company factory. Call (866) 266-9744.

ON THE WEB: Check out more about Morgantown and all over West Virginia online at West Virginia Division of Tourism site: www.callwva.com or call (800) 458-7373 to get a free travel guide to Morgantown from the Greater Morgantown Convention and Visitors Bureau.

ALONG THE WAY: Valley Falls State Park, located about seven miles south of Fairmont, offers 18 miles of trails, a popular whitewater run for hard boaters, a playground, great picnic spots and, of course, scenic views of cascades.

More Cool College Towns

ATHENS: About an hour and a half from Huntington, Athens, Ohio, is a funky and family-friendly college city where "Adventure Happens." That's their motto and it's true even when it's not Halloween. Check out one of the region's coolest skateparks and bike trails. Go online at www.athensohio.com.

BEREA: One of the only colleges in America where all the students work for the school in exchange for tuition, Berea College has put its open-minded stamp on the city ever since it was founded in 1855 as the first interracial and co-educational college in the South. About two hours southwest from Huntington, Berea, the folk arts and craft capitol of Kentucky, continues to be an inspiration with sustainable living practices as a model for the way life, colleges and cities could be. Call (800) 598-5263.

CHARLESTON: OK, it's more suits and lawmakers than students in flip flops, but University of Charleston knows how to rev it up. The campus pops to life every June for the FestivALL Charleston. The lawn at UC hosts Blues, Brews & BBQ and Wine And All That Jazz on back-to-back nights. Catch the river taxi at Haddad Riverfront Park for great nights of national-act jazz and blues. Go online at www.festivallcharleston.com.

MEMPHIS: Now that Marshall is in C-USA, Memphis, the Mississippi Riverside town all smoked up with the blues and BBQ, is a new road-trip option. Of course, when you get down in the music joints of a remarkably refurbished Beale Street, and up in the alley at The Rendezvous (where they've been smoking the cue since 1948) you might forget all about the game. Families, be sure to check out the Children's Museum and the Memphis Zoo as well. Go online at www.memphisite.com.

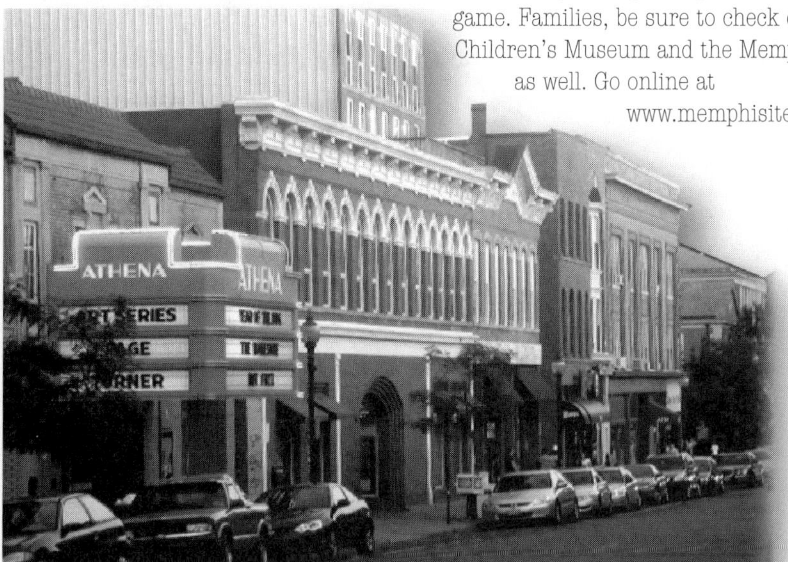

Mountain Stage on The Road

Beckley, West Virginia

It seemed like one of those teachable moments.

The "Mountain Stage" crew was flying about plugging in this, grabbing and whisking away that, and getting the next band ready to take to the air, when I leaned over to our 3 1/2-year-old and slowly whispered, "They are taping this, and people can hear this later all over the world on the radio."

Miles: 115

Original Trip November 2003

Jacob's face looked blank, but then he shot back, "I know that."

OK, knee-high, smarty pants but maybe somebody else would like to know - or at least be reminded - that the longest running live performance public radio program in the country – "Mountain Stage" – is recorded on many given Sundays just a short drive away at the Cultural Center Theater in Charleston.

Or as was the case that Sunday at a beautiful spot somewhere in the Mountain State.

With the temperatures in the low 80s, one good glow-stick left from trick-or-treat, and "Mountain Stage" landing a hillbilly deluxe show (featuring Doyle Lawson and Quicksilver, Natalie MacMaster, Jim Costa, bohola and Gandydancer) at Tamarack, the Dave Trippin' wagon fired back up and hit a weekend of camping, hiking and gorging on great music, weather and grub down in Fayette County.

For those not familiar with the Mountain State's coolest musical export, nearly 197,000 fans tune into "Mountain Stage" on 94 public radio stations across the United States while Voice of America's Music Mix satellite service airs "Mountain Stage" in 46 countries.

It's nothing but fun to see a Mountain Stage live taping on the road. We catch up with the Mountain Stage family at Tamarack, the mothership of WV arts and crafts.

"Mountain Stage" - which has hosted such artists as R.E.M, Los Lobos, Alison Krauss, Phish, Wilco, The Indigo Girls, Norah Jones and Ali Farka Toure - is also seen on more than 200 public television stations, including eight of the Top 10 U.S. markets.

In fact, Mountain Stage, which has been on TV since 2001, debuted several great shows in 2007 in high-def including national specials to celebrate the 75th anniversary of the Bristol Sessions as well as a program celebrating the legacy of the Guthrie Family.

With ticket prices feverishly low (they start at $10.50 in advance for some shows), the live shows are an inexpensive and real musical treat, since the shows are filled with five musical acts that each play a half dozen or so original songs whose flavors run the gamut and the globe.

"Mountain Stage," which first went on the air in December 1983, tapes 26 shows a year with heavy scheduling in October and November, again in February and March and usually in the month of August, says executive producer Andy Ridenour.

Most of those are recorded at the Cultural Center Theater at the Capitol Complex in Charleston. Several times each year, though, Mountain Stage goes on the road to share the fun and spread the word on visits that have included Boston, San Diego, Kerrville, TX (Kerrville Folk Festival), Winnipeg (Winnipeg Folk Festival), Boise, Charleston, S.C. (Piccolo Spoleto Festival), Walt Disney World, Washington, D.C.,and Toronto.

In the region, Mountain Stage has taped shows regularly in most of West Virginia's cities (including Morgantown and Huntington) as well as regular tapings in Athens, Ohio, and at resorts such as Snowshoe and Class VI River Runners.

For newcomers, Ridenour and host and musical director Larry Groce make the crowd at home explaining the show's quirks before the show starts.

"Once we start, there is no intermission - just sneak out and back in," Groce said. "There's no pauses."

While on radio the show runs exactly 1:58; live it usually runs about two hours and 15 to 20 minutes. Although Tamarack with its Greenbrier-trained chefs was certainly the exception, there's no food or concession stand at the Cultural Center Theater.

Ridenour always warms up the audience, something he said he picked up in the early days of "Mountain Stage" from Lewisburg resident Johnny Olson, who was the announcer for "Let's Make a Deal" and Jackie Gleason's TV shows.

"Is anybody here from outside West Virginia?" Ridenour asked the sell-out

crowd of 500 inside Tamarack's new Conference Center that Sunday. "Ohio? That's not out of state. ... Sweden? What county is that in?"

It is that living room feel from Ridenour and then Groce, a Grammy-nominated artist who has sold more than 10 million records himself, and the 20 or so folks it takes to put on a "Mountain Stage" show, that put audience and artists at ease.

Layered with some of the best music anywhere, that vibe creates magical moments at the live tapings, such as roaring standing ovations for the crisp four-part harmonies of Quicksilver to "Mountain Stage" band vocalist Julie Adams getting lost in the music, dancing up a storm beside the stage to Gandydancer's set-closing romp, "Looking for the Bully of the Town," at Tamarack before she stepped on stage with the band to sing a tune by West Virginia songwriter Colleen Anderson.

Since they don't Ted Nugent you with the volume, since they keep ticket prices so low, since they don't sell big gulps of beer and since the start time is a kid-friendly 7 p.m., "Mountain Stage" has always been a draw for families who can't afford the $45 average concert ticket but who can pluck down $12 to $15 for richer, deeper roots music.

At the Tamarack show, Megan Jeffus and her mother, Bev Seale, brought Megan's 2-year-old, Tobias, and 3-month-old, Willow. Megan was surprised at the number of children at the show in an audience that looked to range from about 3 months to 90.

Jeffus, who grew up in the live music rich city of Austin, Texas, said it was a real treat to get to go to her first "Mountain Stage" show since moving to West Virginia.

"It's really nice to be here and to feel it and to hear the audience respond to it," Jeffus said. "There are very few radio shows out there for the people that make a difference."

If You Go

WHAT IT IS: Started up in 1983, Mountain Stage, celebrating 25 years in 2008, is one of the longest-running music programs on radio. Distributed by Public Radio International®, XM Satellite Radio and on Voice of America's Satellite Service, it's heard weekly 'round the world by hundreds of thousands of listeners. Since 2001, Mountain Stage has also been shown on more than 200 PBS stations around the country.

CATCH IT LIVE: Catch a "Mountain Stage" show in person at the Cultural Center Theater at the State Capitol Complex in Charleston at the corner of Greenbrier and Washington streets. Mountain Stage tapes about 26 new shows each year. Some of those are road shows all over the United States, from Smokey's On the Gorge in Lansing W.Va., and the Paramount theaters in Ashland, Ky., and Bristol, Tenn., to Town Hall in New York City.

GETTING TO THE CULTURAL CENTER: From Huntington, take I-64 east to Charleston, and take Exit 99 off of I-77/I-64. Normally, box office opens at 6 p.m., doors at 6:30 p.m. and show at 7 p.m. (which is a new start time as of 2008).

TICKETS: Tickets are usually $10.50 in advance and $15 at the door unless otherwise noted. The price goes up with a really big national act on the bill. Call 1-800-594-TIXX (8499) or go online at www.mountainstage.org.

IF YOU GO: Remember there's no food concessions at Mountain Stage. The show usually runs about 2 1/2 hours and there's no stopping the show once it starts. There's normally five acts that play about half a dozen songs or so. The show is boiled down to the two-hour radio show which usually airs a few weeks after it is recorded.

SOME PAST GUESTS HAVE INCLUDED: Martina McBride, Phish, Muzikas (Hungary), Sarah McLachlan (Canada), Buddy Guy, Ali Farka Toure (Mali), The Neville Brothers, The Kronos Quartet, Bill Monroe, Barenaked Ladies (Canada), Randy Newman, Chucho Valdes (Cuba), Ralph Stanley, John Cale, Wilco, The Indigo Girls, Joan Baez, Lucinda Williams, Joshua Redman, Loudon Wainwright III, Bruce Hornsby, Norah Jones, Los Lobos and R.E.M. have been featured. West Virginia artists who have appeared include Kathy Mattea, Melvin Wine, Tim and Mollie O'Brien, Nat Reese, Gandydancer and Brad Paisley.

More Live Radio Shows

FUR PEACE RANCH: Rock and Roll Hall of Fame member Jorma Kaukonen's Fur Peace Ranch in Darwin, Ohio (just north of Pomeroy, Ohio, hosts rootsy concerts that are taped for Ohio University public radio (WOUB-FM, Athens). Check out such artists as G.E. Smith, Roger McGuinn, and of course, the legendary guitarist Kaukonen with a host of friends including Hot Tuna. Go online at www.furpeaceranch.com or (740) 992-6228.

WOODSONGS OLD-TIME RADIO HOUR: Folk singer Michael Johnathon's Woodsongs Old-Time Radio Hour is taped live at the Kentucky Theatre, 214 Main St., in downtown Lexington, Ky. The Americana-style radio show is heard around the world on public radio, XM Satellite Radio and online. Doors open at 6:30 p.m. Show at 7 p.m. Tickets are usually $10 and $5 students. Concert lasts about an hour and 15 minutes. Go online at www.woodsongs.com.

AMERICANA CROSSROADS: Only taped a few times a year, Americana Crossroads is a roots music program recorded by Morehead State Public Radio, WMKY-FM, 90.3. Doors open at 6:30 p.m. Music at 7 p.m. Admission is $5 or $20 for a family pack of five. Children 12 and under get in free. Shows are taped at the Morehead Conference Center in downtown Morehead Ky. (an hour west of Huntington). Call (800) 286-9659.

THE DAWG'S SATURDAY NIGHT JAMBOREE: A radio revival of the original Saturday Night Jamboree, WDGG-FM, 93.7-FM tapes a number of live concerts a year at the Jean Carlo Stephenson Auditorium at Huntington City Hall. Concerts are usually mixed with gospel, bluegrass and country. They also play shows around the region. Go online at www.saturdaynightjamboree.com and www.wdgg.fm.

BLUEGRASS SHOWDOWN: D28 + 5, the long-running Sunday afternoon bluegrass show on WOUB-FM, Athens, Ohio (Ohio University Public Radio) hosts a live bluegrass and/or old-time concert on the first Sunday of each month (except holiday weekends) at the Front Room in Baker Center on the Ohio University campus. The show is broadcast live on the air at 1 p.m., but you can attend in person. There is no admission charge. The new Baker University Center is located at the junction of Mulberry Street, Court Street, and Park Place. Go online at www.woub.org.

AMERICA'S BLUEGRASS: The nationally syndicated radio show and TV show America's Bluegrass tapes its TV programs live about three times a year, usually at the Paramount Arts Center in Ashland, Ky. The TV show is then aired later on WSAZ-Newschannel 3 and statewide on KET in Kentucky. Go online at www.amerricasbluegrass.com for more info about live tapings.

Snowshoe
West Virginia

Miles: 238

Original Trip December 2005

We go poking around Pocahontas County and explore the wild and wonderful village of Snowshoe Mountain. Thanks to Split Rock Pools, some killer barbecue, skiing out our back door, and fun under the Big Top.

As we tiptoed toward Christmas in mid-December, the weather forecast couldn't have been any better.

The winter weather advisories blared across the channels, sending folks frantically scurrying to the grocery stores to line their carts with all the eggs, milk and bread they could carry (an occurrence we call the French Toast Syndrome).

But once again, we lowlanders here in the Ohio River and Kanawha River valleys got nothing but the cold spittle of winter rain.

Jonesing for a snowflake blast, we loaded up the Dave Trippin' sleigh with some dusty skis – and at least one pair of matching mittens – and blasted off east toward the Potomac Highlands.

Now, it's a well-known fact that folks like to come to West Virginia to ski.

Last season, more than 850,000 skiers carved the powder at West Virginia's five ski resorts, but few of those folks were actually from West Virginia.

In fact, more folks from Florida come up to ski at **Snowshoe Mountain** than do people from West Virginia.

And while my idea of winter sports has often meant roping up an inner tube to the back of an ATV and ripping through an inch or less of snow, I was determined to get our Griswold family a good taste of the wild and wonderful winter sports in the state.

Since **Winterplace**, the closest ski resort to Huntington at two hours away (just south of Beckley), was just in the process of opening, we decided to roll the four hours over to the **Potomac Highlands**. That is where you can hit **Timberline** and **Canaan Valley**, just north of Elkins, and Snowshoe Mountain, south of Elkins.

As it does anytime you roll through the majestic mountains of West Virginia, the drive alone sent spirits skyward.

While Ricky Skaggs and Tim O'Brien took CD turns wearing out the mandolin, our trusty Saturn galloped over the majestic hills of Interstate 79 as snow began to pour. We caught a sighting of that rare winter beast, the snowplow.

Juiced by the increasing winter wonderland, we rushed onward and upward over east through Elkins and then down Route 219 to Snowshoe Mountain, where in the past 10 years Intrawest has been dropping coin (about $200 million) like P. Diddy drops names.

Asleep about half the trip, our 5-year-old son Jake woke up just as we were driving into the super-sized mountaintop resort and added a well-stated, "Wowie, kazowie," and "Holy smokes."

Dropping the bags at one of the hotel rooms in Snowshoe's mountaintop Village, we roamed what reminded me of a Swiss town and got into a raging snowball fight on a big pile of snow on the brick streets before retreating to Foxfire Grille that promised "Views, Blues and BBQ."

It more than delivered all three, and at Applebee's-like prices.

Of course, we were just thankful to be inside for a spell, because the temperature outside at 4,848-feet-or-so was a brisk 12 degrees.

After loading up on the deep-fried pickles and sampling five barbecue sauces from across the South, we figured we better get some exercise.

Why not some outdoor swimming?

Built just a few years ago, **Split Rock Pools** is an indoor/outdoor water park that's free for guests and open until 10 p.m.

Our little fellows, Jake and Will, flipped for the indoor slides, fountains and giant water bucket. Like us, they were mesmerized by the otherworldly experience of swimming under a divider and into the outdoor heated pool, where steam rose to meet the moon. Coldplay's "Rush of Blood to the Head" came pouring out of pool-side speakers and where we felt like we were exploring a galaxy far, far away from Huntington.

The next day, my wife Toril took to the slopes since she grew up in Syracuse (200 inches of snow annually) and learned to ski soon after she could walk.

Meanwhile back on the bunny slope Skidder, I (hillbilly Dave) somehow managed several hours of swooshing without falling and hurting anyone else, or any of my own tender parts, and praised Jake's first forays into skiing that were about as graceful as Disney's Goofy.

Working up the appetite of a family of grizzlies, we made tracks to the newest family friendly playground, of sorts, at Snowshoe: the just-opened 15,000-square-foot **Big Top**, located adjacent to the pub and restaurant-filled **Shavers Centre**.

Inside the sprung structure of the Big Top, we scarfed some pizza then headed for the smorgasbord

of fun, diving into everything from some of the 60 arcade games to ping pong and the Eurobungy (imagine jumping on a trampoline but being suspended by giant rubber bands).

The family-friendly touches on the mountain make taking little kids skiing not easy (unless you really enjoy dressing and undressing wee tots in five layers) but definitely manageable and a heck of a lot of fun.

After more skiing and fun on the mountain, it was time to wrangle off the boys' snow gear (something akin to calf roping and wrestling). We opted to make a dinner run to **Wildcat Provisions**, for sandwiches, a movie rental and snacks.

While you can get as fancy as you want at Snowshoe, there's also a wide range of places to eat and stay that don't require a family on a budget to leave the youngest child behind to do dishes until spring.

In the morning, we hopped across the Village bricks and into the **Starbucks**, which sports an indoor and outdoor gas fireplace that makes for a cozy stop to get stoked on the bean before or after you hit the slopes.

After scraping off the windshield with the working end of Scoop, a Bob the Builder toy fished in desperation out of the back seat, I could see clearly now.

Flipping on the radio and getting a surprising homegrown dose of classic rock from the Tri-State-based WRYV-FM, 101.5, I had to again agree with Jake who said, "Let's come here another day" and "Let's put this on the West Virginia map."

Right on, little man. Let's do that.

Maybe we didn't carve up the double black diamonds like Bodie Miller, but we can't let those Palm Beachers have all the mountain-grown fun right in our own back yard.

If You Go: Snowshoe

WINTER KIDS PROGRAM: West Virginia's ski resorts have kids programs to help children enjoy the slopes. Snowshoe has Kids World for ages 4 up to 12. Costs for the full day program are about $90 (lunch included) and $60 for half-days.
BABYSITTING SERVICES: The ski resorts in West Virginia have child care services to help parents get a day out on the slopes. Prices at Snowshoe are $12 hourly (two-hour minimum) at Snowshoe Area, and $15 an hour at Silver Creek Area at Snowshoe.
TUBE IT: So you can't ski, so what. Each of West Virginia's ski resorts has tubing parks including Winterplace, which has the state's largest tubing area, and Canaan Valley, which just added airboarding. Find out more info at www.callwva.com and click on Skiing.
BEYOND THE SLOPES: There's also a wide variety of fun things to do with the kids off the slopes. At Snowshoe, you can enjoy horse-drawn sleigh rides, snowmobiling, snowshoeing, snowcat tours, dining, Split Rock Pools, the family-fun center called Big Top (home to an arcade and movie nights) and much more.
A GOOD TIME TO GO: Check out some of the great weekend deals and special events at West Virginia's ski resorts online at www.herald-dispatch.com. Click on Entertainment and then Outdoors.
ON THE WEB: Go online at www.wvwintersports.com. The West Virginia Ski Areas Association web sites are www.goskiwv.com and www.westvirginiaski.com.

More Places For a Natural High

VIA FERRATA IN THE GORGE: Torrent Falls Family Climbing Adventure, Campton, Ky., in the Red River Gorge. Open 9 a.m. until dusk daily. Torrent Falls is one of the first European style via ferrata or iron path rock climbing centers in the United States. Climbing rates are $29 and $26 for ages 10 to 18. Call (606) 668-6613 or go online at www.torrentfalls.com.

PINNACLE ROCK: At Pinnacle Rock State Park, located off of U.S. 52, near the Virginia border, near Bramwell, W.Va., take stone stairs up the mountain for a glorious panoramic view of the world below this sandstone outcropping that sits 3,100-foot above sea level. Call (304) 248-8565.

BALD KNOB VIA CASS: Get a great view the easy way, by letting the locomotive do all the work. Cass Scenic Railroad offers trips up to Bald Knob which, at an elevation of 4,842 feet, is the second highest point in West Virginia. Located 11 miles up the mountain from Cass, the train ride round-trip takes five hours. The Bald Knob area has a spectacular view from atop the overlook where you can see into two states. The train will stop at Whittaker station. Call (304) 456-4300.

ROCK CLIMBING TOWER: By reservation, the Tri-State Area Council Climbing Program at Camp Arrowhead in Ona, W.Va., is open to in-council troops ($17 a person); out-of-council troops ($25) and non-scouting groups ($35). There must be a minimum of eight climbing participants and no more than 24. Call (304) 523-3408.

BY HOT AIR BALLOON: Since 1978, you've been able to catch a hot air balloon ride with Fox Fire Balloon Promotions. Catch a ride at Foxfire Resort in Milton, W.Va. Hot air balloon flights usually last about 1 hour or more. Gift certificates are available. Costs start at $250 for one person. Call (304) 743-4588.

GRANDVIEW: The Grandview area of the New River Gorge National River is so well named. Get panoramic views of the upper New River near Beckley. The park is open year-round but the visitors centers at both Thurmond Depot and Grandview operate seasonally from Memorial Day to Labor Day. Thurmond Depot's seasonal hours are 10 a.m. to 5 p.m. Grandview is open seasonally noon to 5 p.m.

ROTARY PARK TOWER: Climb up into the tower at Rotary Park in Huntington for a great view of Huntington's east end. Go online at www.ghprd.org.

Kentucky

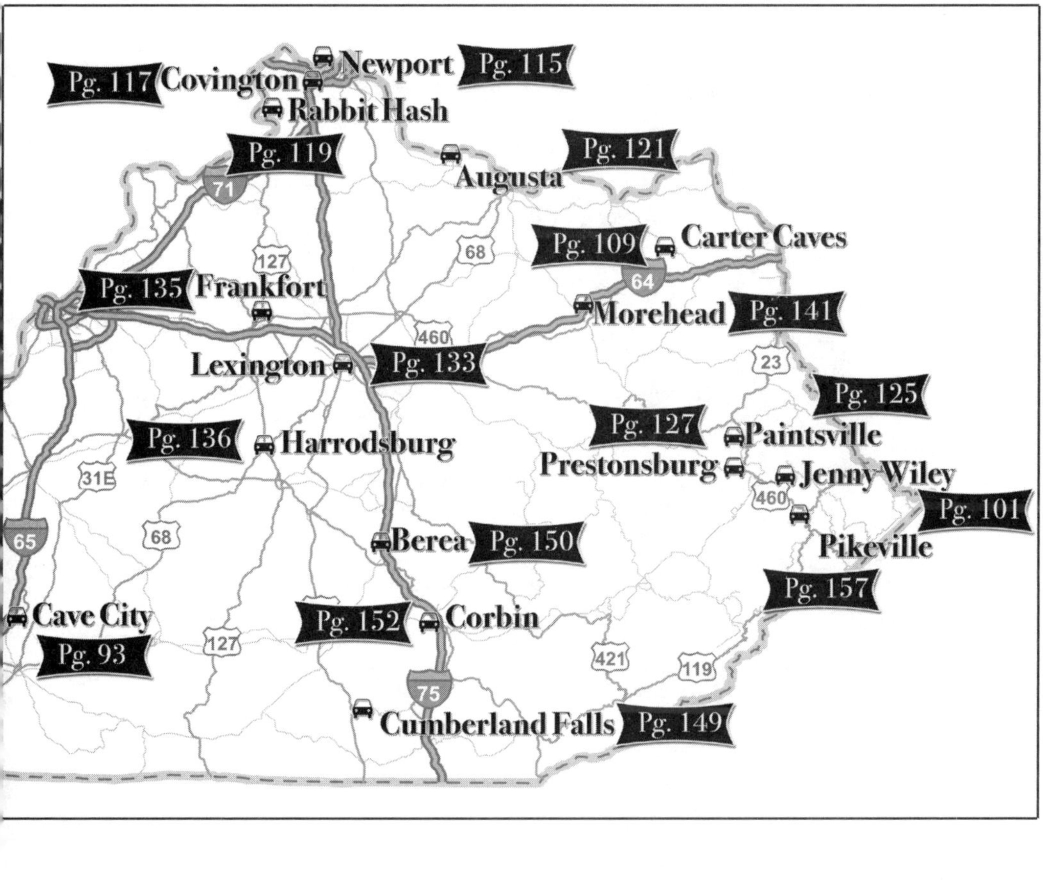

Pg. 117 Covington
Newport Pg. 115
Rabbit Hash
Pg. 119
Pg. 121
Augusta
71
127
68
Pg. 109
Carter Caves
64
Pg. 135 Frankfort
Morehead Pg. 141
460
Lexington
Pg. 133
23
Pg. 125
Pg. 127
Paintsville
Pg. 136
Harrodsburg
Prestonsburg
Jenny Wiley
31E
460
Pg. 101
65
68
Berea Pg. 150
Pikeville
Pg. 157
Cave City
Pg. 93
Pg. 152
Corbin
127
421
119
75
Cumberland Falls
Pg. 149

Cave City
Kentucky

Miles: 250

Original Trip January 2005

The Dave Trippin' crew gets a little lost in time, in Cave City, Ky., home to the world's longest cave system, fields full of dinosaurs and a place where you can stay in a wigwam village.

Last year, I was trying to hang on and hold out. Hoping to get a couple of weeks off during summer, I didn't take much of a break during winter and spring.

By the time I zombied into summer, my mind, spirit and body had the consistency of a McDonald's french fry forgotten under the heat lamp.

Not this year.

When we heard one of our good buddies was going to be playing in the International Blues Challenge in Memphis, we knew we had to be on the bricks of Beale.

And like anyone who travels with kids and relishes some sanity, we also eyeballed a good halfway point that would make a refreshing stop on the way up and back.

Located just under four hours from Huntington, Cave City, Ky., is that and more. It is home to **Mammoth Caves National Park (270-758-2180)**, the world's longest cave system at 365 miles and counting, since the surrounding counties in this karst topography are thought to hold as many as 800 caves.

Not a bad place to hang out and hide out.

Like Niagara Falls (also a day's drive from Huntington), Mammoth Caves dates back to one of the first vacation destinations in the United States – and for good reason.

The park is home to 14 cave tours that explore about 10 miles of the cave open to the public, not to mention 53,000 acres above ground with some really neat hiking, biking, and canoeing .

Like many longtime natural tourist stops, an odd collection of attractions (wax museums, alpine slides and wildlife museums) have sprung up around Mammoth Caves, making it a fairly inexpensive but diverse destination spot for spring breaks or for a long weekend.

With two critters in the middle of their peak dinosaur years (ages 3 and 5), we figured we'd better go straight to **Dinosaur World (270-773-4345)**.

Located a stone's throw off of Exit 53 of I-65, the recently developed Dinosaur World is an outdoor and indoor museum whose calling card is a ½-mile trail filled with more than 100 life-size dinosaur models.

After being in the car for a couple of hours, the boys got out on the trail and hit a full sprint.

Placed chronologically, the dinosaurs pretty quickly start towering over you. It's hard not to feel very humbled, since our species would have been nothing more than a chicken wing on a buffet if the dinosaurs had survived.

Thank God and good meteorites for extinction!

Although I don't care for many things located right off interstates, the constant roar of the 18-wheelers and swiftly rolling clouds seemed to bring the giants to life.

"It looks like they just crashed through here," Jacob said.

Yes, indeed.

Since it cost $37 (for four) to get in to Dinosaur World, we were thankful there were other things to do, including a fake cave/movie theater that continually ran a dinosaur documentary, a dino playground, a dino dig for fossils and a nice museum.

About dinosaured out after a couple hours, we went looking for our hotel room. It wasn't hard to find.

Although there are more than 1,000 hotel rooms in Cave City, we couldn't pass up the chance to "Sleep in a Wigwam" at the historic **Wigwam Village #2 (270-773-3381)** that was built in 1937.

Listed on the National Register of Historic Places, the quaint, old-school motel grounds are filled with a semi-circle of 15 teepees.

Located on 31-W, the old highway strewn with that era of motels, the Wigwam Village is immaculately preserved and gave the kids a great space to roam.

Rested and ready, we decided to do one of the 14 cave tours at Mammoth Cave.

Just a warning for parents with little kids – backpacks aren't allowed inside the cave.

Although my wife Toril and I have done many of the tours there, we took the shortest one, the Mammoth Cave Discovery Tour, which is an easy ¾ mile round-trip hike and 1¼ hours long.

It was only $10 for all of us, and it was a treat to be underground with NPS park ranger Joe Duvall, a local retired school teacher who had first worked at the cave in 1961 when he was in college.

Though just a short walk, it doesn't take long to soak in the spectacular size and idea of it all.

The first big room, the Rotunda Room, is 140 feet directly below the hotel lobby. The room is ½-acre in size, making it only the sixth largest room in the cave. The largest is 1.8 acres.

Since there was no way I was carrying our son Will to the Snowball Room (the cave's dining hall located 267 feet below the ground), we returned above ground to the Mammoth Cave Hotel and Restaurant, whose walls are filled with historic photos of 189 years of being a show cave, as Duvall called it.

Although you can certainly spend several days at Mammoth Caves and not see all the 14 tours, there are six other private caves in the area, each with their own unique formations and stories.

Certainly, **Bowling Green's Lost River Cave (270-393-0077)**, an underground boat tour, is a natural selection for families, as is **Hidden River Cave and American Cave Museum (270-786-1466)**.

We saved Hidden River for a much-needed stop for the return trip from Memphis.

Located in Horse Cave, Ky., just two miles from Interstate 65, the Hidden River Cave (located right under the town's main drag) is a must-see-and-learn experience.

The cave museum was first-rate and the subterranean river was filled with those eyeless crawdads that cave guides always talk about but you never see.

That the cave has any critters is a great testament to the ecological cleanup that has taken place at Hidden River, which was just reopened in 1993 after being closed for 50 years because of groundwater pollution.

The cave guide and the American Cave Museum's multi-floors of presentations gently drove home the story of this remarkable recovery and how what we do above ground impacts everything below the surface as well.

With a Sunday of sunshine warming us, we climbed back in the car, filled with lingering echoes of the Beale Street blues, the joy of Hidden River's redemption song and filled with the fact that, forget the calendar, on this 60-degree January day, we felt like we've already indulged in a spring break.

If You Go: Cave City

ALONG THE WAY: There's a lot of cool stops located off of the Bluegrass Parkway, including the Kentucky Railway Museum in New Haven (south of Bardstown), where you can catch a scenic train. Call (502) 549-5470.

A GOOD TIME TO GO: The campgrounds at Mammoth Cave National Park open March 1. March and April are good times to go, since it is a bit warmer there and you miss the super-sized summer crowds that make it tough to get on a cave tour. There are 14 cave tours underground and 53,000 acres above ground to hike, bike and canoe. Check the Web site at www.nps.gov/maca.

UNDERGROUND: In addition to Mammoth Cave National Park (the world's longest cave system), there are also six other commercial caves open for walking tours, wild caving tours and the Lost River Cave underground boat tour. Call (270) 782-0800.

YOU GOTTA SEE: At Kentucky Down Under, you get a cool hands-on adventure that explores the animals and culture of Australia, as well as get to see Kentucky Caverns. Call (800) 762-2869.

ON THE BIG SCREEN: Kentucky native and Hollywood director Cameron Crowe put "Elizabethtown" (located about 30 minutes northeast from Mammoth Cave) on the map, so to speak, in 2005 when the movie of the same title was widely released. The DVD features clips of Crowe talking about coming back to his native state of Kentucky to film.

LIVING ON HART COUNTY TIME: You gain an hour as you cross into Hart County, Ky., on Interstate 65, since that is the start of Central Standard Time. Remember to factor that in, especially on the drive back.

SOME FUN FREEBIES: Bowling Green, located about 15 to 20 minutes south of Cave City off of I-65, has six disc golf courses. They are all free and open to the public. Go online at www.pdga.com to get directions to the courses.

More Places to Crave the Cave

CARTER CAVES STATE RESORT PARK: Public cave tours daily throughout the year at Carter Caves State Resort Park in Olive Hill, Ky. In winter, take guided tours of X-Cave and Cascade Cave, the largest of nearly 200 caves in Carter County. Also take self-guided trips into Horn Hollow and Laurel. In 2008, Laurel was closed in winter because of hibernating bats. In summer, take guided tours of Bat Cave and the historic Saltpetre Cave as well. Those caves are also closed in winter due to hibernating bats. Cost is $6 and $3 for children for X-Cave and $8 and $4 for Cascade. Guided wild caving tours of Bat Cave and Saltpetre are also available in the summer. Call (606) 286-4411.

CRAWLATHON AT CARTER CAVES: The ultimate weekend backstage pass to some of the best of the 200 caves in Carter County, Ky., Crawlathon is the last weekend in January at Carter Caves State Resort Park and draws cavers from around the world. Learn rappelling, try the Squeezebox, and see how dirty you can get after hours of caving. More than 100 different trips for all skill levels. Go online at www.crawlathon.com.

LOST WORLD CAVERNS: Open year-round in Lewisburg, W.Va. Cave tours run 10 a.m. to 4 p.m. daily. Closed on holidays. Exit 169, off of I-64. Admission is $10, $5 for children 6-12 and free for children younger than 6. Wild caving tours also offered. Advanced registration needed for those trips. Call (866) 228-3778. Go online at www.lostworldcaverns.com.

SENECA CAVERNS: Open daily 10 a.m. to 4 p.m. Also, offers gemstone mining and on-site restaurant. Located three miles east of Riverton, W.Va. near Canaan Valley. Call (800) 239-7647 or go online at www.senecacaverns.com.

SMOKE HOLE CAVERNS: Open year-round with guided tours every half-hour on Route 55 near Spruce Knob and Seneca Rocks. Motel, Wildlife museum, restaurant and log cabins, on site. Call (800) 828-8478.

Jenny Wiley State Resort Park
Kentucky

Sometime in those toddling two's and not too long after rolling out "mama" and "dada," our oldest child Jacob would say, "Play Paptain Hook," then proceed to place a plastic bucket on his head, grab the nearest, sharpest stick, and come dashing at his "dada" like I was that clock-ticking croc.

Thank you, Walt Disney!

With one obvious "Peter Pan fan" already on board, we loaded up the Dave Trippin' wagon and rolled down U.S. 23, "The Country Music Highway," and "Into the Woods" at Jenny Wiley State Resort Park outside Prestonsburg, Ky., for a weekend of fun being "Lost Boys," tromping trails, making sand monsters and walking sticks, riding the waves of Dewey Lake like pontoon pirates and soaking up two starry nights of shows at Jenny Wiley Theatre.

Hit by a near biblical flood in late May 2004, the Theatre and Park have bounced back this summer with the spirit and courage of the park's namesake - Jenny Wiley, the legendary pioneer who, after 11 months of captivity, escaped from the Indians who had killed her brother and five of her children and simply walked back hundreds of miles to home.

Celebrating its 40th season and nestled up high in a hill-rimmed holler at the state park, Jenny Wiley Theatre has carved out its own living legend in the entertainment world.

Miles:
73

Original Trip
July
2004

The Lavender crew gets a refreshing summer-time splash of outdoor theatre at the renowned Jenny Wiley Theatre, and the weekend's topped off with great hikes, a pontoon cruise and even a Sunday morning church service coming down in a one-room school house.

The Theatre has been proving ground for a long list of accomplished actors including Tony Award-winning Huntington native Michael Cerveris ("Assassins"), Paige Davis (host of TLC's "Trading Spaces") Randy Jones (of The Village People), Jim Varney (the "Ernest" movies) and more than 1,150 other actors, dancers, musicians and technicians.

Over the years, JWT, one of the nation's leading outdoor amphitheaters, has put on more than 135 productions that have been seen by more than 625,000 people.

That the theatre's shows ("Into the Woods," "My Way," "Peter Pan," "Legend of Jenny Wiley" and "Jenny Wiley Theatre - 40 Years in Revue") continued was a miracle in itself because of the flood.

Managing director Martin Childers let folks know about it in a real, immediate way as he introduces each show.

"Is anybody sitting in row I?" asked Childers before Peter Pan. "We had water up to your knees. We lost about $75,000 in sound equipment. If it had not been for our friends we would not be here this season."

A flood of record in Eastern Kentucky, which devastated many counties, still had left its muddy mark on the park where work was being done on the campgrounds, the golf course, and the Lakeshore Trail.

"The shows are top notch and everything went well together," Childers said, of the shows that are filled with actors from around the country. A few are local, but most are culled from professional casting calls in New York and Atlanta. "All the music fits the voices, the sets look phenomenal and nobody is here. The season's attendance is really off this year , and it's not because we're not doing good productions."

Complete with a live, 12-piece orchestra tucked to the side among a grove of trees, the magical and G-rated production of "Peter Pan" with a simply wonderful set and stand-out cast kept our critters spellbound with eyes as big as quarters, waiting for the next band of dancing pirates, Lost Boys or Indians to come racing through the woods.

A nice ending every night at JWT is that after the bows, the cast disappears from the stage and somehow beats the crowd out to the entrance where they line up to greet folks and give autographs, hugs and high-fives.

Filled with the lingering energy of the youth and joy and freedom-filled flying of the production of "Peter Pan," we got right back to the park Saturday morning to check out some of the park's diverse educational and crafts programming.

If you're staying the weekend, make sure you pick up one of the park's programs. The programs are either free or ridiculously cheap to do a little bit of everything from boat rides to crafts and hikes.

We arrived just a few minutes into park naturalist Ron Vanover's show featuring snakes at the park's Nature and Interpretative Center.

We were quickly mesmerized with Vanover's quick wit during a slide show and his hand-curling cache of uniquely marked live snakes such as the Eastern Milk Snake.

With our fill of live reptiles in close quarters occupied by a couple dozen kids, we decided to stretch our legs and head for the hills.

The park has dozens of miles of trails, including a unique trail that actually starts inside the amphitheater.

We shifted gears and our gang of air-gasping mountain goats chugged up, up, up through the hills for some nice overlooks of the theater along the 1.3-mile loop Moss Ridge Trail.

We did some double-time on the way back to make tracks down again to The Nature Center where they were making a quite timely craft for our troops - a sand monster to put on your bed to scare away the monsters since our little man Will just recently had started to fear things that go bump in the night (usually the cat who's been booted out of bed).

We came back a third time on this cloudy day to make a really cool Kentucky souvenir – $5 got us all the materials to make walking sticks from tobacco stakes complete with burned etchings and roped beads.

And before the park's crafts corps probably thought of booting us out, we ambled back out into what was becoming sunshine.

While "Lost Boys" napped, I enjoyed my requisite pilgrimage (with my sister Jen who lived in West Van Lear) to the nearby Webb's Grocery and Loretta Lynn's homeplace of Butcher Hollow to visit and get the latest dish from Loretta's brother Herman and her niece Madonna, who runs the general store in Van Lear.

After that quick side trip, it was a quick cleanup of the crew and a slingshot back to JWT for another wonderful night of theater out under the stars to see

"Into the Woods," which Childers describes as his hands-down favorite show in a long-time at the theatre.

He's right and the giants and the wee people in our crew loved JWT's great take on Stephen Sondheim's modern basket filled with the classic fairytales.

Having stayed up until the other side of midnight, I was almost persuaded to hit the inner snooze button.

But the temptation to worship at the Josie D. Harkins Schoolhouse, Kentucky's last one-room schoolhouse, was too great.

Parked up on concrete blocks within a stone's throw of the campground, is the little white schoolhouse that operated for 68 years in Daniels Creek and up until 1987 when the elementary was consolidated.

For the past 12 years it has served as a Sunday morning, non-denominational campground ministry hosting worshippers from 36 states and three countries.

When we pulled up, tired spirits rose as "Love Lifted Me," wafted through open windows.

Spirits continued to rise when we went inside to see a full house of sleepy, happy folk stuffed into little wooden desks to hear the word of the Lord preached in front of the portrait of George Washington and to see an old-school, coal-truck-sized blackboard.

With a Sunday afternoon open and the sun actually peeking through the clouds we thought it was high time to ride the waves of the 1,100-acre, hill-rimmed Dewey Lake.

At the Marina, we rented a pontoon boat ($30 for two hours and $15 for gas and oil) that could sit up to 12 people and took turns diving and driving in the many inlets and fingers of the lake.

We had a great time soaking up the sun and swimming.

And if you've got a pretty good crowd, it's a great way to get out on the lake for an afternoon.

Heading back with two exhausted boys and a car full of Appalshop's WMMT-FM, we felt soul-full as can be. The path and hills of home for Jenny Wiley made a wonderful summer weekend.

If You Go: Jenny Wiley Theatre

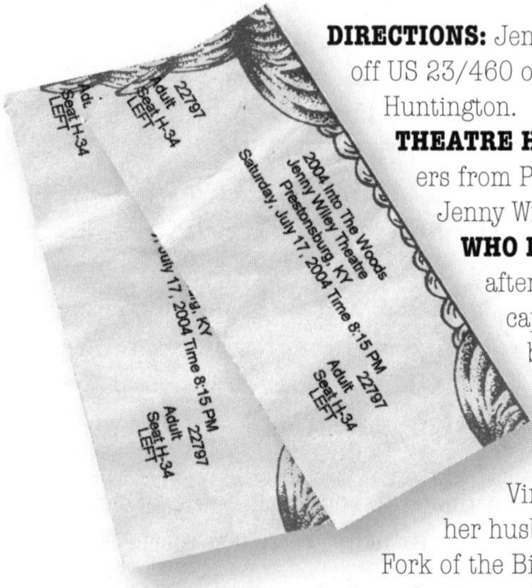

DIRECTIONS: Jenny Wiley is located in Prestonsburg, Ky. off US 23/460 on KY 3. It is about 90 miles southwest of Huntington.

THEATRE HISTORY: In 1964, a small group of players from Paintsville, Ky., presented "South Pacific," Jenny Wiley Theatre's first show.

WHO IS JENNY WILEY: The park is named after legendary pioneer Jenny Wiley, who was captured in 1790 by Indians who killed her brother and five of her children. Wiley escaped after 11 months and walked a couple hundred miles back home from near South Shore, Ky. to southwestern Virginia. In 1800, Jenny Sellards Wiley and her husband Tom moved to the banks of the Levisa Fork of the Big Sandy River. After returning from captivity, she bore five more children.

WHO'S PLAYED JENNY WILEY THEATRE: More than 1,150 aspiring actors, singers, dancers, musicians and technicians have worked at JWT including Michael Cerveris, Tony-Award-winning actor and Huntington native.

GET TICKETS: Tickets to JWT are about $21; $19 for seniors (ages 55 and older) and $13 for youth (under 21). There's also dinner theater prices as well.

CONTACT: For more information or for tickets call (877) 225-5598. For more info on the park, call (800) 325-0142.

WHERE TO STAY: On site at Jenny Wiley State Resort Park is May Lodge, which has 49 rooms. There are also 1 and 2-bedroom cottages. The campground has primitive and RV sites. Hotels in nearby Prestonsburg and Paintsville run specials for JWT tickets and a one-night stay. Go online at www.jwtheatre.com.

WHERE TO EAT: The dining room in May Lodge serves an excellent buffet and has a regular menu as well. On show nights, arrive about two hours before the show. Cost was about $12 each and free for small children.

FUN AND FREE: Jenny Wiley State Resort is home to one of the area's newest 18-hole disc golf courses. The course is free and open to the public to play.

OTHER SHOWS: In the summertime, check out the weekend Branson-style variety music shows by the Kentucky Opry and the Kentucky Opry Jr. Pros at the Mountain Arts Center in Prestonsburg, Ky. Call (888) MAC-ARTS. Go online at www.macarts.com.

ON THE WEB: Go online at www.jwtheatre.com. For more information on the park, go online at http://ky.gov.parks and click onto Jenny Wiley State Resort Park.

More Outdoor Theater

HUNTINGTON OUTDOOR THEATRE: Nestled in the hills of Huntington's Ritter Park, Huntington Outdoor Theatre, H.O.T., has been a tradition for more than a decade. Shows run weekends in July. Musical shows also include a pre-show and children's pre-show. Go online at www.hotwv.org.

THEATRE WEST VIRGINIA: Located at the beautiful amphitheater at Grandview near Beckley, Theatre West Virginia runs June through August with a variety of productions including, the nation's oldest running Civil War drama, "Honey in the Rock," as well as "Hatfields and McCoys." Go online at www.theatrewestvirginia.com.

TECUMSEH: Located at the Sugarloaf Amphitheater just north of Chillicothe, Ohio, "Tecumseh," written by Allan W. Eckert, with musical soundtrack by the London Symphony, is one of the most popular outdoor dramas in the U.S. since more than two million people have seen it in nearly 40 years. A cast of 100 with live horses, musket and cannon fire make it a realistic drama of the life of "Tecumseh" and the plight of the Native American people. Go online at www.tecumsehdrama.com.

ARACOMA STORY: Located at the Liz Spurlock Amphitheater at Chief Logan State Park in Logan, W.Va., "The Aracoma Story," is a unique outdoor drama that Spurlock and company have been putting on since the mid 1970s. There's also three other stage productions that take turns running June through August at the park. Go online at www.thearacomastory.com.

TERROR OF THE TUG: Featured on the History Channel in 2007, the McArts Fine Arts Organization in Welch, W.Va., in McDowell County, has breathed new life into the historic story of the region's mine wars that came to a head on Aug. 1, 1921, when Matewan's Chief of Police Sid Hatfield and Ed Chambers were shot to death at the Welch Court House. Come and see "Terror of the Tug," a play about the epic struggles between the miners and the coal companies. Go online at www.mcartswv.com.

SOMETHING IN THE WATER: An original musical written by Mickey Fisher, "Something in the Water" has a limited stint at the new amphitheater at Greenbo Lake State Resort Park, located near Greenup, Ky. There's also a wide array of concerts and other theatrical events at the region's newest amphitheater that opened in 2007. Go online at www.parks.ky.gov and click onto Greenbo.

Crawlathon

Carter Caves, Kentucky

Miles: 46

Original Trip January 2007

For years, Christy Board and her 12-year-old son, William Seiter, have made the two-hour trip from Northern Kentucky to **Carter Caves State Resort Park** to get back to the Earth – literally.

The mother and son were two of a record-breaking crowd of 740 cavers from all over the country who came together at Carter Caves to take part in the 26th annual **Crawlathon**.

"It's about being able to be on a guided trip but one that's not lighted and that has crawling that lets you get down in the Earth," Board said of the lure of the wild caving event.

Like the ultimate backstage pass to Carter County's wealth of caves, the three-day Crawlathon, is a family friendly affair that offers educational programs from some of the country's top biologists and cave experts, unique indoor sports from the Squeezebox and the Mammoth Corrugated Cave and about every type of cave trip imaginable, from canoeing and advanced cave pit plunging trips to simple walking tours.

"It's an experience you really can't get in other parts of the country," said Linda Pollock of Anderson City, Ky.

Pollock and her husband Don who have been involved with Crawlathon from the beginning, would know.

She started bringing her daughter Leia Curphey, 28, when she was just a child, and

Part of the Dave Trippin' crew checks out the house of slithering at the Crawlathon, one of the world's largest winter-time caving events held each year at Carter Caves State Resort Park in Olive Hill, Ky. Check out this crawl through Middle Earth and even through the cardboard, too.

Curphey now brings her husband and two kids, including 3-month-old Fiona.

"This is the most family-oriented caving event that you will find, from the bat crafts to the Caving Let's Do It Right program," Pollock said.

Hanging at the Lewis Caveland Lodge on Saturday, Pollock couldn't wait to have her fun on Sunday when she got to try out her latest creation, a 3-D cavers version of the board game "Clue" in Cascade Cave, a live murder mystery to find out who killed Sir John Karst.

That kind of creative spirit pervades Crawlathon.

In the basement of the Caveland Lodge, Steve Duncan's cardboard masterpiece, the Mammoth Corrugated Cave, stumped even the best cavers with its maze of boxes twist-tied together in a giant maze that had two levels, fake cave formations, bats and even a live cam that folks could watch by the fireplace upstairs.

"That was a lot of work you all put into that," said a tired Jennifer Tislerics, 33, a Detroit-area resident who was the first person to get through the cardboard cave on Saturday morning.

Too busy reporting about the bizarre cardboard cave, I realized that my 7-year-old son Jake slipped into the labyrinth.

I got that queasy, uneasy feeling that, like a cat in a tree, someone would cry for help about halfway through or, worse yet, in front of the live cam broadcast into the main lodge entrance.

And someone less brave and who probably ate more cookies than should be legal for breakfast (moi) was going to have to crawl through confining cardboard boxes.

Thank God for the power of emergency prayer, a big furry mop of red-hair and laughs came tumbling out just minutes later.

In the Fields Room, the famous Squeezebox, a wood box to test your crawling skills, drew a large crowd on Saturday night to see how low they could go.

Although he stands 6'5" and weighs over 201 pounds, Marshall student Jamie Dzierzak won his third straight heavyweight division in the Squeezebox competition.

Somehow, Dzierzak, who doesn't look like he could fit comfortably in a regular-sized car, pulled himself through the Medieval-looking contraption at 7 ½ inches height.

If you're wanting a visual, that's just a wee bit higher than a dollar bill's length of six inches.

Dzierzak was just one of the 28 people associated with Boy Scout Troop 762 (out of Huntington) who were attending Crawlathon.

The Cabell County crawlers did a number on the Squeezebox with sisters Sarah Thacker, 9, and Erin Thacker, 11, winning first place in their age division with squeezes of 6 ½ inches and 6 ¼ inches, respectively.

Beth Thacker took third place in the 126-157 pound division, and Seth Spurlock took second place in the 7-year-old division.

Park naturalist Sam Plummer has been at Carter Caves for 25 years and has been a part of all 26 Crawlathons.

Plummer said he attributes good organization and publicity and a good time as factors to why Crawlathonistopping record numbers.

"The word has finally gotten out after 26 years," Plummer said, laughing. "I think part of it too is that the fall of the year and the first part of the winter have been very mild. We just have a lot of people who just want to get out and explore."

On Saturday, Lisa Pruitt-Thorner, president of ESSO Grotto and a veteran caver, guided two dozen cavers through the sopping wet passages of Rimstone, Horn Hollow and Laurel Caves.

"This is the fun part. Now we get to crawl on our bellies backward," Pruitt-Thorner said teasing the group of mostly Boy Scouts from Troop 111, out of Lexington, Ky., after they just completed a 50-foot crawl called the Connection.

John Alcorn, the troop leader, said they brought 41 kids this year after getting hooked on the event that is geared for all skill levels and teaches so much about the ecology of caves and that is just so much fun.

Alcorn burst into laughter as his scouts emerged soaked from the Surprise Dome Passage, a short but extremely wet crawl.

"I knew if anyone would have to get completely wet it would be you," Alcorn said to Nick Thompson, 11.

"It was worth every second of it," Thompson said.

If You Go: Carter Caves

DIRECTIONS: Take I-64 west to Ky. 182 north. Carter Caves State Resort Park is about 30 miles west of Ashland, Ky.

WHERE TO STAY: The Lewis Caveland Lodge has 28 rooms; there are also 11 cottages with up to four queen beds each as well as 89 campsites, About 30 of those are primitive. There are also group camps as well.

WHERE TO EAT: Tierney 's Cavern (named for retired naturalist John Tierney) is located in the bottom floor of the Caveland Lodge. It has a kid-friendly and Kentucky-grown menu with fresh local produce in season and Kentucky favorites like a Hot Brown, Derby Pie and cornbread and beans.

WHAT ELSE: Carter Caves is full of other activities including one of the few state parks in the area that offers horseback riding, 9-hole golf course, mountain biking, canoeing (on Smokey Lake and Tygart's Creek), 18 holes mini golf, tennis, and 26 miles of hiking trails.

THE TRAILS: Carter Caves has more than 26 miles of trails taking you past some of the largest natural bridges in Kentucky and in some odd rock structures such as the sheer cliffs of Box Canyon located at Cascade Cave State Nature Preserve near Carter Caves.

ON THE WILD SIDE: Carter Caves offers guided wild caving trips in the summer in such caves as Saltpetre and Bat Cave (both of which are closed in the winter). Also, Carter Caves is part of the state-wide Backcountry Adventure Series that includes such excursions as overnight backpack trips, canoe trips and a wild caving trip as well. Adventurers participate in three out of the four types of excursions offered and receive a $50 Kentucky State Park Gift Card. Go online at www.parks.ky.gov for more info.

A GOOD TIME TO GO: Aside from Crawlathon, some other fun events at Carter Caves include the annual Fraley Fest Mountain Gathering each September. The amphitheater and lodge also have other shows as well throughout the year. In Carter County, some other cool events include the U.S. 60 Sale (first weekend of August), as well as several good summer-time bluegrass festivals including Rudy Fest in Grayson and the Carter County Shrine Club Bluegrass Festival in Olive Hill.

WHERE ELSE TO PARK IT: Carter County also boasts another unique Kentucky State Park, Grayson Lake, a 1,512-acre lake walled by majestic sandstone cliffs. Also home to Hidden Coves Golf Course, rated by Golf Digest as the #4 new course in the country in 2005.

ON THE WEB: Go online at www.parks.ky.gov and click onto Carter Caves or go online at www.heartoftheparks.com for the tourism office in Grayson.

FREE CRAWLING: Outside of Crawlathon there are regular guided tours at Carter Caves, and wild caving in Laurel and Horn Hollow that can be explored for free (unguided) with a permit obtained at the Welcome Center. Call (800) 325-0059 or (606) 286-4411

More Fun and Free Activities

In addition to its guided tours, Carter Caves has free, un-guided cave trips, year-round. Here's a few more of our favorite free things to do and see:

SALT ROCK PETROGLYPHS: Dating back to about 1550 to 1650 A.D.,The Salt Rock Petroglyphs were first featured by the Smithsonian Institute in 1848. This significant rock art is located 13 miles from Huntington. Take WV 10 through Salt Rock. Take a right on the first gravel road past the bridge. It is about a mile or so down that road over a small embankment. A great place for a picnic and Geocaching.

HUNTINGTON MUSEUM OF ART: Located on 52 acres, the Huntington Museum of Art, 2033 McCoy Road, has a number of free things including Kids Art Saturdays. Also, on Tuesdays, the Museum is free and open late. The Nature Trail is a perfect short hike for small children and adults. Be sure to check out the koi ponds and orchids in the C. Fred Edwards Conservatory, a tropical plant conservatory. Call (304) 529-2701.

DISC GOLF: Once you buy a disc, playing any of the region's disc golf courses is free. Disc golf courses in the region include: two 18-hole courses at Rotary Park in Huntington, Songer Whitewater in Lansing, W.Va., Jenny Wiley State Resort Park near Prestonsburg, Ky., Great Seal State Park in Chillicothe, Pike Lake State Park (near Bainbridge, Ohio), Flat Rocks in Lancaster, OU-Chillicothe, Rocky Fork State Park in Hillsboro, Ohio and Forked Run State Park in Meigs County, Ohio. Go online at www.pdga.com for more courses.

RITTER PARK ROSE GARDEN: Yes, life is short, yes, you should stop and smell the roses at the Ritter Park Rose Garden in Huntington. It has more than 2,000 plants under the loving care of Truman Watts, who has planted about 500 to 700 of the plants at the garden which was started in 1934. Go online at www.ghprd.org.

MODEL TRAIN SHOW: Held at Greenbo Lake State Resort in Greenup, Ky., and sponsored by the Collis P. Huntington Railroad Historical Society, this free weekend event each March features tons of model trail layouts, and model-scale steam engine rides. Go online at www.parks.ky.gov or www.newrivertrain.com.

Newport
Kentucky

As we peered through a telescope across a high, muddy Ohio River, the shiny, sparkling new Cincinnati Reds stadium looked, well, great and American.

But on this particular Sunday, the Philadelphia Phillies were spanking the Reds 13-1, and we (two friends, one wife and two wild kids) thought it safer if we just anchored down in Newport and Covington.

Boasting one of the largest waterway investment projects in the nation (with an impact exceeding $5.4 billion), Greater Cincinnati has worked marvels with its riverfront.

Nowhere is the buildup more striking than in Newport. Once a bit seedy and rundown, this small, riverside city now boasts Newport on the Levee, a $210 million shopping and entertainment complex that draws 6 million people annually.

While there is an IMAX theater, Shadow Cabaret, GameWorks and countless restaurants, the real draw worth driving for with young'uns is the **Newport Aquarium, (800-406-3474)** a habitat to more than 11,000 aquatic species.

Inside the Aquarium, the momentum builds as you walk and learn ("Sea More, Know More"), reading quick facts and watching fish from the world's rivers, the Ohio Riverbank and the world's shorelines.

Miles: 115

Original Trip November 2003

You can see a little bit of anything in Northern Kentucky. We find one of the area's biggest aquariums, the remains of Woolly Mammoths, the awesome Rabbit Hash General Store, and the world's largest stained glass window.

Classical music piped in at various exhibits, including the Jellyfish Gallery (set up like an art gallery), only added to a peaceful Sunday morning.

While we've been to several aquariums, one of the things that is way cool at Newport (besides it being only 2 1/2 to three hours away) is a series of seamless clear acrylic tunnels that put you nose-to-nose with critters of the sea.

Only 2.5 inches separates you from three species of shark, stingrays, giant loggerhead turtles and scores of colorful schooling fish that swim under, beside, and over you as you contort your head to follow their path.

In the aquarium for two hours, we emerged into the sunlight of Newport at noon, an excellent time since it is then that the World Peace Bell, the world's largest free-swinging bell, tolls daily.

For those who like live music and the arts, one funky and historic night stop-off right across the street from Newport on the Levee is **The Southgate House (859-431-2201)**. Built by the inventor of the Tommy Gun, the historic house hosts live music seven nights a week, featuring a wide spray of music from punk to pop to such national act singer-songwriters as Larry Cordle and Robert Earl Keen.

One of my favorite places to eat in the Greater Cincy area is only a few blocks from Newport on the Levee, and it carries a Huntington connection of sorts.

Pompilios, 600 Washington St., (859-581-3065) is a good, inexpensive ($6 to $10 per dinner) family-run Italian restaurant that has been around since 1933.

It was here they filmed the "Rainman" scene where Dustin

Hoffman's character (based upon Huntington's own Joseph Sullivan) drops the toothpicks and counts them.

As much as I love Pompilios, we were jonesing for some German food, so we sniffed around the Hofbrauhaus, but the $15 million German brewery and authentic German restaurant was not open, so we headed to Covington in search of sauerkraut.

While the Greater Cincinnati area's thick German heritage can be seen in pockets around the city, including Over the Rhine on the Ohio side, Covington is home to one of the best concentrations. **The MainStrasse Village (859-491-0458)** area in and around Main Street is five blocks of a restored German village that has flavors of the old world and the new, from Triple-A-Skateboards to unique shops such as Gothic Edge, a Renaissance store. There are also plenty of coffee shops, bakeries and restaurants such as **Dee Felice, 529 Main St., Covington, (859-261-2365)** a good jazz club and New Orleans-style restaurant.

With the sun warming things up to the low 80's, we wanted to be outside so we followed the mesmerizing bells of the 43-bell Carroll Chimes Bell Tower, which fittingly has mechanical figurines depicting the story of the Pied Piper.

We parked our double stroller and entourage on the patio of **Wertheim's Restaurant, 514 W. 6th St., Covington (859-261-1233)**. There, we filled up on good German food before heading just a block away to the base of the bell tower, which sits beside the 6th St. Goebel Park Playground where we let the 3-year-old run and romp.

Having already spent a couple clams (lunch was $45 for five), my nose for free fun lit up – ironically next to the sign boasting that Covington was home to Haven Gillespie, who composed "Santa Claus is Coming to Town."

Although it was a Sunday afternoon, I informed

my posse we were walking 10 blocks to church, **Cathedral Basilica of the Assumption, 1140 Madison Ave., Covington (859-431-2060)**, which has 82 stained glass windows, including the largest hand-blown stained glass window in the world, measuring 67 feet by 24 feet.

Amazingly, our 3-year-old was quiet for the 30 minutes or so that we walked around, dumbfounded by the beauty of afternoon light pouring in through thousands of colorful panes of stained glass.

Of course, that silence was broken when we all knelt to say a simple, yet fervent prayer, "Please, Lord, don't let the Cincinnati Bengals draft our beloved Byron Leftwich."

One of the things I really love about Northern Kentucky is that you can get country real quick if you need it, and sometimes you do.

So on Monday morning, we loaded up the van and pointed the nose toward Rabbit Hash, Ky., a historic Ohio River town about 22 miles south of Covington and across the river from Rising Sun, Ind., now famous for its casinos.

Although it only lands as No. 38 on the 101 Things to Do in Northern Kentucky, a trip to **Rabbit Hash General Store, (859-586-7744)** around since 1831, ranks a whole lot higher on my list.

A favorite of bikers, campers at nearby Big Bone Lick State Park, tourists and locals, the store is filled with just about anything you can imagine: art, milk, videos, cold pop (including Ale-8-1, ginger ale out of Winchester, Ky.), Harlan Hubbard books, antiques and lots of other stuff that has been accumulating for 170 years.

Mary Ellen Pesek, who was working the store (and who is, by the way, wife of Milton native Mark Lawhorn), said they don't get much business from the gambling boats just across the Ohio River, but the boat's assistant captain canoes to the store. Once inside, he radios over to have the casino blow its whistle.

Since dinosaurs are at the top of any kids' list of really cool things, we figured we better hit nearby **Big Bone Lick State Park, (859-384-3522),** one of the premier paleontological sites in the United States and no doubt one of the oddest named state parks in Kentucky or anywhere.

And it is only a hop, skip and jump (about 10 miles or so) from Rabbit Hash along Big Bone Lick Scenic Highway.

Visited by such historic figures as Daniel Boone and Mary Ingles, the park, which is only 512 acres, is where thousands of extinct mammals such as the 5-ton mastodon, the giant ground sloth, and the woolly mammoth came to lick the salt, fell into the swampy, marshy ground and couldn't get up.

Although the animals' bones are in museums around the world, there is still a nice collection here. A small museum, closed Mondays and Tuesdays, contains many of the large-scale bones. There is a paved walkway that features life-size models of the creatures, including the kid-favorite Woolly Mammoth (Ray Romano's voice not included).

Also featuring a real buffalo herd, the mile or so walk is an interesting creek-side stroll back in time as you read of wagon loads of fossils ranging from 12-foot-tusks to 20-pound teeth being removed in 1868.

Boxes of replica bones lay about, giving kids the hands-on connection that "Ice Age" is – believe it or not – more than an animated movie. It was here once, right in our backyard.

If You Go: Newport/Covington

PLACES TO STAY: Radisson Hotel Cincinnati Riverfront, 668 W. 5th. St. If you are heading to a Cincinnati Reds game and want to stay close, Covington is a cheaper option than downtown Cincy, and you can take the Reds Riverboat ferry over from Covington Landing for only $2. The Radisson is a neat place to stay that is close, and it features the Riverview Revolving Restaurant, which provides a wonderful panoramic view of the Cincy skyline. You may want to make reservations for a game night when the city is lit up and when sometimes fireworks fill the night sky when the Reds hit a homerun.

THE WILDWOOD INN TROPICAL DOME AND THEME SUITES, 7809 U.S. 42, Florence, Ky., You can stay in an African Safari hut, a boat, a cave, a `59 Cadillac or in the Old West in one of the hotel's themed rooms. You can also stay in a regular (and reasonably priced) room and take advantage of the Tropical Dome, which features an indoor heated pool, waterfall hot tub, games, video gameroom and a sundeck in a tropical setting. For a discount, check a rest stop for Interstate Coupon books or go online at www.motel-coupons.com and print out a coupon to get a room for about $45.95 Sunday through Thursday or $56 for Friday through Saturday. Call (859) 371-6300 .

ON THE WAY: Depending on where you live in the Tri-State, there are several good routes to get to the Greater Cincinnati area. We took I-64 west to Grayson, hit Ky. 9 north to Maysville and the AA Highway (Ky. 10). You can also take the AA from its start near Lloyd, Ky., in Greenup, Ky. Do not speed on the AA, a known speed trap. Although the AA is the quickest route, hitting some slivers of Ky. 8, which runs right along the river, is essential if you aren't in a hurry.

The stretch from Maysville to the quaint and historic Ohio River town of Augusta is nice and includes (just about 200 yards off Ky. 8) a covered bridge on Lee's Creek Road near Dover, Ky.

AUGUSTA: home to the late star Rosemary Clooney, who lived along Riverside Drive, has a bunch of neat shops and eateries, including the Beehive Tavern, which dates

back to 1796. We ate at the, uh, new place in town, the General Store, which began business in 1850. Lunch for three was only $10.50, and the store is only a stone's throw from the Ohio River,.

FERRYING ACROSS: At Augusta, you can hitch a ride on the *Jenny Ann*, a ferryboat that crosses the Ohio River (a five-minute and $5 ride) up to 90 times a day. The ferry spits you out on U.S. 52, which is perhaps my favorite route to Cincinnati since I grew up near U.S. 52 in Franklin Furnace. We have traveled that river road many times heading to see the Reds play.

GRANT'S HOME: There are several neat stops along U.S. 52, including President U.S. Grant's birthplace in Point Pleasant, Ohio. Call (513) 378-4222. That tiny home and museum is part of the nearby Land of Grant tours, which includes tours of Grant's boyhood home and his school in nearby Georgetown and Ripley. A Grant Birthday Remembrance is always planned each April, and the Ohio Bicentennial Presidents Weekend usually happens in May.

QUILT BARN TRAIL: Adams County, Ohio, birthed the first Quilt Barn Trail when Donna Sue Groves put up a quilt block of her mother (Nina Maxine Groves). There's 22 quilt blocks on barns in Adams County. Call (877) 232-6764 or go online at www.adamscountytravel.org.

ON THE WEB: For more information about traveling in Northern Kentucky, go online at www.kentuckytourism.com or try www.staynky.com for a look at 101 Things to Do in Northern Kentucky. Call (800) STAY-NKY.

Other Heavenly Sites

If you thought the world's largest stained glass window in Covington was cool, Here's some other faith-inspired sites.

FATIMA SHRINE: A quiet roadside Catholic shrine with gorgeous mosaics depicting the life of Christ. Located near Haverhill, Ohio, on Old U.S. 52 just west of Hanging Rock. Take U.S. 52 west to Haverhill (west of Ironton, Ohio) and follow the signs.

BLENKO GLASS MUSEUM: Located just off of James River Turnpike in Milton, the world-famous Blenko Glass may be known for its tableware, but it is also one of the world's last makers of hand-blown glass used for stained glass. See incredible stained glass art at the Blenko Glass museum, located on the second floor of the Visitor Center. Call (304) 743-9081 or go online at www.blenkoglass.com.

HOLY CROSS MONASTERY: This monastery moved to Wayne, W.Va. in 2000. The Russian Orthodox Church Abroad monks support themselves by making hand-rolled incense, painting icons and making homemade goat's milk soap. Church services for visitors are at 5 p.m. daily. Go online at www.holycross-hermitage.com.

SHAKER VILLAGE: America's largest restored Shaker community is a 3,000-acre National Historic Landmark. Shaker Village at Pleasant Hill located just south of Lexington, Ky. Go online at www.shakervillageky.org. Call (800) 734-5611.

WEE HOUSE O' WORSHIP: Our Lady of the Pines, in Horseshoe Run ,W.Va., has been promoted for more than 50 years as the smallest church in 48 states. Seating for 12. Located north of Canaan Valley, off Route 219.

CREATION MUSEUM: A state-of-the-art, 60,000-square-foot museum that brings the pages of the Bible to life with special effects. Cost is $20; $10 for children. Go online at www.creationmuseum.org.

PASSION TRAIL: Paradise Island in Christian, W.Va., is a Christian retreat campground that hosts many annual events at its base on Route 80 in Logan County, W.Va. "Footsteps of Jesus," is a 1/2-mile trail with 40 Biblical scenes with actors. Also, be sure to see "Christ in Rock," a unique 60,000 lbs. rock. Call (304) 583-2825.

Country Music Highway

Kentucky

"We're looking for Herman," Sylvia Myers announced, camera in hand, poking her head into the front door of Loretta Lynn's cabin homeplace in Butcher Hollow.

"If you've found a good-looking man, then you've got Herman," said a smiling and winking Herman Webb, with his hands in his pockets.

Making their way from Winterhaven, Fla., to Columbus, Ohio, Sylvia and her husband, Don, found out on the Internet that part of U.S. 23 is called the Country Music Highway.

Driving through Eastern Kentucky, they dropped in to see if the road of almost mythical musical proportions was for real. Could they scare up the ghosts of country music past, present and future along U.S. 23, whose 144 miles of four-lane highway are designated the Country Music Highway, National Scenic Byway?

The answer is a resounding yes.

The Myers, after several lost minutes driving these curvy-as-a-copperhead roads off U.S. 23 and back to Butcher Hollow, found Herman Webb and his sweet embrace of country music memories of his older sister, Loretta Lynn, who has celebrated over 40 years as a recording artist.

You don't have to look or listen long to taste that seemingly eternal talent spring that has sent down from the mountains to national stardom the likes of Patty Loveless,

Miles: 99

Original Trip June 2003

With the radio on full blast and the windows down, the Lavender posse goes a singing down The Country Music Highway looking for the ghosts of country superstars past and a listen to the next generation of stars.

Ricky Skaggs, Dwight Yoakam, Billy Ray Cyrus, The Judds, Ralph Stanley, Tom T. Hall, Keith Whitley, Gary Stewart and more recently, Rebecca Lynn Howard.

Since we'll wear out a muddy cowpath between Huntington and Ashland during Kentucky Music Trail, we figured we would load up our two cookie-crunchers in the station wagon and take a 90-mile ride down the famous Country Music Highway to visit the Paramount Arts Center's sister venue in this eight-week concert series – the Mountain Arts Center in Prestonsburg.

Built in 1997, the 1,000-seat Mountain Arts Center, also known as the MAC, is perhaps best known for its Kentucky Opry.

The Opry and the Kentucky Opry Junior Pros is the living dream of Billie Jean Osborne. She taught music and band in Floyd County Schools for 30 years. When she retired, "Miss Billie Jean" formed the Branson or Pigeon Forge-style variety musical troupe, which consists solely of local talent.

A visit on opening night at the Kentucky Opry, which runs on Friday nights throughout the summer, proves these hills are still very much alive with the sounds of all kinds of music.

With its kicking house band, the Kentucky Opry showcases Eastern Kentucky's best young performers who bare their mountain soul, singing everything from disco and country to gospel, movie-theme music and bluegrass – all performed with a sensational light show.

"This is a show much like you'd see in Branson except that all of our performers are from right here in Eastern Kentucky," said emcee Keith Caudill to the crowd. "We hope you will share some of the pride that we have in Eastern Kentucky. If you like our show, go home and tell your friends. If you don't like it, keep it to yourself."

It was hard not to enjoy the almost three-hour show.

Nearly 30 members of the Kentucky Junior Opry Pros put an angelic, harmonic presence on the '80s-classic, "We Are the World." During the nonstop regular show, Fred Goble, or "Munroe" (a homegrown comedic character), kept the crowd rolling, constantly poking fun at Caudill.

Munroe and the Mud Daubers And One Girl (the standout multi-instrumentalist Angie Carriere)

put a bluegrass breakdown on everything from "I Can't Get No Satisfaction" to Grandpa Jones' "Mountain Dew."

"That's not bluegrass," Caudill yelled storming on stage about a verse into the Rolling Stones' classic.

"Hey, man, I don't come down to the Tasty Freeze and bother you on the job," Munroe said.

Jokes aside, the music (under the direction of David Kazee) is the focus, and it would be a long, long drive to find a more talented and entertaining young pianist than Caudill's 17-year-old son, Kory, who sent the nearly full house crowd jumping to its feet with a killer Jerry Lewis-style workout on a black baby grand.

Since the MAC has a state-of-the-art recording studio (which has pressed some national releases including IIIrd Tyme Out's "Live at the MAC") there are CDs of the Kentucky Opry and many of the artists in the gift shop.

If you go down to hit a Kentucky Opry show at the MAC, you may want to make a weekend of it, since just about 10 minutes away is **Jenny Wiley State Resort Park**, which is one of a half dozen state parks tucked right off of U.S. 23 in Eastern Kentucky.

The park, which sits on the beautiful **Dewey Lake**, is perhaps best known for its outdoor theater shows. While we hit the park on an off weekend, there are about four shows each summer, including a number of popular musicals .

The state park also features plenty of other live music on the weekends, including square dancing in the campgrounds on Friday and Saturday nights and on Sunday mornings, a nondenominational church service at the old one-room schoolhouse at the park.

Jenny Wiley, who heroically endured being captured by the Cherokee and then escaped in 1790 to reunite with her husband Tom, is buried just off of U.S. 23 in River, Ky.

If you swing over on Route 302 to visit Loretta's homeplace, then you will want to learn more about Jenny Wiley at one of the region's coolest independent bookstores.

Run by retired highway engineer Jim Tramel and his wife Ann, the white-block building store, **"Words 'N' Stuff," 1246 Route 302**, is a treasure trove of a regional bookstore featuring music from along the Country Music Highway, maps and thousands of new and used books that range from genealogy, coal mining, railroading and Appalachia to cooking, health, the classics and children's books.

The store also happens to have, attached to swinging doors, three huge maps that pinpoint the important places in the life and incredible journey of Jenny Wiley as she escaped the Cherokee.

Jim Tramel said it is a book store that has room for a wide range of authors, including many native writers such as Linda Scott DeRosier whose memoir "Creeker" (about growing up about 10 miles away from the bookstore) caught national attention to Walter Preston's "1930 Federal Census of Johnson County, Vol. 1."

"I wanted to have a place in Van Lear that is a regional book store," Jim Tramel said. "You meet the best people. We have a whole lot more friends than before we started this place."

If You Go: Country Music Highway

TURN YOUR RADIO ON: Here are some cool stations to listen to on a Country Music Highway road trip. If you want to hear a lot of blasts from the Highway 23 past, your best bet may be WZAQ-FM, 92.3. We heard a lot of gems such as Ricky Skaggs' "Country Boy," a rare Billy Ray Cyrus cut and Roger Miller's "Dang Me."

If you want a real taste of old-time music and some eclectic fare, WMMT-FM, 88.1, an Appalshop station out of Whitesburg, Ky., is a real treasure. It's worth listening to WMMT just for the station IDs, which give out the colorful town names located their listening area. "This is WMMT, broadcasting for Candlewax, Johnny and Pappaw."

MORE THAN MUSIC: Out of a local library and at gift shops, you can check out and/or buy "More Than Music: A Heritage Driving Tour of Kentucky's Route 23" narrated by Ricky Skaggs. The three-CD set points out great tourist stops along The Country Music Highway and the country roads off of it.

AT THE MAC: The Mountain Arts Center in Prestonsburg hosts concerts year-round including the Kentucky Opry and Kentucky Opry Junior Pros each summer. Call (888) MAC-ARTS for more info,

OTHER PLACES TO SEE LIVE MUSIC AND MEMORABILIA: There are many restaurants - and even gas stations - tucked off U.S. 23 that have live music, and/or memorabilia from the Country Music Highway. Just a few of those places include:

THE PAVEILLON: U.S. 23 in Louisa. Some live music on the weekends. The five-story tall store displays items from a couple dozen stars of the Country Music Highway, including Larry Cordle, Ralph Stanley and Melvin Goins. The Exxon Marketplace also features a Taco Bell (also with memorabilia), a Baskin Robbins, a gift shop, a mini-mart and some cool public art (five giant painted Gibson guitars) from Nashville. Call (606) 638-9999.

EAST KENTUCKY EXPO CENTER: A new 7,000-seat arena in downtown Pikeville. Hosts national-act shows such as Z.Z. Top, Kid Rock and others, as well as regional bands and events. Go online at www.eastkyexpo.com.

MCDONALD'S IN PRESTONSBURG: At the McDonald's in Prestonsburg you can find Nemo and Hylo (the late, great bluegrass star Hylo Brown). One of Brown's stage jackets hangs between the men's and women's restrooms. In the dining area, there is a nice Country Music Highway collection of memorabilia, including one of the brown signs and some rare 45s, such as Letcher County native Gary Stewart's "Life's a Game" from 1984 on Red Ash Records.

MOUNTAIN HOMEPLACE: The Mountain Homeplace at Paintsville Lake State Park often hosts bluegrass and gospel singing in season.

Go online at www.mountainhomeplace.com.

ON THE WEB: For more information about tourism in Eastern Kentucky, go online at www.kytourism.com and at www.countrymusichighway.com.

For more information about the Country Music Highway, National Scenic Byway, go online at www.byways.org.

More Cool Live Music Venues

PARAMOUNT ARTS CENTER: 1300 Winchester Ave., Ashland, the Paramount is awash in live music from its annual season that brings in diverse entertainment from symphonies and the latest Broadway shows to jazz/blues from Dr. John. There's also a healthy dose of national–act bluegrass as well home-grown country superstars such as Wynonna and Billy Ray Cyrus. Call (606) 324-3175.

KEITH-ALBEE PERFORMING ARTS CENTER: An exquisite Thomas Lamb-designed theater, the Keith opened in Huntington in 1928 and hasn't slowed down. Home to the Marshall Artists Series and the Huntington Symphony Orchestra, the Keith has also been used for a wide range of concerts from Mountain Stage to Taylor Swift. Go online at www.keithalbeearts.org.

MOUNTAINEER OPRY HOUSE: Located in Milton, W.Va., the Mountaineer Opry House has been hosting national-act bluegrass bands most Saturday nights since the early 1970s. The concrete-block building, located just off of I-64, has a cozy atmosphere that is family-friendly (smoke and alcohol free). Call (304) 743-5749.

CULTURAL CENTER THEATER: Located in Charleston at the Capitol Complex, this theater seats about 550 and is famous for hosting Mountain Stage that has been taping here for a couple decades. Catching a live Mountain Stage taping is always a treat and often unforgettable. Go online at www.mountainstage.com. The Cultural Center also hosts the FOOTMAD concert series and the Vandalia Gathering. Go online at www.wvculture.org.

BLUE RIBBON FOXHUNTERS LODGE: Located just south of Cannonsburg, Ky., on Blue Ribbon Road, the Foxhunters Lodge has been bringing in regional and national-act bluegrass for years. All shows at 7 p.m. Children under 12 get in free and tickets are $12 to $15 for adults. Call (606) 928-9984.

STUART'S OPERA HOUSE: Located in 52 Public Square, Nelsonville, Ohio, Stuart's sat empty for 50 years. In spite of a fire in 1980, it was restored. It re-opened in 1997, and has gained a knack for getting in some top-shelf Americana acts including The Avett Brothers. Go online at www.stuartsopera-house.org.

Lexington
Kentucky

As the Monarchs lined up on our back yard butterfly bush filling up for their flight to Mexico like truckers at a Waffle House, we loaded the redheads into the station wagon and headed west to the Bluegrass to my old Kentucky college home.

Miles:
135

Original Trip
October
2003

It is fall, and everything is in flight or on the run.

As we found out on a weekend in Lexington and central Kentucky, if it ain't nailed down then they're racing it and somebody's got a couple nickels riding on the outcome..

This glorious weekend in October, we crossed over into the commonwealth where in central Kentucky alone, the Red Mile Harness Track and the Keeneland Race Course were off and running, not to mention the 12th annual Great Outhouse Blowout races near Gravel Switch and the fourth annual Battle of the Barrels, a bourbon barrel racing contest in Frankfort.

We couldn't TiVo time, but two out of four ain't bad in a weekend on a budget, and who really wants to be in the racing infield when an outhouse racer goes astray?

Not wanting to battle the 15,263 folks (most of whom dressed in 1930s attire to pay homage to "Seabiscuit") at the opening day of Keeneland, our first of three days in Lexington found us just driving around.

And what a drive it is.

An autumn trip to the unique Bluegrass region of Lexington where the thoroughbreds are running, the paddlewheels churning and the barrels racing. Get a family's look at Keeneland and driving tours of the central Kentucky horse farms.

Home to 450 horse farms, the Lexington area (which rightfully claims title as the Horse Capital of the World) is a wonderful place to just go and drive.

Get off the manic interstates and always-clogged New Circle Road and wind your way to the small towns around Lexington – such as Paris, Frankfort, Harrodsburg, Nicholasville, Georgetown, Versailles and Richmond – on miles of tree-lined roads flanked with beautiful black plank fences holding in horses of all types grazing on the bluegrass.

Only two hours away, it is truly another world.

And we had a map for it. We were armed with a central Kentucky map obtained at the Huntington AAA office that listed all the major horse farms in the region. We spent some time every day just driving, making me fall in love again with such roads as Old Frankfort Pike, Russell Cave Road, Ironworks Pike and Newtown Pike.

Home to lots to see and do – including the relatively new Lexington Center-based **University of Kentucky Basketball Museum, 410 W. Vine St., (800-269-1953), the Lexington Children's Museum, 440 W. Short St., (859-258-3256) and the Lexington History Museum, 215 Main St. (859-335-6637)** – downtown has continued to evolve while holding onto its heritage.

Walking, we enjoyed a great public art display called "Dynamic Doors: Portals to Creativity." The display is 200 doors that Lexington Arts and Cultural Council volunteers removed from the Bluegrass/Aspendale housing project before its demolition and then put their own personal art stamp on. Scattered about town, the exhibit was a nice touch if you happened to be coming downtown anyway.

One of my favorite historic spots in downtown Lexington is the very much alive and kicking **Kentucky Theatre, 214 E. Main St. (859-231-6997)**, which hosted the world premiere of "Seabiscuit."

Fred Mills, who runs the theater and was behind the counter when we were there, keeps the main theater (the Kentucky) and its smaller kid sister theater (the State) filled with an incredible range of film, live performance and art.

There's cult classic midnight movies such as Monty Python's "Holy Grail," old flicks from the likes of beloved actors such as Bob Hope, new documentary and art house flicks, as well as art exhibits.

Like most cool-movie-deprived twenty and thirtysomethings saddled with the chocolate milk-moustached gang, my wife Toril and I were thrilled to sit down to a funky, first-run movie: the Oscar-nominated and gorgeously photographed documentary "Winged Migration."

With the wild winds blowing cold through downtown Lexington, we watched in awe as birds from the bald eagle to the arctic tern (which migrates 12,500 miles) made the flight of their lives with that beloved promise to return.

We, too, made that promise, since the Kentucky Theatre is also home to **Michael Johnathon's Woodsongs Old Time Radio Hour (859-252-8888).** Heard in syndication around the world and in Huntington on WTCR-FM, Woodsongs is taped at the Kentucky on selected Mondays. Like Mountain Stage, it features an eclectic range of musicians and singer-songwriters from around the world..

With more than 80 restaurants scattered about downtown and campus, dining was a tough choice. A few blocks from campus we found just the former Jewish synagogue of our culinary choice, Joe Bologna's, 120 W. Maxwell St. Although you can't ring up any "Kentucky steak" at Joe B's in spite of its name, you can ring up some great breadsticks and a pretty good pizza pie in an atmosphere colored by pastel-shaded stained glass and deep, comfy booths.

After an all-the-Cheerios-we-could-munch continental breakfast Saturday, we headed out for a real Bluegrass breakfast, at **Rebecca-Ruth Candy Inc., 112 E. Second St., Frankfort, (502-223-7475)**, where you can take a free candy factory tour and sample some of those world-famous pecan-topped, chocolate-smothered bourbon balls.

With a nose on for a good race, we had caught wind of the fourth annual Battle of the Barrels, a bourbon barrel race at **Buffalo Trace Distillery, 1001 Wilkinson Blvd., Frankfort, (502-696-5926)** and we had to check it out.

After playing on the playgrounds and walking the lush gardens at Buffalo Trace, we watched the intense competition in which men and women teams tried their darnedest to roll and wrangle 55-gallon barrels around a U-shaped course.

After watching Buffalo Trace worker Obie Kemper do a Harlem Globetrotteresque dribbling workout on the barrel, we decided with armfuls of sleepy kids that we had seen it all. Since bourbon isn't exactly our cup of tea, we cracked open a couple Ale-8-1's (ginger ale made in Winchester, Ky.) and pointed our plastic Tennessee stud (a Saturn) down toward Shaker Village.

Like the horse farms, the majority of the world's bourbon – about 95 percent – is made in central Kentucky. There are six other distilleries nearby. Tours are free, and the grounds usually filled with trails and places to picnic.

Since we were so close, we headed down U.S. 127 to Harrodsburg, one of the first settlements in Kentucky.

Shaker Village at Pleasant Hill, seven miles east of Harrodsburg, **(800-734-5611)** is the largest historic community of its kind in America and another unique stop in the Bluegrass.

The peaceful, communal society was started in 1805 and by the 1920s there were 500 Shakers living here.

The society, which loved to make furniture and music, but not love, started fading away in central Kentucky in the 1860s.

Operated by a nonprofit, educational organization, Shaker Village is home to 34 original 19th-century buildings on about 3,000 acres.

With two cookie crumblers (who are perhaps a bit too rowdy for the white bonnet crowd), we decided to just hit the Shaker Village's historic sternwheeler, *The Dixie Belle*, which plies the Kentucky River through the Palisades for an hour-long cruise.

Leaving three times a day through Oct. 31, (noon, 2 and 4 p.m.) the *Dixie Belle* at $7 a piece (and free for kids under 6) was a wonderful way to spend an afternoon soaking up the waning sun, the region and its river.

On a sunny Sunday afternoon, we loaded up a picnic and parked beneath the towering oak trees at **Keeneland Race Course, 4201 Versailles Road (859-253-0541)**. A National Historic Landmark, which you see as Baltimore's Pimlico race track in the movie "Seabiscuit," the track is simply one of the world's most beautiful racetracks.

Like **The Kentucky Horse Park, 4089 Iron Works Parkway, (800-678-8813)**, located just north of Lexington in Georgetown, Ky., the races, which run spring and fall, are a great spend-the-day destination for horse lovers.

Having only been a handful of times to the races in college, I was surprised at how kid-friendly Keeneland was. There are changing tables in all restrooms, and kids can nuzzle up to the track and the paddock area where they get a great look and sometimes even pet the horses before or after a race.

The track, which costs $3 and is free for kids, also hosts Breakfast With the Works, a $5 buffet breakfast each Saturday with kids activities including pin the tail on the (fake) horse, free temporary tattoos and pictures made in pint-sized jockey silks.

We soaked up the sun and the colorful, neck-craning crowd that roared to life when the thoroughbreds came rumbling 'round to the end.

After a photo finish and our pockets a wee bit lighter for tossing a couple Washingtons on a horse named Chuck Yeager (who couldn't seem to keep it on the runway), we piled the sleepy kids in the car, heading to the hills of home, leaving Lexington richer since our souls were filled with newly plowed memories.

If You Go: Lexington

GETTING THERE: Take I-64 west for about two hours or until you start seeing horse barns that are nicer than people houses.

PARKING IT: The 1,200-acre Kentucky Horse Park, located just north of Lexington on Iron Works Parkway, is dedicated to horses of all breeds. Tour the working horse farm with its two museums, gift shops, riding trails and more. Go online at www.kyhorsepark.com.

HORSING AROUND: Grab a horse farm map at your local AAA office and take a driving tour of Lexington's famous horse farms. You can also take a van tour of Calumet Farms that has produced nine Kentucky Derby winners. You may recognize the red and white buildings from the movie, "Seabiscuit." Call (859) 231-8272.

HORSE BY TRAIN: The Blue Grass Railroad Museum runs 5 1/2 miles of tourist train track through Kentucky horse farm country between Versailles and the Kentucky River. Call (859) 873-2476. Go online at www.bgrm.org.

RIDE A HORSE: You can ride horseback through 1,000 acres of lush bluegrass at the Big Red Stables, 1605 Jackson Pike, in Harrodsburg, Ky., just south of Lexington.

WHERE TO STAY: A unique place to stay is The Inn at Shaker Village of Pleasant Hill (south of Lexington). Kids 17 and under stay free, and even offers boarding for your horses. Call (800) 734-5611.

WHERE TO EAT:

ALFAFA'S RESTAURANT: 141 E. Main St., Lexington. Doing the vegetarian thing since the 1970s, it's a cool spot for the veggie lover and the meat lover as well. Call (859) 253-0014.

ATOMIC CAFE: A cool and colorful Caribbean restaurant at 265 N. Limestone St. Call (859) 254-1969.

JOE BOLOGNA'S: Great pizza and breadsticks in a building (former church) on the National Register of Historic Places at 120 W. Maxwell St. Call (859) 252-4933.

RAMSEY'S DINER: Located at 496 E. High St., this home-style cooking restaurant has all the Kentucky favorites from Hot Browns to Derby pie. Call (859) 259-2708.

THE PARKETTE: Authentic 1950s drive in with Kentucky Poor Boy and great onion rings. Located at 1230 New Circle Road. Call (859) 254-8723.

Other Great Factory Tours

LEE MIDDLETON DOLLS: One of the top baby doll manufacturers in the U.S., Lee Middleton Dolls is located at 1301 Washington Blvd., Belpre, Ohio (across from Parkersburg, W.Va.). Visit the factory and the Doll Home Store and Legacy Museum. Call (740) 423-1717 or go online at www.leemiddleton.com.

ROSSI PASTA: Kids love spaghetti and they'll love seeing how it's made. Located at 114 Greene St., in Marietta, Ohio, the Rossi Pasta Factory is open for tours. Call (740) 373-5155. Go online at www.rossipasta.com.

BLENKO GLASS: Hand-made in Milton, W.Va. since 1921, the colorful and historic Blenko Glass is a blast to see made with the company's six-man teams gathering, blowing and finishing all sorts of glassware. See it made from an observation deck during week-day work hours. Also, visit the museum and Visitors Center. Call (304) 743-9081. Go online at www.blenkoglass.com.

HEINER'S BAKERY: Located in the historic Old Central City district in Huntington, W.Va.'s west end, Heiner's Bakery has been baking up fresh bread since 1905. You can tour the factory from 9 a.m. to noon, Wednesday through Friday, Oct. 1 through May. 31. Reservations are required and visitors must be 6 or older and group cannot exceed 30 people. Call (800) 776-8411. Go online at www.heinersbakery.com.

ALE 8-1: Take a backstage look at the making of one of the region's only sodas, Ale-8-1 at the Winchester, Ky.-based bottling plant. Tours are Friday and by appointment. Call (859) 744-3484. Go online at www.ale-8-one.com.

CORVETTES: You can take a one-hour, and one-mile-long guided tour of the only production site for the Corvette at the General Motors Bowling Green (Ky) Assembly Plant. Don't miss the Corvette Museum with more than 75 Corvettes. Call (800) 558-3883. Go online at www.corvettemuseum.com.

LOUISVILLE SLUGGER MUSEUM AND FACTORY: Located on 800 W. Main St., in downtown Louisvile, the Louisville Slugger factory is where they make the official bat of Major League Baseball. Also, check out the museum with interactive exhibits. Call (877) 775-8443. Go online at www.sluggermuseum.org.

Morehead
Kentucky

Miles: 75

Original Trip November 2003

A splashdown at the region's largest lake, Cave Run, located just west of Morehead. We also check out the always colorful and cool Kentucky Folk Art Center.

Although it's only an easy hour away, cruising Interstate 64 west, Morehead is a place I hadn't been to in probably at least a year.

A trip to this ever-blossoming Mecca for everything from bluegrass to Kentucky-fried blues music, musky, and whimsical folk art, was long overdue.

Oddly enough, the seed for the need for going was planted at the new grass festival Appalachian Uprising, when we met a Morehead State University grad who lives in Dayton.

He spoke about the rock climbing, trails and fishing at **Daniel Boone National Forest** and **Cave Run Lake** with such energy that we knew the Dave Trippin' crew had to go drink in the views and experiences of our region's largest lake, Cave Run, and the little college town just east of the lake in Morehead.

It's a good thing our Johnny Morehead Seed was such a vocal disciple, because it's an easy place to buzz by at 65 or 70 mph when you're Lexington bound. At the rest stop on I-64, there was not even one brochure to let you know you might want to get off at this exit. But, you might want to consider it, because you are approaching the largest lake in the region (8,270 acres), one of the country's greatest collection of folk art at the **Kentucky Folk Art Center** and the land of giant festivals, including Poppy Mountain

Bluegrass Festival, the Cave Run Storytelling Festival and the Cave Run Rock 'n' Blues 'n' BBQ Festival.

Since we arrived right before the crack of noon, we decided it was high time for another cup of coffee. We found just the right place in the heart of downtown.

Opened earlier this year in a historic building that was once a bank (and still has the vault and the ultra cool vault room to prove it), **Grounds and Sounds** is a great lunch or live music stop.

With be-bop jazz grooving from suspended Peavey speakers between suspended stage lights, and everything from banjos to congas on the stage, it was comfortable and clear that Grounds and Sounds takes both seriously.

Behind an 8-foot or taller Norfolk Pine was hidden the street sign, "Live Music - Stage Open to All." That truly is the case.

While such well-traveled local troubadours such as Eddie Riffe and Rob McNurlin have taken the stage, so has Mike Seeger - thanks to Grounds and Sounds' well-connected neighbor, the **Kentucky Center for Traditional Music** that was established in 2000 at Morehead State University. It promotes traditional music and teaches university courses in one of Appalachia's greatest gifts.

The **KCTM, 149 E. Main St., (606-783-9001)** and Don Rigsby, its director and internationally known bluegrass artist, are also working on some exhibits. They will include an interactive Instrument Petting Zoo that will allow kids to pick and play fiddles, banjos, mandolins and guitars.

We enjoyed a game of checkers and some excellent sandwiches, including the kids' favorite, a rarely seen peanut butter and fluff sandwich. I had a Kentucky Hot Brown on grilled bread. We could have easily camped at Grounds and Sounds for a few more hours, but the Lavender boys wanted a closer look at Cave Run Lake.

Not being in charge, the boys got to accompany mom and dad for a quick pitstop at the **Kentucky Folk Art Center, 102 W. First St. (606-783-2204 and www.kyfolkart.org)**. The center boasts more than 900 pieces of regional folk art. That summer's exhibit was Mark Anthony Mulligan's 50-piece, "You Must Withstand the Wind: Transformation of the Urban Landscape."

A colorful, quirky and hand-drawn-and-written powerful blast on urban sprawl and the McDonaldilization of America, the exhibit showcases Mulligan's knack for putting the microscope to his hometown of Louisville. In doing so, he gives quite a commentary on modern America.

Mulligan's exhibit includes colorfully painted road signs. Some are real and a bit surreal like the once-here "Ashland Oil" to the maybe even more real fictional place, "Bacon Toast Hospital." The paintings were augmented by a collection of his hand-written songs, including my favorite, "Thank God for Captain D's" sung to the tune of "Thank God I'm a Country Boy."

With John Denver now planted in my head for the weekend, we decided to head the few miles west to Cave Run Lake.

Any trip with kids to Cave Run Lake should include a quick stop at the **Minor E. Clark Fish Hatchery**. Located at the top of the lake, the hatchery (one of the largest warm-water hatcheries in the United States) is free and open weekdays 7 a.m. to 3 p.m. **(800-858-1549)**.

Cave Run, which has become the "Musky Capitol of the South" and has

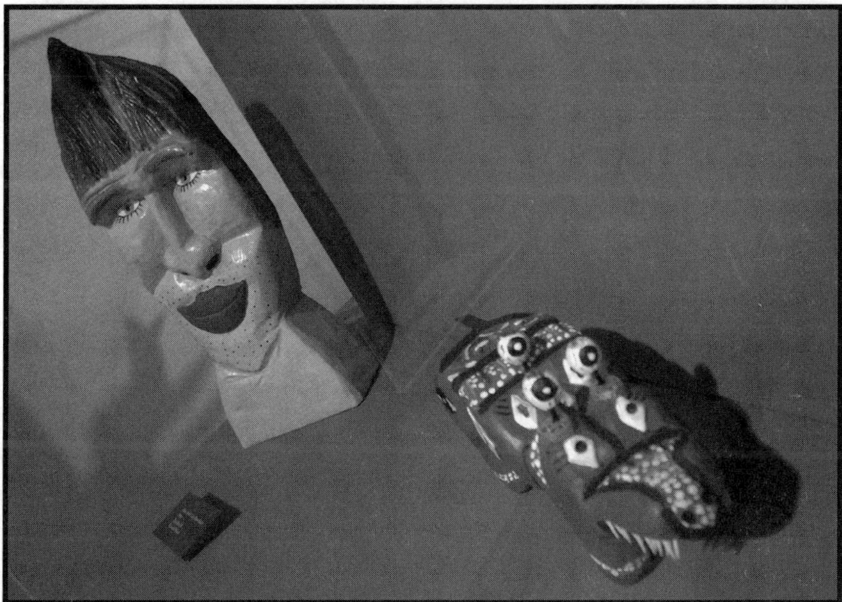

the hundreds of happy fish-holding photos to prove it, is armed with this not-so-secret weapon.

With the afternoon sun hotter than a Karl Rove e-mail, we decided to forgo walking to the more than 100 ponds on the property and instead checked out the fascinating round display pool in the shade that had layers of fry, fingerlings and full-sized fish ranging from the bizarre gar to carp and bass.

Busting down Kentucky 801, we made a beeline to **Twin Knobs Campground (877-444-6777)** and did so just in time.

Although it was a Friday morning (and the campground is good-sized), we got one of last camping spots for the weekend.

After putting up our teepee tent (in the shade again and not on the government-approved gravel pad), we made a beeline to the main attraction at this wooded peninsula on Cave Run: a 2,000-foot beach that could fit our local Beech Fork beach in its back pocket.

Soaking up the sun and fun of the beach, we were hoping we would see a sailboat or two come blowing down the lake, since it has its own sailing club (online at www.caverunsailing.org).

After several hours, and ready to almost eat the beach sand, Toril fired up the campsite coals to grill fish and our garden veggies while I took the boys to enjoy one of Morehead's main courses when it comes to tourism: fishing.

With a sunset striping orange across the dark blue waters, the Lavender boys (Will, 2 and Jake, 5) got into some serious bluegill battles that, of course, are just a laughable fishing appetizer for the folks who come to Cave Run to throw out lures the size of Chad Pennington's cleats for those famous Cave Run Musky.

There is plenty of cool stuff to get into around the lake from Cave Run Bingo and sky diving to putt-putt golf and plenty of antiques. We decided to break on through to the other side of the lake and drive the 11-mile Zilpo Scenic Byway that lies on the west side of the lake. It winds up at the more secluded 355-acre peninsula that houses the **Zilpo Recreation Area**. There, you can find another, quieter campground, hiking and jogging trails, another large sandy beach and spectacular views of Cave Run.

Along the scenic byway, there are eight stops you can make, such as **Clear Creek Lake** (a small, quiet lake) to access the 269-mile-long **Sheltowee Trace National Recreation Trail** that's named after Daniel Boone (who was called "Sheltowee" or "Big Turtle" by the Shawnee).

We wanted to see the world from the window up above, so we stopped at **Tater Knob Fire Tower**, which was first erected in 1934 and refurbished in 1993.

The last fire tower left in the **Daniel Boone National Forest (606-784-5624)**, the 35-foot-steel-tower is a fun, moderately easy climb (if you've chalked up a few frequent hiker miles). Even 5-year-olds could do it, although they may require a horsey ride down the many, many, many steps as Jake did.

Seeing the expansive rolling green quilt of our national forests from up above makes you realize that man really doesn't improve on God's original interior decorating.

With the warm voice of longtime WMKY-FM DJ Sandy Knipp and his "Bluegrass Diversions" show carrying us homeward bound, we easily rolled east on I-64, back across the Big Sandy River border, determined to make a point to come back to Morehead sometime soon.

If You Go: Morehead

GETTING THERE: Turn off the GPS and go west on I-64 (about an hour from Huntington) until you hit the Morehead, Ky. exit. Whew, that was hard.
GOOD TIMES TO GO: Morehead has lots of cool festivals. The Cave Run Rock 'n' Blues 'n' BBQ Festival, at Poppy Mountain, 8030 U.S. 60 East (10 miles east of downtown Morehead). is held in July. Call (800) 654-1944 or www.caverunblues.com.
POPPY MOUNTAIN BLUEGRASS: Poppy Mountain also hosts one of America's largest traditional bluegrass music festivals each September. It runs for a full week with more than 100 acts taking the stage. You can camp, hike and fish at Poppy Mountain throughout the year. Call (606) 784-2277 or go online at www.poppymountainbluegrass.com.
TELLING STORIES: The fish tales are big at Cave Run and get even bigger each September, during the annual Cave Run Storytelling Festival, a full slate of national-act storytellers at Cave Run Lake. Enjoy ghost and fireside stories by the beach on Saturday evening. Family camping within walking distance of the festival. Call (800) 654-1944 or go online at www.caverunstoryfest.org.
TOURISM INFO: Call the Morehead Tourism Commission at (606) 780-4342. Go online at www.moreheadtourism.com.

Other Cool Lakes

SUMMERSVILE LAKE: The 2,790-acre lake in Summersville, W.Va., is known for its super-clear, deep water (25 to 40 feet visibility in the summer). That makes it a diving hotspot that *Skin Diver* mag calls, "The little Bahamas of the East." Call Sarge's Dive Shop at (304) 872-1331.

YATESVILLE LAKE: Located just about 40 minutes from Huntington, Yatesville Lake, near Louisa, Ky., is a tributary of the Big Sandy River. The shoreline measures 93 miles. There's lots to do on and around the lake, including the 18-hole Eagle Ridge Golf Course. Call (606) 686-2361.

GRAYSON LAKE: Known for its spectacular cliffs, Grayson Lake (1,510-acre, 20-mile long) is also home to the 10,000 acre Public Wildlife Refuge where you can hike, bird and ride horse trails. Call (606) 474-4513.

SENECA LAKE: North of Marietta, and south of Cambridge, Seneca Lake, at 3,550 acres of water is Ohio's third largest inland lake in Ohio, and the largest south of I-70. A nice stop if you're going up to The Wilds since there's 513 campsites. Call (740) 685-5831.

BEECH FORK LAKE: Only about 10 miles south of Huntington, Beech Fork Lake has a state park on one end (with W.Va's largest campground) and a developed U.S. Army Corps of Engineers' site on the Lavalette side with a beach, hiking trails, a marina, picnic facilities, and a wildlife museum. Call the State Park at (304) 528-5794. Call the Corps at (304) 525-4831.

LAKE VESUVIUS: Located just north of Ironton, Ohio, the 143-acre Lake Vesuvius is an intimate lake with lots of recreational opportunities. A wheelchair accessible trail leads to Rock House, and a wheel-chair accessible boardwalk cuts across the lake, providing easy fishing access. The Ohio University Southern Nature Center hosts educational programs and rents boats from canoes and kayaks to johnboats seasonally. Call (740) 532-4600.

Cumberland Falls
Kentucky

On the first Dave Trippin' of 2004, we thought we'd take the Elmo wranglers to see something you can't see anyplace else in this hemisphere.

Since our 4-year-old Jacob is a certified moon spotter with a penchant for howling (a trait he began while backpacking him under full moon through the wilds of Manhattan at age 2), we figured we'd try again to catch the elusive moonbow.

With our Dave Trippin' budget more Zanesville than Zimbabwe, we figured we best bypass Victoria Falls and gas up the station wagon – destination: south-central Kentucky and **Cumberland Falls State Resort Park**, home to the only moonbow in the Western Hemisphere.

The Cliff notes (yes, bad pun intended) are that the Cumberland River's 125-foot wide curtain of water called "The Niagara of the South" cascades 68-feet into the rocks below, creating enough mist to produce the magic of a moonbow that can be viewed during clear evenings with a full moon (and the two evenings before and after the full moon).

Knowing well that we could drive 3 ½-hours and only see snowy nights of white haze, we still set out in great spirits because the land where Daniel Boone once romped is chock full of fun.

Miles: 225

Original Trip February 2004

We take a quest to see the only Moonbow in the Western Hemisphere at Cumberland Falls State Resort Park. Along the way we bump into the Kentucky Music Hall of Fame, the original KFC, Daniel Boone, Yahoo Falls, and one of the coolest little colleges anywhere.

With Morehead State University's WMKY-FM cranking, we barreled down I-64 to Ky. 627, and our first stop of **Fort Boonesborough State Park (859-527-3131)**.

The replica of the 1775 fort built along the banks of the Kentucky River "by beavers" (Jacob's revisionist history) is quite impressive, though we found it silent in winter. The place is hopping alive in spring and summer, though, with craftspeople and 18th century re-enactors.

Snaking our way south, we jumped back on I-75 and made a beeline for Berea, a small town with the well-deserved title of "The Folk Arts and Crafts Capital of Kentucky." It's home to the quirky **Berea College (800-366-9358)** where they are, for good reason, darn proud of Basketweaving 101 and where "Skittles" is not just a colorful candy treat, but a cool, ancient wooden game students make.

Berea College – where Huntington native and Black History Month founder Carter G. Woodson got his bachelor's degree – is one of the few colleges in the country where students work for the school (often in the Appalachian craft industry) in lieu of tuition.

A Mecca for Appalachian artists since the 1800s, Berea got an additional tourism boost when the 20,000-square-foot **Kentucky Artisan Center** opened in July 2003.

We loved the exposed-beam construction and the display of local arts and crafts in a kinder, gentler, Tamarack-lite setting.

But we also hope it never replaces a visit to downtown Berea, home to dozens of arts and crafts shops and the student-run **Log House Sales Room (859-985-3226)**, where we bought an awesome harbor bell made by students; **Boone Tavern, (800-366-9358),** a historic hotel and dining room built in 1909, is also run by the students.

Since our 1-year-old Will calls everything "ball" before chucking forks, knives and anything his paws can grab off a table, we retreated from the too-quiet Boone Tavern and walked a few doors down at **Papaleno's Pizza**, where the students hand-toss pizza dough high into the air.

After a good brisk walkabout and fired up with a Pinnacle Blend coffee from **Coffee Conspiracy (859-986-8597)**, we boogied down I-75 for a long overdue trip to the **Kentucky Music Hall of Fame and Museum (877-356-3263)** in Renfro Valley.

Opened in May 2003, the Kentucky Music Hall of Fame and Museum is a wonderful, tourist-drawing neighbor to **Renfro Valley Entertainment Center (800-765-7464)**, which hosts headliner concerts (from March through December), festivals and four nights of homegrown country, bluegrass and gospel music weekly through December.

Ten cents of music history here is that they've been sending out the Renfro Valley Barn Dance over the airwaves since Nov. 4, 1939, on WLS. That makes it one of the oldest music radio shows in the country.

The Hall of Fame and Museum has a wonderfully rich tie to its neighbor, since the exposed-beam building was once a horse barn owned by John Lair, the radio man who started the Barn Dance.

While Jacob danced on the wood slats stage where the museum hosts live music, we stood and were amazed by "The Ol' Homeplace Exhibit," the wood-carved names of 350 Kentucky music artists in coats of paint of many colors.

The multimedia museum features its Hall of Fame with video biographies of folks such as Loretta Lynn and Rosemary Clooney, a 6 ½-minute video about Kentucky and its music, artifacts such as a 1931 Ford produce wagon as well as George Gibson's incredible banjo collection from African gourd instruments up through 1900 and more.

You can even cut a CD, singing karaoke of famous Kentucky songs.

Feeling a rumble in our tummies, my wife Toril and I skipped a karaoke Judds duet of "Why Not Me" and headed back out on I-75.

We couldn't resist a trip to "Eat Where it All Began," a visit to the **Harland Sanders Café and Museum (606-528-2163)**.

One of the few fast-food places on the National Register of Historic Places, Col., Sanders' original restaurant in Corbin, Ky., appears just as it did in the 1940s, complete with the Colonel's open kitchen, his model motel room and tons of quirky Col. Sanders' memorabilia and artifacts. I'm still kicking myself for not snatching the Col. Sanders Mandolin Orchestra doing gospel favorites on vinyl for $5.

After a flurry of family photos with the Colonel (whose plaster image is sitting on a bench in the restaurant), we loaded back in the wagon at dark to go the final 20 miles to our destination – licking our sticky, greasy-good chicken fingers all the way to the falls and still thinking about those 11 secret herbs and spices.

The timing was ripe for moonbow viewing – just a small problem, though. Snow, snow and some more snow.

Alone at the falls that night, I made a wish on a fallen flake for clear skies the next night.

Found in 1780, Cumberland Falls has been attracting streams of tourists since 1875.

Kentucky's third state park, opened in 1931, Cumberland Falls State Resort Park does tourists right. Each weekend around the full moon cycle, the park hosts two days of workshops, photo seminars as well as field trips to some awesome nearby places.

Having missed the Saturday field trip to **Yahoo Falls and Natural Arch** in the adjacent 100,000-acre **Big South Fork National River and Recreation Area**, we decided to make the trip ourselves on Sunday. Boy, was it worth it.

Armed with our Kentucky Atlas and Gazetteer (which we needed), we made the 30-minute drive west, parked and hiked back 1.5 miles to the arch and then doubled back and down below to get what I called the "backstage pass" (under the cliff and behind the falls) to the highest waterfall in Kentucky, Yahoo Falls, which is 113 feet high.

Just past the falls, we encountered a seemingly endless steep set of stairs. About halfway up, Jacob who was back in my backpack after hiking quite a bit, asked, "Are we stairmasters?"

"Yes, we are."

With clear skies, we stopped in historic Stearns for lunch. In season (spring through fall), this town is the starting point of an open-car, train ride on the **Big South Fork Scenic Railway (606-376-5330)**, (one of only three tourist railroads in Kentucky). It travels back through deep gorges and along steep cliffs to such abandoned mining towns as Blue Heron.

Back at Cumberland Falls, we enjoyed another meal at the **DuPont Lodge**, built of massive pine timbers cut on property by the Civilian Conservation Corps. The CCC also cut about 20 miles of trails (including the highly recommended trail to Eagle Falls, a trail which offers a great view of Cumberland Falls from the other side of the river).

We took a long dinner at the restaurant with its near floor-to-ceiling windows providing a panoramic view of the Cumberland River gorge below and feeders attracting everything from birds to skunks and raccoons.

Just after dinner on our way back to our Woodland Room, we saw the star of the show – the moon. It was rising, but with a yellow, cloudy fuzz all around it.

As night fell, I made my way to the falls, where I ran into park ranger Doyle Bird, who's worked midnight shift at the park for 18 years, and who's seen the moonbow hundreds of times.

In the empty parking lot, he talked about the beauty of the pastel moonbow on cold, clear nights and of the blessing of being able to work and live near the Daniel Boone National Forest. Bird took one look at the old yellow moon, and the once-starry sky turning to haze, and sadly shook his head.

Even in a world of drive-thru, instant everything, it was sure hard to feel bummed out or cheated.

Even if our eyes were still searching for a night-time rainbow, our souls had been filled with a drink of God's natural beauty and our bellies filled with the finger lickin' good creations of the Colonel.

If You Go: Cumberland Falls

WHAT IT IS: Cumberland Falls has the only moonbow in the Western Hemisphere. The other is at Victoria Falls, Zimbabwe, on the Zambezi River. The moonbow is similar to a rainbow, except it is formed at night. When conditions are right, the arch of white light begins at the base of the falls and continues downstream. Several factors determine the occurrence of a moonbow: a clear moonlit night, sufficient mist from the waterfall, wind direction and velocity.
WHERE: Cumberland Falls is located 20 miles southwest of Corbin, Ky. Traveling south on I-75 from Lexington, take exit 25 and follow the signs. Take U.S. 25 W to Ky. 90. It takes about 3 1/2 to four hours to get there from downtown Huntington.
BEST TIME OF YEAR: Fall is the busiest. Nights can be relatively warm, yet in fall and winter you may see color in the moonbow. Also, leaf peepers can do some great hiking at Cumberland Falls State Resort Park, located within the Daniel Boone National Forest, as well as at Big South Fork National River and Recreation Area and other area Kentucky State Parks such as Levi Jackson State Park.
LODGING: Cumberland Falls State Resort Park has 52 rooms at the DuPont Lodge, as well as Woodland Rooms, cottages and 50 campsites, available April 1 through Oct. 31.
ROLLING ON THE RIVER: Guided whitewater rafting trips are offered on the Cumberland River through Sheltowee Trace Outfitters. Trips daily from May through October (depending on water levels). Call (800) 541-RAFT.
ON THE WEB: For more information about Kentucky State Parks, call (800) 255-PARK (7275) or go online at www.parks.ky.gov. For more info about traveling in Kentucky, call the Kentucky Department of Travel for a free Getaway Guide at (800) 225-8747 from 8 a.m. to 4 p.m. Monday through Friday. Or go online at www.kentuckytourism.com.

More Waterfalls

TORRENT FALLS: Located alongside Ky-11, just north of Natural Bridge State Park, near Slade, Ky., about 2 1/2 hours southwest of Huntington. The 165-foot-tall falls is part of Torrent Falls Resort home to Torrent Falls Family Climbing Adventure. Call (606) 668-6613 Go online at www.torrentfalls.com.

ANGLIN FALLS: A worthwhile sidetrip to Cumberland Falls is Anglin Falls, a 75-foot-tall waterfall at the John B. Stephenson Memorial Forest State Nature Preserve, in Rockcastle County. The waterfall is usually only running in Spring.

HOCKING HILLS: This state park and adjacent state nature preserves near Logan, Ohio, are packed with many waterfalls including Upper and Lower Falls (at Old Man's Cave), Whispering Falls, Cedar Falls, Ash Falls, Conkle's Hollow Falls, Rockhouse, Cantwell Cliffs and Rockbridge. Go online at www.hockinghills.com.

BLACKWATER FALLS: One of West Virginia's most famous falls, Blackwater Falls cascades through 500-foot-deep gorge near Davis, W.Va., at Blackwater Falls State Park. Nice observation deck and lots of hiking trails nearby.

Go online at www.blackwaterfalls.com.

CATHEDRAL FALLS: Located just two miles southeast of Gauley Bridge, W.Va., this 100-foot waterfall drops over a series of overhanging ledges. The city of Gauley Bridge has provided a picnic shelter, parking and a viewing area.

MALL FALLS: For those city-folk in the crew who bristle at the sight of muddy boots, they can enjoy the spectacular indoor cascades at the three-story atrium with lush greenery while sipping a cup of joe from nearby Starbucks inside the Charleston Town Center Mall. Go online at www.charlestontowncenter.com.

Hillbilly Days
Pikeville, Kentucky

Miles: 100

Original Trip April 2005

The Lavender crew loads up the jalopy south for a Springtime run to one of the region's biggest gatherings, Pikeville's Hillbilly Days.

On a sleepy Saturday, our 5-year-old son Jacob jumped up from bed, ran into our room and said his first words for the day: "Can we go on a mini vacation?"

Yes, we can.

With gas prices higher than Spruce Knob, the Dave Trippin' posse hasn't been looking for some place for fun so far away that you have to sell off a kid or two along the route just to pay for the fuel.

So, after a leisurely Saturday morning scooping in cartoons, cereal and the ever-greening scenery outside, we loaded up the wagon for an easy two-hour day trip to the 29th annual **Hillbilly Days in Pikeville, Ky.**

No strangers to the Country Music Highway, the Lavender posse has worn down paths to such places as Prestonsburg, Ky., and the Jenny Wiley State Resort Park, but has rarely kept on trucking down 23 to hit Pikeville, one of the largest cities tucked just north of the southeast corner of Kentucky where Virginia and the other Virginia (the Mountain State) get all tangled together.

One of four National Scenic Byways in the state, U.S. 23 was breaking into full glory with the hills along the highway ablaze with splashes of redbuds and dogwoods.

With just a bite of chill in the air, we motored down to get a refreshing drink of

one of the first big festivals of the season and one of the largest festivals in our region.

Although the Lavender clan was ripping through Louisa, Paintsville and Prestonsburg like Burt Reynolds' Firebird in "Smokey and the Bandit," there are plenty of good reasons to stop along the way.

Not the least of which are a number of good flea markets, such as **Storm Hollow** and **Bull Creek**, that run along the Country Music Highway.

Exactly 62 miles from Huntington, you can also take a good break by jumping off U.S. 23 and hitting **Loretta Lynn's homeplace** in Butcher Hollow in Van Lear, Ky.

As soon as we could get in range, the radio dial went straight to WMMT-FM 88.7 out of Whitesburg.

Operated by **Appalshop**, the media mothership of all things Appalachian, the station and the media center turned 35 in 2005 and is a real treasure, since there isn't hardly a type of music they won't play and any story they aren't afraid to tell in film or on stage.

We were able to wash our souls in the morning musical dew of Ella Fitzgerald and a whole slew of crooners who brought in Saturday nice and easy.

By the time we saw the "Welcome Y'all Hillbillies Back Home to Pikeville" sign, we were laid up in a country state of mind and ready to join what is estimated at about 30,000 or more of our closest hillbilly cousins, since this fest draws more than 100,000 over a weekend.

Even though it's more crowded than New York City sidewalks, there's a great vibe that runs through the year's first big fest. All the wackiness is for a good

cause, since the Pikeville Shriners raise more than $50,000 annually for the Shriners Children's Hospital in Lexington, Ky.

As a veteran parade lover who grew up going to the Ironton Memorial Day Parade every year, I can tell you the parade here is worth the trip.

Tucked in the shade of Azalea Alley off of Pikeville's main drag, we gulped down 32-ounce tin cups of fresh draft root beer, hitting an absolute hillbilly high. We watched a seemingly endless line of jalopies, mini bikes, golf carts and chopped VW bugs and bands cranking music on the back of pickup trucks – all affixed with bumper stickers such as "Honk If Parts Fall Off" that kept you chuckling for what seemed like hours.

After witnessing a working shower on a truck, Christmas wreath hubcaps (actually, those looked pretty good) and Darth Vader and a Stormtrooper slinging Mardi Gras beads from the back of a pickup, we decided we had darn near seen it all, even though there was no end in sight of this parade.

Throughout the day, we found ourselves plopped in the grass listening to a steady stream of old-time and bluegrass music from such bands as Grayson Ratliff and the Sunny Valley Boys.

Although there was a river full of traditional Appalachian music, we refreshingly ran into Delta blues, rock, several flavors of country and even some music from Ecuador going down along the streets of Pikeville.

Though we didn't run into hardly any Appalachian crafters, which surprised us at such a festival, the Hillbilly Days proved that Pikeville, which is building a new 7,000-seat arena and convention center in

its downtown across from the gazebo, knows how to "Git-R-Done" when it comes to festivals.

After staying all night with Kris and Charlie Preston, some musician friends in Pikeville, and their great dogs Buck and Pearl Scruggs, we headed our horse back up north along the Country Music Highway, our eyes feasting again on the glorious redbuds, our ears soaking up some Dwight Yoakam singing "Crazy Little Thing Called Love" on WDHR-FM as we rolled through Betsy Lane and our cups running over with that sweet taste of homemade root beer ... Ahhhh, a wonderful mini-vacation.

If You Go: Pikeville

ALONG THE WAY: A must-stop for music fans is the Country Music Highway Museum, which opened March 5 2005, just off of U.S. 23 at Paintsville. Enjoy the interactive exhibits featuring the memorabilia of Eastern Kentucky born and raised stars such as Tom T. Hall, Loretta Lynn, Rebecca Lynn Howard, Billy Ray Cyrus, Ricky Skaggs and others. Sing karaoke to songs made famous by Highway 23 stars, enjoy the rare Nickelodeon, a full-band player piano made by the Mills Novelty Co. This piano (only one of 17 left of its kind that works) was donated by the estate of Proc Brown of Paintsville, Ky. Cost is $3 and $2 for children.

OTHER SITES IN PIKEVILLE: History buffs will get their fill in Pikeville, since you can check out the historic Dils Cemetery and Garden, where Randolph McCoy is buried. You can also visit the Hatfield-McCoy Feud Site and take a downtown tour. Call (606) 432-5063 or go online at www.tourseky.com.

SOME GOOD TRAILS: Highway 23 is blessed with a bounty of great state parks and places to dayhike along the way. There is Yatesville Lake State Park, Paintsville Lake State Park, Jenny Wiley State Resort Park in Prestonsburg and the Breaks Interstate Park, a park that features "the Grand Canyon of the South." On the way back from our trip, we had a great dayhike at Paintsville Lake State Park, which is also home (since 1995) to the living history farm, the Mountain Homeplace. Go online at www.mountainhomeplace.com. Check out all the state parks in Kentucky at www.parks.ky.gov.

SOME COOL PIKE COUNTY AREA FESTIVALS:

IN MAY: The Apple Blossom Festival in Elkhorn City, Ky., south of Pikeville. Enjoy crafts, music, local art and the splendor of the mountains. Call (606) 754-5000.

IN JUNE: The annual Hatfield-McCoy Festival in Pikeville. Already a Top 20 event by the Southeast Tourism Society, enjoy festivities in Pike County as well as in nearby Wiliamson, W.Va., across the Big Sandy. Call (800) 844-7453 or go online at www.tourpikecounty.com.

IN JULY: Independence Day Celebration at the Breaks Interstate Park (one of only two interstate parks in the United States). Located about 45 minutes south of Pikeville. Call (800) 982-5122.

More Great Fests

CHILIFEST: Held mid September along Third Avenue and Pullman Square in Huntington. One of the oldest and best family-friendly chili cook-offs in the region. It's the annual West Virginia State Chili Championship sanctioned by the International Chili Society. It raises money for Huntington's Ronald McDonald House and is hosted by Chili Willi's, 840 4th Ave. Call (304) 529-4857 or visit www.chilifestwv.com.

MOTHMAN FESTIVAL: Held mid-September, celebrates the internationally-known Mothman. Takes place in downtown Point Pleasant, W.Va. Exhibits, displays, merchandise and guided tours and hayrides of the TNT area. Go online at www.mothmanlives.com.

BRIDGE DAY AT THE NEW RIVER GORGE BRIDGE: Held third Saturday in October in Fayetteville, W.Va. Recognized as a top 100 festival in the country. It is the one day you can walk across the 876-foot-high bridge, rappelers can descend and ascend on fixed ropes and BASE jumpers can parachute off. Call (800) CALLWVA .

GREEK FESTIVAL: St. George Greek Orthodox at 701 11th Ave., on Huntington's Southside toward September's end. Festival has dancing, music and authentic food and pastries. Go online at www.stgeorgewv.org.

FESTIVALL CHARLESTON: Held each June, a now nine-day city-wide arts festival with national, regional and local, art, dance, theater, food, and music in Charleston, W.Va. Go online at www.festivallcharleston.com.

GREENUP OLD FASHION DAYS: First weekend of October in downtown Greenup, Ky. A small-town fest at its best with antique car show, a W-Hollow bus tour, apple butter making, flea market, 6-mile run, square dancing, music, a parade and more. Go online at www.greenupoldfashiondays.com.

WEST VIRGINIA PUMPKIN FESTIVAL: One of West Virginia's largest fests in early October at Pumpkin Park in Milton. Arts and crafts, food, music and, of course, lots of pumpkins. Go online at www.wvpumpkinpark.com. Also, don't miss the Maize at Cooper Farms (located behind Milton Middle School) in September and October.

FESTIVAL OF TREES/TRAINS: Late November, Paramount Arts Center, 1300 Winchester Ave., Ashland, Ky. About 100 trees and magnificent model railroad layout in the balcony. Call (606) 324-3175. Go online at www.paramountartscenter.com.

MULTI-FEST: First weekend each August, free, ethnic celebration at State Capitol Complex in Charleston, W.Va. Blues, gospel, hip hop and jazz performers. Call (304) 347-7663.

ROY ROGERS FESTIVAL: Late May, a celebration of the life of Scioto County, Ohio, native Roy Rogers and all things western. Held in downtown Portsmouth. Go online at www.portsmouthcvb.org.

X-FEST: The region's largest heavy metal festival. Held at Harris Riverfront Park in Huntington late summer. Hosted by WAMX-FM, 106.3. Go online at www.x1063.com.

APPALACHIAN FILM FESTIVAL: Mid-April at the Keith-Albee Performing Arts Center in downtown Huntington. Enjoy indie films from the Appalachian region that range from feature-length and documentaries to shorts, videos and student films. Also, check out workshops and the annual awarding of the Appys. Go online at www.appyfilmfest.com.

IRONTON MEMORIAL DAY PARADE: Memorial Day weekend, the nation's longest continuously running Memorial Day parade is so big it spawns a homecoming that spills out all over downtown Ironton. Check out events at St. Joseph High School and other places downtown. Call (740) 377-4550

SUMMER MOTION: A nationally-recognized week-long fest taking place over July Fourth in Ashland, Ky. Enjoy a weekend of live music and entertainment in Central Park, and then nightly double-shots of national-act concerts at the Ashland Boat Ramp.

WEST VIRGINIA HOT DOG FESTIVAL: Late July at Pullman Square in downtown Huntington. Check out one of the coolest new festivals in the state with all the classic Huntington-area hot dog vendors including Stewart's, Midway, Frostop, and Hillbilly Hotdogs. There's hot dog eating, root beer chugging, and bun stacking competitions as well as wiener dog races. Call (304) 525-7788.

POAGE LANDING DAYS: Mid-September, in downtown Ashland, Ky. Features a weekend of live national and regional musical acts, arts and crafts, a fiddle contest and much more. Call the Ashland Convention and Visitors Bureau at (606) 329-1007 or (800) 377-6249 or go online at www.visitashlandky.com.

JESSE STUART WEEKEND: Third weekend in September in Greenup, Ky. A weekend at Greenbo Lake State Resort Park honoring the late, great Greenup County author and poet, Jesse Stuart. A look at the memory of Stuart the poet laureate of Kentucky, through a tour of his homeplace, W-Hollow, through film, book discussions and more. Call Greenbo at (606) 473-7324 or the Jesse Stuart Foundation at (606) 326-1667.

BOB EVANS FARM FESTIVAL: October at the 1,000-acre Bob Evans Farm in Rio Grande, Ohio. Musicians from around the country and the region, square dancing tractors, nearly 1,000 cloggers, chainsaw carvers, and many demonstrations including blacksmithing and glassblowing. Call (800) 994-3276.

WEST VIRGINIA BOOK FESTIVAL: Mid-October at the Charleston Civic Center in Charleston, W.Va. The event features readings, workshops, book signings, as well as activities and programs for kids. Call (304) 343-4646.

GUYANDOTTE CIVIL WAR DAYS: The first weekend in November, celebrate the reenactment of the raid on Guyandotte in this historic Ohio River-side Huntington neighborhood. Check out period music, sutlers, craft displays, food, tours of the historic Madie Carroll House and daily re-enactments of the battle. Call (304) 736-9381.

APPALACHIAN UPRISING: The first weekend in June in Scottown, Ohio (Lawrence County) at the Eden Valley Farm. National-act bluegrass and progressive acoustic bands annually including Sam Bush, Larry Keel and Natural Bridge, host Melvin Goins and many others. Go online at www.appalachianuprising.net.

Ohio

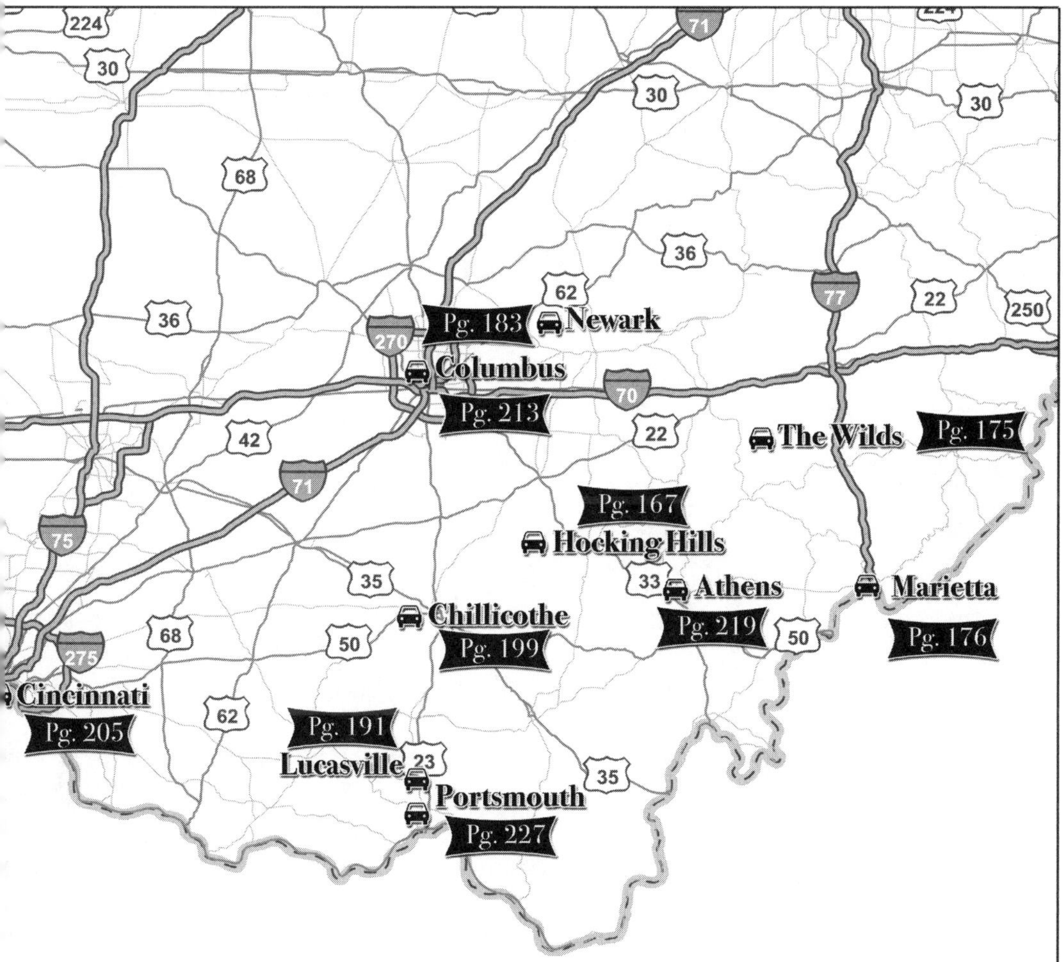
Pg. 183
Newark
Columbus
Pg. 213
The Wilds
Pg. 175
Pg. 167
Hocking Hills
Athens
Marietta
Chillicothe
Pg. 199
Pg. 219
Pg. 176
Cincinnati
Pg. 205
Pg. 191
Lucasville
Portsmouth
Pg. 227

Hocking Hills
Ohio

One of my favorite Southern Ohioans of all times is Emma "Grandma" Gatewood.

Gatewood, at age 67, left her Gallia County home in 1955 after reading about the Appalachian Trail in a magazine and hiked the entire trail that runs from Georgia to Maine.

Gatewood – who through-hiked the Appalachian Trail two more times and the Oregon Trail at age 72 – also had favorite trails in Southern Ohio, and they were almost all in Hocking Hills.

So, with the campaign fins circling again in our town, we decided a great Grandma-inspired recipe for the weekend would be to load the Dave Trippin' wagon and to find the peace of wild things in these nearby hills.

Filled with some of Southern Ohio's great natural features from **Rock House** and **Old Man's Cave** to **Conkle's Hollow** and **Rock Bridge**, Hocking Hills provides some great hiking and a smorgasbord of other things to do – from canoeing and rappelling to a ride on the **Hocking Valley Scenic Railroad**.

Less than two hours from Huntington, Hocking Hills is now known as the "Hot Tub Capital of Ohio," as it is filled with more than 500 cottages, cabins, cabooses, castles, yurts and other cool places to stay, as well as plenty of quirky and good places to get a meal.

Miles:
142

Original Trip
September
2004

A ride on one of the area's tourist railroads, waterfall-filled hikes, a lunch spot crazy for lunch boxes and a great getaway in the Hocking Hills region of Southeast Ohio.

Since I still tote my Buck Rogers metal lunchbox to work, we knew a first stop in Hocking Hills had to be at **Etta's Lunch Box Café, Ohio 56, in the big city of Starr, Ohio**.

Formerly residents of German Village in Columbus, LaDora Ousley and her partner, Tim Seewer, made a break from the big city by establishing a mom-and-pop general store and café that houses, among other things: Ousley's collection of more than 400 lunch boxes, Seewer's art work scattered about the place and their dog, Elwood.

While I sipped on a Gem yellow cream soda (bottled right down the road in Wellston, Ohio), my eyes took a great waltz down memory lane as I looked for all the lunch boxes of my childhood from "Punky Brewster" and "Six Million Dollar Man" to "Mork and Mindy" and "Grizzly Adams."

In this true general store (Tim's saying is "We have everything, if I can find it") we had a ball browsing, and, of course, found something we, uh, needed – a couple of kites for the kids.

Fueled with the warmth of a belly filled with good food and the energy of these two cool folks plowing their own path in these hills, we headed off to hike at Old Man's Cave at Hocking Hills State Park.

You can't go wrong hiking here or at nearby **Ash Cave**, **Cedar Falls**, **Rock House** or **Rock Bridge**, **Cantwell Cliffs** or **Lake Hope State Park**.

Although I usually prefer to be alone in the woods, I must say walking the well-trod paths at Old Man's Cave on Sept. 11 with a good number of friendly quiet folks seemed right.

Never with a watch, we became immersed in an afternoon of waterfalls (there's a lower and upper falls to hike to near Old Man's Cave), wading, rock skipping and listening to the comforting muffled words of families talking and walking which echoed softly through this spectacular gorge.

With the lingering human touch of Hocking Hills (where the Adena culture inhabited first more than 7,000 years ago), we headed up into the nearby hills for a good dinner.

Since my wife Toril and I had both spaced out and forgot our anniversary the week before, we headed to a pretty nice place, the **Grouse Nest and Ash Cave Cabins (740-332-4501)** to eat.

In the evening sun, we made puppet shows on the table, enjoyed the company of the owner's 13-year-old dog Sebastian and enjoyed some pretty fine dining. We had grilled mahi-mahi and ribs, and our two boys had pasta. This ridge-top restaurant has its own herb garden and adjacent cabins.

With the sun fading on Sept. 11, our 4-year-old said, "Everything is quiet in this world."

We said nothing, but smiled at him and at each other.

Yes, at least sometimes, for a little while, in some places.

Although we love to camp out, we decided to try one of the cool places to stay at Hocking Hills that is kind of like camping but a bit better.

We stayed for a couple of nights at the **Yurt at Salt Creek Retreats (614-397-3422)** a secluded, round canvas-cabin of sorts that was about a 15-minute drive from the heart of Hocking Hills. It was tucked away but close enough to still roll back into "town" (the state park) to check out some of their great kids programs.

Hosting weekend programs year-round, the **Hocking Hills State Park (1-866-644-6727)** has great guided activities such as canoeing and hiking, as well as night-time movies in the campgrounds and naturalist shows.

We caught one most-informative show, "Ohio's Birds of Prey," by a man with the best name in the bird business, Pat Quackenbush. Pat brought out Ruby, a red-tailed hawk, and an owl named Ivan, and answered more questions than you can imagine and graciously opened up his cozy "Naturalists Cabin" filled with snakes, fins and fur and even an interesting animal "scat" exhibit that the boys loved, of course.

On Sunday afternoon, we decided to take our little knee-high, rail-nuts over to **Hocking Valley Scenic Railway** in nearby Nelsonville **(800-967-7834)** for a little choo-choo fix.

It was a good call.

We had a delightful outing on the train, which is perhaps best known for its all-caboose trips, as well Santa trains and even a fireworks shuttle train.

Although you can't beat West Virginia tourist railroads for scenery, we did enjoy the HVSR trip on which we saw such odd things as a purple backhoe in someone's back yard. We also met fellow passengers Mike, Bonnie and Cody Walters of Proctorville, Ohio, and we all enjoyed a delightful (but not quite long enough) 30-minute stopover at **Robbins Crossing**, an 1850s-era village on the Hocking College campus.

On the weekends, the Crossing is a pioneer village. Volunteers such as Junior Acord bring the place alive – the schoolhouse, a blacksmith, a spinner and even, I guess, "pioneer snakes" such as a Mexican boa constrictor.

For those into the outdoors, you'll want to hoof it over to **Rocky Shoes and Boots, (740-753-3130)** which is located right in front of the train depot.

The boots and shoes are made right there at the factory, which has a nice outdoors gear store and an honest-to-God factory outlet where you are in for a serious deal or two.

After much-needed naps 'neath the shade trees at Rock House, we had an absolute ball climbing through Rock House, the only true cave at Hocking Hills, and a grand series of tunnels that sit halfway up a 150-foot-high sandstone cliffs.

After a quickie stop at **Hocking House, 29580 Big Pine, Road, Logan (740-385-4166),** the garden art shop of clay artist Jean Magdich, and one of dozens of artist hot spots in Hocking Hills, we rumbled over to **Rempel's Grove** in Logan.

Located past the Mc/Wal-Mart complex, Rempel's Grove has been known as a picnic ground for more than 100 years, and is now that and much more.

Sort of like an Amish supercenter of sorts, Rempel's Grove features an **Amish Furniture Outlet**, the **Logan Antique Mall**, the **Hocking Hills Craft Mall**, the **Hocking Hills Canoe Livery**, an 18-hole **Adventure Golf**, an ice cream and candy shop and the **Olde Dutch Restaurant, 12791 Ohio 664, (740-385-1000)**. The Olde Dutch features a buffet and better yet, Amish family-style dinners where everybody passes the dishes around just like they do at home.

We tore into the mashed potatoes and fresh-roasted chicken and then enjoyed a free petting zoo outside – although you couldn't pet the animals, you could toss corn at the goats gathered around.

With the weekend waning and all of us and the station wagon smelling like we'd had been wallowing in the creek, we decided to drive south and home, everybody happy from having tromped up Grandma Gatewood's way.

If You Go: Hocking Hills

DRIVING THERE: Drive time is about 1 hour, 45 minutes or so north. You can take West Virginia 2 to Point Pleasant, to U.S. 35 west and then take Ohio 93 up into the Hocking Hills region. If you're driving up during the week, you might want to take Ohio 327, which goes through Wellston, home of the Gem Bottling Company, which still bottles up Gem sodas, Ski and Double Cola.

COOL PLACES TO STAY: You will want a travel guide or a visit to the Hocking Hills' Web site to sift through this, since choices in the "Hot Tub Capital of Ohio" range from Ravenwood Castle (where you can also stay in a gypsy wagon) and the Steep Woods Caboose to Hopping Turtle's traditional Sioux teepees to Salt Creek Retreat's Yurt. Call 1-800-HOCKING or go online at www.1800hocking.com.

COOL PLACES TO EAT: There's a load of good places to eat in these hills from Etta's Lunch Box Café in Starr to the Grouse Nest, the Inn at Cedar Falls, the Hocking Hills State Park lodge, the Pizza Crossing and the Olde Dutch Restaurant.

AMERICAN MADE: The Hocking Hills region is filled with wonderful artists and mom-and-pop crafts shops. It also is home to at least a couple American factories: The Columbus Washboard Company, in Logan, is the last washboard maker in the United States. It's open for free tours Monday through Friday. The Washboard Music Festival is held each June. Call 1-800-343-7967.

ROCKY SHOES AND BOOTS: Rocky Shoes and Boots has a cool outlet store with all kinds of rugged gear from Rocky (made right there in Nelsonville) as well as Columbia, Teva and other outdoor gear. Call (740) 753-3130 or go online at www.rockyboots.com

ON THE WEB: www.1800hocking.com and www.hockinghillspark.com.

Ride The Train

HOCKING VALLEY: The Hocking Valley Scenic Railway in Nelsonville offers trains on Saturdays and Sundays that leave the Nelsonville depot for a 14-mile or 22-mile round trip ride. During the Paul Bunyan Days, enjoy the all-caboose shuttle to nearby Hocking College. Call (800) 967-7834 or on weekends at the depot, call (740) 753-9531 or go online at www.hvsr.com.

CASS SCENIC RAILROAD: One of the only state park railroads in the country, the world-famous Cass Railroad, in Cass, W.Va., draws in rail fans from around the world as it is pulled by the steam-powered Shay locomotive up to Bald Knob for spectacular views at 4,842 feet. Unique accommodations also include a Caboose and a company house. Call (304) 456-4300 or (800) CALL-WVA.

NEW RIVER TRAIN EXCURSION: Leaving out of Huntington, the New River Train does trips from Huntington to Hinton in the New River Gorge in October during peak fall foliage. The train also stops in St. Albans and Montgomery. Cost is about $125 per person (round-trip coach) and $90 for kids. Premium and private cars also available. Go online at www.newrivertrain.com.

DURBIN AND GREENBRIER VALLEY RAILROADS: With departures from various towns in West Virginia, the Railroad includes a number of unique trains including the open-air Cheat Mountain Salamander, the Durbin Rocket, the New Tygart Flyer and the Mountain Explorer (dinner train). The trains pass through unspoiled mountains, climb to 4,000 feet, burrow under Cheat Mountain (via an 1,800-foot tunnel) and negotiate the two of the sharpest mainline railroad curves in the U.S. Trips from two hours to two days. Go online at www.mountainrail.com.

BIG SOUTH FORK SCENIC RAILWAY: Stearns, Ky., traveling through the Big South Fork National River and Recreation Area with steep cliffs and deep gorges. Train tickets include admission to the Stearns Museum. Prices are about $18; $9 for children. Go online at www.bsfsry.com.

MY OLD KY DINNER TRAIN: Five-course meals for all 125 passengers at Bardstown, Ky. tourist train. Go online at www.kydinnertrain.com.

MYSTERY TRAIN: Speciality travel trips by train out of Huntington. The Mystery Train features all inclusive trips. Weekend train trips include weekend excursions to D.C., Chicago, fishing and rafting trips. Meals and hotel included with price. Call (866) 529-6412.

The Wilds
Cumberland, Ohio

Miles: 154

Original Trip July 2006

We go to where the wild things are. The Wilds, the largest conservation facility in North America, located just north of Marietta. Also, some rambling 'round the historic river city of Marietta.

To celebrate Independence Day weekend, we thought it would be a great idea to express our freedom by loading up the Dave Trippin' mobile and going where the wild things are.

No, we're not talking about City Hall, and certainly not Washington, D.C. (too many donkeys and elephants frothing at the mouth there). We were on the road to **The Wilds**.

Located about 150 miles or so from Huntington, and just off of I-77 north of Marietta, Ohio, The Wilds, in Cumberland, Ohio, is a less than a three-hour trip that whisks you off the interstate and onto country roads that take you by sun-drenched savannahs and still waters teeming with more than 25 species of exotic animals.

One of the largest conservation education facilities in North America, The Wilds provides food and shelter mostly in grasslands and lakes for an array of mostly endangered species that include zebras, giraffes, gazelle's, wild horses and rhinos.

Incorporated in 1984 as a non-profit, The Wilds, started releasing endangered animals (Hartmann's mountain zebra, scimitar-horned oryxes, and Przewalski's horses) into open range habitat in 1992 on part of the 9,152-acres of strip mined land that was donated by American Electric Power.

In the years since, more species have been added including the red-crowned crane, Persian onagers, white, black and greater one-horned rhi-

noceroses, Bactrian camel and deer, Sable antelopes and many others.

Since we had an open air safari set for the morning, we figured instead of wrestling our tiny men in superhero PJs into carseats at the crack of dawn, we would overnight at one of our favorite Ohio River towns – Marietta, located just 50 miles south of The Wilds.

Although they have often paid the price for it, Marietta's riverfront is sans floodwall and strolling it again in the shadow of the historic **Lafayette Hotel (740-373-5522)** was a grand drink of summer. In the warmth of the evening sun, we soaked in a surround-sound, river-rolled musical lesson with live Dixieland jazz just a block or so away from wailing electric blues smoking out of the 12th Annual Red, White and Blues festival.

We didn't want to be fenced in at the crowded fest (whose proceeds all went to beautifying the city), so we went strolling in downtown which is a great thing since it isn't far before you run into the River Trail, a walking/biking path that goes along the Muskingum River as it joins the Ohio.

Along that trail is the B&O Harmar Bridge, built as a covered bridge in 1856 and which has been open to foot traffic since 1962.

Draped with giant hanging baskets, the bridge provides sweeping views of the Marietta harbor and the mouth of the Ohio and the Muskingum, which is filled with the rare sight of area rowing teams in season and where now the *Becky Thatcher Showboat* sits silently and for sale.

On the other side of the bridge, we were delighted to find the historic Harmar Village, which has a surprisingly eclectic blend of shops that included the "Pampered Reptile," where they were working on a "home" for a 7-foot-alligator. Crikey!

All of us river rats fell immediately in love with **Hartel Shipyard, 116 Maple St. (740-374-SHIP)**, where owner and artist Barbara Hartel showcases her artwork depicting the working boats of the river and her warm, welcoming spirit.

We felt a tinge of city riverboat envy when the **Valley Gem Sternwheeler (740-373-7862)**came joyously slapping water out to the Ohio. It got us jonesing for a good river ride. Maybe all of us can get one in the fall since the **Ohio River Sternwheeler Festival** rolls each September in Marietta.

After a nice refueling with a round of house-made draft root beer at the **Marietta Brewing Co. (740-373-2739)** and a good night's sleep, the Dave Trippin' posse was ready to roll up to The Wilds and again to do our part in celebrating the 50th anniversary of the Interstate Highway – 47,000 miles and no traffic lights (just lots of orange barrels).

Our open-air safari tour was set for late morning, which left us more than an hour to hit a couple trails at **The Wilds, (1-866-444-WILDS).**

There's more than 15 miles of hiking/mountain biking trails on the spacious grounds as well as some unique places to walk to, including a butterfly habitat (wildflowers gone wild) and a Windharp, located on the hill above the Welcome Center.

After a nice walk, we stopped in to rent some binoculars for the trip.

Since many of the animals can be far away (what endangered species wouldn't feel a little uneasy around homo sapiens?) you'll want to either bring binoculars or you can rent some fine ones for $5 for the trips into the open range.

Even before the trip began, we had a great time in the field high above range, tracking dragonflies zipping on near invisible wings through the goldenrod and grass and then below zooming in to see what bizarre animals (seemingly drawn by Dr. Seuss) that we could locate in these Southern Ohio hills.

If you like the A/C and don't care for a bit of dust, which can get kicked up on the gravel roads of The Wilds, you might want to take a regular tour in an enclosed bus.

We hopped on the open-air bus that was pretty wild itself, looking like Xzibit and crew had pimped out this ride, chopping out some of the sides to give prime viewing on the tours that run 10 a.m. to 4 p.m. Wednesday through Sunday.

You can also catch Sunset Safari tours on Saturdays June through September.

Showing off some pretty good wheel skills, the school bus driver, Jamie Guernsey, was also the tour guide, giving us the lowdown on The Wilds, which has more than 37 conservation and science projects underway with partners such as **The Columbus Zoo** and **The Ohio State University**.

Driving the curvy gravel roads, Guernsey was the straight talk express about humans' impact on many of the world's flora and fauna, including the American bison, which had been totally killed off from Ohio by 1808. There are now about 200 at The Wilds.

Driving up to The Lake Trail, where we had a 15-minute stop to walk to the lake to see the majestic Trumpeter Swans, we happened by a Indo-chinese Siki deer, a species native to Asia.

"Whoa, back up on the left," a passenger hollered.

"We have 200 here in the wild," Guernsey said. "That's about 20 percent of the world's population."

After a hike at The Lake Trail, we toured The Wilds' special animal management area where the eight -person medical staff gives each of the animals out on pasture in the summer a complete physical each winter thanks to something called "The Tamer," which allows for examinations with minimal use of drugs.

We all loved this part of the tour, a real behind-the-scenes look and touch session as we passed around part of a giraffe tail (as tough as fishing line) as well as skulls and a number of shedded racks and horns from the various animals.

The extended open-air tour was a wee bit long for our youngest one Will, who was starting to fade in the heat of the afternoon and was pretty much ready for a nap when the rest of us met Bubba, the 5,000 pound One-Horned Rhino who needs a lot of care since he came to The Wilds after a life of zoo living.

Although not much is made of the fact, on the way back to the trip's end, Guernsey mentioned that part of The Wilds' land conservation efforts since it is located on nearly 14 square miles of quite bizarre looking landscape that was strip-mined for decades.

She pointed out an Ohio State experiment in which they are trying to see what native trees can work well and grow fastest on the reclaimed strip mine land on which The Wilds had to erect shade shelters to give the animals in the field some reprieve from the sun.

"If we could grow trees we would grow trees but the soil is too poor," she said.

Just down the road from The Wilds, you can even stop off at nearby AEP Re-Creation Land and see the bucket of "Big Muskie," once the world's largest dragline that could take away the equivalent of a 12-car garage in one bite.

We sure didn't have the time or the stomach for that, knowing good chunks of Kentucky and West Virginia's beautiful, irreplaceable mountains are being blown up and hauled away as we speak, as coal keeps the lights on.

Like the dream-like baseball players who stepped back into the corn after playing baseball in "Field of Dreams," as we slipped away from The Wilds, we were a bit fuzzy-headed thinking of it all.

The Wilds is an ever-evolving ecological and sociological experiment – an odd collection of beasts and the people who love them coming together on forsaken and forgotten soil in this quiet place, a world somewhere between a zoo and the open range, and so close to home.

If You Go: The Wilds

WHAT IT IS: North America's largest conservation facility filled with mostly endangered species, include scimitar-horned oyrx, Cuvier's gazelle, Asian Przeswalski's horses, Hartmann's mountain zebras and other.
WHEN: Open 10 a.m. to 4 p.m. Wednesday through Sunday, June through August; and 10 a.m. to 4 p.m. Saturdays and Sundays in May, September and October. Special programs slated for off-season called Winter on The Wilds.
WHERE: Cumberland, Ohio (north of Marietta). Take I-64 east to Charleston and I-77 north to Exit 28 (Belle Valley). Take Ohio 821 North to Ohio 340 West.
TOURS: Tours are $14 and $9 for kids 4 to 12; Open Air Safari Tours are $20; There are also special Sunset Safari Tours as well on Saturdays only (June through September).
WHERE TO STAY: Marietta and Parkersburg are full of motels and hotels. Go online at www.mariettaohio.org. Also, if you have a group, The Wilds has a lodge that sleeps up to 12. There is also camping nearby at many state parks as well as the AEP Re-Creation Land.
WHAT ELSE TO DO: There are 15 miles of mountain bike trails at The Wilds, as well as guided fishing excursions on the almost-famous Wilds' lakes, which have been featured on some nationally televised outdoor shows.

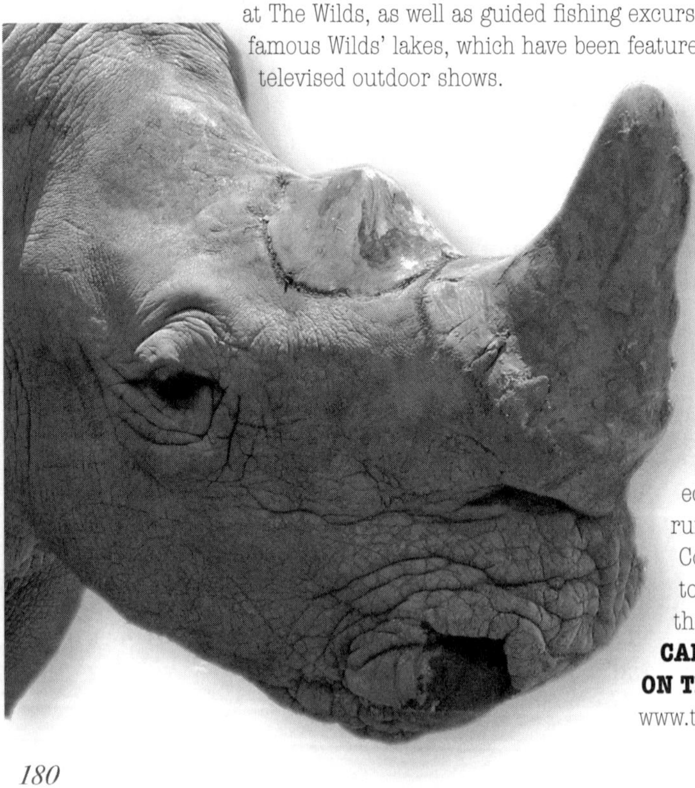

NEW AT THE WILDS: In July 2007, The Wilds opened up its 60-acre Carnivore Conservation Center that houses cheetahs and African wild dogs.
CAMP: The Wilds has week-long nature education camps that run through August. Cost ranges from $275 to $410 per camper for the week.
CALL: (740) 638-2286.
ON THE WEB: Go online at www.thewilds.org.

Where More Wild Things Are

COLUMBUS ZOO AND AQUARIUM: More than 80 years old, the Columbus Zoo is one of the largest zoos in North America. It is nationally recognized since it was operated from 1978 to 1992 by Jack Hanna, who started his TV show "Jack Hanna's Animal Adventures" in 1993. That TV show is seen around the world. Go online at www.colszoo.org, Call 1-800-MONKEYS

CINCINNATI ZOO & BOTANICAL GARDEN: Recognized by *Child Magazine* as one of "The 10 Best Zoos for Kids," the world famous Cincinnati Zoo & Botanical Garden was rated the No.1 attraction in Cincinnati and one of the top five zoos in the nation by Zagat Survey. It has more than 500 animal and 3,000 plant species. Go online at www.cincyzoo.org, Call 1-800-94-HIPPO

THREE RIVERS AVIAN CENTER: Located in the New River Gorge, in Brooks, W.Va. Three Rivers Avian Center is an animal shelter for injured and endangered wild birds, raptor rehabilitation, and raptor environmental education programs. Though they travel extensively doing educational programs, you can still visit the center in Brooks as well. Go online at www.tracwv.org.

KENTUCKY REPTILE ZOO: More than 100 species of reptiles, including many species of venomous snakes. Located in the Red River Gorge in Slade, Ky. Call (606) 663–9160:

ELK TOURS: See a few of the 5,700 majestic elk re-introduced to Eastern Kentucky after a 150-year-absence. Tours are at Jenny Wiley State Resort Park in Prestonsburg, Ky., and at Buckhorn Lake State Park in Buckhorn, Ky., as well. Cost is about $20 and $10 for children. Call Jenny Wiley at (800) 325-0142 and Buckhorn Lake at (800) 325-0058.

HAND-FEEDING HUMMINGBIRDS: A popular and unique summer-time activity at Lake Hope State Park in Zaleski, Ohio (just south of Athens). Call (740) 596-4860. Go online at www.lakehopestatepark.com.

KENTUCKY DOWN UNDER: A unique destination in Horse Cave, Ky., where you can hand-feed birds, pet kangaroos and learn about the many different animals, as well as the culture of Australia. Also, a great cave there as well. Call (800) 762-2869. Go online at www.kdu.com

NEWPORT AQUARIUM: A water wonderland in Newport, Ky., open year-round with thousands of aquatic creatures from around the world. Call (800) 406-3474.

Columbus Burbs
Ohio

Ever since I was knee-high to a plastic Santa Claus, there's been a trip to Columbus for the holiday season with the fam.

For years, my Aunt Linda, who I think is still recovering, would graciously open up her house hosting her six brothers and sisters and all their wild young'uns.

Sometime after scarfing the roast beast, wrestling and roughing up some fine shag carpet and riding my cousin Kim's totally cool riding toy shaped like a Heinz ketchup bottle, the kids would get rounded up for some holiday shopping at Lazarus.

Although a shopping weekend has about as much appeal to my Lavender crew as seeing Hannah Montana on Ice, we cruised up to Columbus recently for some other kinds of family fun.

After giving a proverbial Archie Griffin stiff-arm to the many malls, we took a walk on its wild side at one of its indoor water parks, **CoCo Key Water Resort**, and at the world-famous **Columbus Zoo and Aquarium**.

After just seeing Jack Hanna's sold-out show at the Keith-Albee Performing Arts Center a few weeks before as part of the Marshall Artists Series, we were jonesing to make a long-overdue trip north to see what Hanna said is now one of the largest zoos in America

Miles:
210

Original Trip
November
2007

The Columbus Zoo and Aquarium just north of Columbus in Powell, is a sprawling, growing complex that is full of life. The Columbus Zoo and Aquarium just north of Columbus in Powell, The Columbus Zoo and Aquarium just north.

and to see more of these beautiful, and oft-crazy looking critters that have made Hanna a household name.

OK, and yeah, what young man cub didn't want to see Fluffy, the world's largest snake in captivity?

Celebrating its 80th season, **The Columbus Zoo and Aquarium (614-645-3550),** just north of Columbus in Powell, is a sprawling, growing complex that was full of life in mid-November in spite of the shrinking temperatures and with its popular Wild Lights still a week away.

With our two nephews (Colin and Cameron) also along for the ride, the wild pack of four boys set out at a full sprint into the zoo.

It was no secret where they were headed first: Penguins. Thanks to films in which they surf and rock out, penguins have waddled past nearly every animal in the kingdom onto the top of the popularity pedestal.

On the way to see the wide array of little blues, rock hoppers and other penguins, the boys stopped to stare at a flock of flamingos perched in a pond, oddly enough in front of a mirror.

"That's how they mate, That's how they mate," Jake said loudly repeating what Hanna told the crowd in Huntington about the use of the mirrors at the Zoo.

Thank you and TMI, Jack.

With faces as red as parrots, we hurriedly ducked inside a number of exhibits from the reptiles to the Manatee Coast, where Stubby (1,995 pounds) and Holly (2,100 pounds) swim about amongst the fish.

Although Columbus can be crushing with crowds, we found this off-season for the Zoo to be refreshingly sparse with humans and refreshingly alive with animals out and about and active.

Open 9 a.m. to 5 p.m., seven days a week, the Zoo's winter months are a great time to visit since many of the North American animals (moose, bison, wolves, eagles and puma) love this time of year, and indoor sections, like the not-to-miss Asia Quest, are open with silvered-leaf langurs, a water monitor, sun bears and giant fruit bats that snacked upside down on apples while scrapping with each other.

Asia Quest also houses Fluffy, the 300-pound, 24-foot or 31-kids-long reticulated python that is right up there with the penguins for being the star of the show.

Whether it's the actual "Time Running Out" exhibit in Asia Quest or the signs at the exhibits to show how endangered an animal is, it is also hard not to miss and to understand the need for the Zoo's conservation mission.

In the past five years, the Zoo has donated $3.3 million for field conservation from helping save mussels in Ohio to gibbons in Borneo. The work being done at its sister facility The Wilds in Cumberland, Ohio (just north of Marietta) deserves mention.

On the day we were there, they got a couple dollars more. Colin, our seven-year-old nephew who had lost a tooth the night before, pulled a hard-earned crumpled tooth fairy-given dollar out of his pocket to hand over to the manatees.

A few minutes later, without hesitation, he pulled his last dollar out to give to the elephants.

Like Camden Park, the Zoo is cool with folks bringing lunch and we did.

Topping off the day with a frugal souvenir stop by buying four pressed pennies (cost 51 cents per kid), we saved some coin and energy for the rest of this long weekend.

Since the kids had Monday off school, we decided to trip on over to **CoCo Key Water Resort at Cherry Valley Lodge**, located 25 miles east of Columbus.

Opened Dec. 14 2006, CoCo Key is a great winter-time tropical-tinged oasis for folks headed up that way.

Upon laying eyes on it, Jake declared this indoor water haven a "dream come true."

Yep, a kid's dream and a trend come true.

CoCo Key is just one of seven new indoor water parks that have sprung up around the Buckeye State in the past couple of years.

Tucked a bit away from the usual people-packed madness of Columbus, the 50,000-square-foot CoCo Key waterpark is a wonderland of water packed with play areas for kids of all ages.

We soon found out why it was ranked by *Nick Jr. Family* magazine as one of Top 7 Trips for '07.

Like the outdoor water park in Jackson, Ohio, we liked the size of CoCo (capacity 242) that was not too big, but just right, and packed for ultimate play.

There's a 274-foot long Coconut Grove Adventure River (a lazy river to the rest of us), three super-sized water slides (Shark Slam, Gator Gush and Barracuda Blast), a Dip-In Movie Theatre (a pirate's sail projection screen TV that was showing the Sunday NFL games), a Coral Reef Cavern pool (a deeper pool with basketball and lilypad jumping) and the Parrot's Perch, a monstrous kids' play gym packed with slides, water cannons and a 300-gallon bucket that when filled to the tipping point brought the water thunder from above.

Tag on a family hottub, and an adult hot tub that, like Split Rock Pools at Snowshoe Mountain, goes outside as well, and you've got a whole day's worth of full-bore fun and for the kids especially a night's rest like no other.

While you could do the park in a day and motor back, there's no reason not to spend the night.

Weekend day-passes are $35 a piece ($140 for four) while you can score package deals as low as $144 a night for a room at Cherry Valley Lodge plus four water passes.

Looking like a stone-built ski lodge, Cherry Valley is one of the nation's only hotels that's also an officially sanctioned arboretum and botanical garden.

It sits on 18 acres with rooms circling around the rustic lodge, and its complex has four restaurants and bars that range from a Pizza Hut Express (near the pool) to Sunflowers, an upscale restaurant similarly priced to say, Rocco's in Ceredo.

The unusually large rooms (with a microwave, refrigerator and flat-screen TVs) have sliding glass doors that open to a landscape that looks like a team of John Marras were set loose on this probably one-time farm field.

A path lit at night with lanterns goes back to the lodge circling a lake complete with a cascading waterfall among healthy plantings of herb beds, prairie grasses, perennials and trees of river birch, sweet gums, and a glorious October Glory red maple that did not pay any mind to the calendar.

And nor had we.

If You Go: Columbus Zoo

WILD LIGHTS: The light displays at the Zoo run daily from around Thanksgiving through Jan. 1. Closed Dec. 24 & Dec. 25. Zoo Opens at 9 a.m. Wildlights Activities start at 5 p.m.

HOW MUCH: $10; $6 for children 2 to 11 and free for children under two. Seniors (60 and up) $8, and parking is $5.

ALSO AT THE LIGHTS: An ice rink, the Wildlights Model Train Railway and of course, the zoo's historic carousel.

REGULAR ZOO HOURS: Open 365 days a year. 9 a.m. to 5 p.m. Labor Day through Memorial Day. Summer hours: 9 a.m. to 6 p.m. Memorial Day weekend through Labor Day. The Zoo is also open until 9 p.m. on Wednesdays mid-June through August.

GETTING THERE: From I-270 outerbelt around Columbus, take Exit 20 Sawmill Road, and follow the signs. The Zoo is located northwest of Columbus at 9990 Riverside Dr., Powell, Ohio.

FOR MORE INFO: (614) 645-3550 or go online at www.columbuszoo.org.

ALONG THE WAY: The ultra-cool, Sumburger Drive-In, dates back to 1953 in Chillicothe. Take the last Chillicothe exit (North Bridge Street) and take a left to this landmark drive-in at 1487 N. Bridge St. On the web at www.sumburger.com. Call (740) 772-1055.

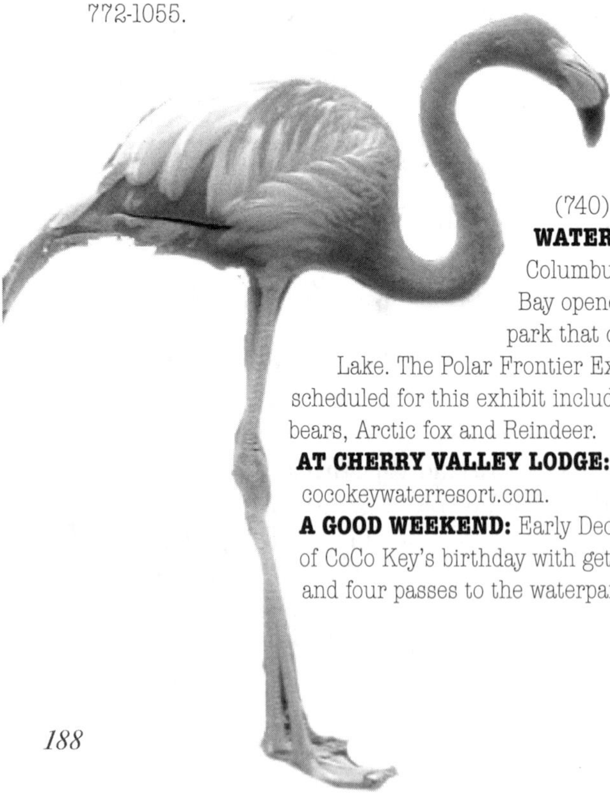

ANOTHER GREAT FOOD STOP ALONG U.S. 23: The Emmitt House, 123 N. Market St. Waverly, Ohio, (right on U.S. 23) that dates back to 1861. Call (740) 947-2181.

WATERPARK AT THE ZOO: At the Columbus Zoo and Aquarium, Zoombezi Bay opened in 2008 – a 22.7 acre water park that occupies the past home of Wyandot Lake. The Polar Frontier Exhibit opened in 2008. Animals scheduled for this exhibit include: Polar bears, Alaskan brown bears, Arctic fox and Reindeer.

AT CHERRY VALLEY LODGE: Call (800) 788-8008 or www.cocokeywaterresort.com.

A GOOD WEEKEND: Early December is the annual celebration of CoCo Key's birthday with getaways starting at $144 for a room and four passes to the waterpark.

More Water Adventures

WATERWAYS: Located in Julian, W.Va., outdoor waterpark with water slides, pool, archery and go kart. Located off of U.S. 119 in Logan County. Go online at www.waterwayspark.com. Call (304) 369-6125.

WAVES OF FUN: Located in Valley Park in Hurricane, the largest outdoor wave pool in the region. Open Memorial Day through Labor Day. Also, several water slides, putt putt, volleyball and more. Call (304) 562-2355.
Go online at www.putnamcounty.org/parks.

SPRAYGROUND AT APRIL DAWN PARK: The region's first sprayground is a water-breathing dragon, located in downtown Milton, W.Va., at April Dawn Park. Go online at www.ghprd.org. Open spring through early October,

INDIAN ACRES AQUATIC CENTER: Located in Marietta, Ohio, this is a $3.3 million aquatic center with a lazy river, water slides and more. Go online at www.mariettaquaticcenter.com. Call (740) 373-2445.

CAMDEN PARK: Located five miles west of Huntington, the historic family-run amusement park (operating since 1903) has some fun water attractions including the West Virginia Log Flume Company and the Swan Lake Pedal Boats. Call (304) 429-4321 or go online at www.camdenpark.com.

CASTAWAY BAY AT CEDAR POINT: A 38,000-square-foot indoor waterpark, a day spa, fitness center, 6,000-square-foot state-of-the-art arcade, a craft and child activity center and three restaurants. Go online at www.castawaybay.com

FORT RAPIDS INDOOR WATER PARK: in Columbus, a western-themed indoor resort with 12 water slides and a four-story interactive water play structure with a 1,000 gallon tipping bucket, gliding down the Cowboy Creek Lazy River or soaking in the 30-person hot tub. Go online at www.fortrapids.com

GREAT WOLF LODGE MASON : A sister resort to the Great Wolf Lodge property in Sandusky, Great Wolf Lodge in Mason features a 79,000-square-foot indoor water park, and a water roller coaster. Next to Paramount's Kings Island, the lodge also boasts 11 waterslides, six pools and a four-story treehouse waterfort. Go online at www.greatwolflodge.com/Locations/Mason

KALAHARI RESORT: Kalahari Resort is the largest indoor waterpark in Sandusky, Ohio and boasts 80,000-square-feet of African-inspired excitement. Surf or boogie board on the five-foot ocean-like waves of FlowRider®, ride the Zip Coaster uphill roller coaster slide or just chill out on the lazy river or at the spa. Go online at www.KalahariResort.com

SPLASH HARBOR: Splash Harbor's 6,000-square-foot tropical-themed atrium lets the sunshine stream in and keeps the cold out during the winter months just north of Columbus. There are plenty of water activities to enjoy including a 49-foot looping water slide that shoots more than 600 gallons of water per minute. Go online at www.qualityinnbellville.com.

Lucasville
Ohio

Just a dot on a state road map, Lucasville, Ohio, is one of those places that you usually never think of visiting and that you sure as heck don't want to be sent to in a car with bars.

Lucasville is home to Ohio's most notorious maximum security prison where they aren't afraid to flip the switch on 'Old Sparky' or the death-producing equivalent.

Outside of the acres of barbed wire, life "Over The Hedge," so to speak, is nothing but a good time since Lucasville is also home to a couple unique attractions certainly worth the drive.

When we had caught wind that the **Scioto Breeze Twin Drive-In, 9959 U.S 23, (740-259-2881)**, was open for the season we just had to load up the Dave Trippin' mobile and get this delicious slice of summer before the mosquitoes brought their families.

Located just about an hour from Huntington, the Scioto Breeze is one of the last remaining double drive-in movie theaters in the country, and it is the second closest drive-in to us, since the Kanauga Drive-In just north of Gallipolis, Ohio, on Ohio 7, is still open for business (and even hosting country concerts too).

Some folks have the misconception that drive-ins only play second-run fare, or use those bad speakers on a wire, but that was so 20 years ago.

Miles: 56

Original Trip June 2006

A visit to one of the nation's last twin drive-in movies in Lucasville, and a must-see trip to the already regionally famous Swap Meet at the Scioto County Fairgrounds.

On opening night we had the choice of seeing "Da Vinci Code" or "Over the Hedge" as the first shows and then "Mission Impossible 3" and "RV" for the second shows – not bad for $6 per adult and free for children.

I've not been overly concerned about Opie (Ron Howard) and the actor from "Big" (Tom Hanks) shaking my faith and I enjoyed "The Da Vinci Code" book, but since "Over The Hedge," which features William Shatner as a talking possum got superior reviews, we headed for the tiny screen in the back.

The front screen is an incredible 85-foot-wide and 60-feet-tall while the back one is a bit smaller and, hear this now and believe it later, but since the 35-mm projector can't clear the roof, the movie is shot 400 feet through mirrors, said Mike Adkins, who has managed the Scioto Breeze since 1980.

I didn't have size envy for long. The back screen is set to the West and we had a sunset of painted sky amongst swirled clouds that left us breathless.

Or maybe that was caused by all the Frisbee throwing. One of the great things about the drive-in is that it's OK to play before the show. There's room to romp (respectful of other cars and people of course). We jumped out, found a good free patch of grass and tossed around a Frisbee (not exactly a regular theater-approved activity).

Adkins, who gets a helping hand from his 12-year-old son Scotty, said the Breeze tries to be as family-friendly as possible with policies of no alcohol, the ability to use credit cards and debit cards, and a policy that lets patrons

bring in any drinks and food they want, although there's everything from theater food (popcorn, candy, etc.,) to cheeseburgers at the concession stand.

Toss in the sightings of some bats overhead and three shooting stars, and the fact that Toril and I also got to see a movie on the big screen that didn't showcase the talent of talking squirrels, it was a most memorable night and a great slice of summer not often tasted.

Since Lucasville is a bit of a drive, especially with children, it's nice to find a good spot to hit before the show to make a day of it.

We found just that spot.

Since I moved back to the area I have been getting an earful about how great the **Southern Ohio Poultry Association Swap Days** is from Abner Webb, who works in the H-D pressroom, and who hardly misses a Swap Meet at the Scioto County Fairgrounds in Lucasville.

He's got good reason to crow about this super-sized event that is held only three times a year. Swap Days run 7 a.m. to 3 p.m. the second weekend in April, June and October.

Featuring lots and lots and lots of livestock (most of it exotic) and seemingly anything legal for the right price, the Swap Meet, which is free but costs $2 to park, is like the Super Bowl of flea markets.

Be prepared to do lots of walking, be prepared to be blown away by the sheer size and scope of flea market on steroids, be prepared to enjoy and be prepared to stare – at least a few times.

Also, there are some cool locally-owned restaurants along the way including the **Mault Brothers Portsmouth Brewing Company** (one of the only brewpubs in the region) and **The Scioto Ribber** (one of the region's best rib joints).

Since my youngest sister lives within a stone's throw but had somehow never been to **Dick's Pizza (740-776-6231)**, located on the Ohio River in Sciotoville, we decided to stop by one of my favorite riverside restaurants anywhere.

The restaurant's drawing card is about 10 different specialty pizzas (BLT or Buffalo Wing Pizza, anyone?) and the atmosphere is as refreshing as the menu selections.

When we rolled up we heard the familiar slap of the corn bags on the wood as someone was playing Cornhole at the campground next door and knew we were home – laid back on the river.

Dick's backyard is filled with beautiful flower beds, shuffleboard, a small playground for wee tots and a yard full of tire swings for kids of all ages.

Called the Picnic Area, it is open until 8 p.m. daily, and it's a great place to let kids (and adults) run free without causing the kind of havoc that can happen in a confined space inside a restaurant.

Under a surround sound grove of speakers pouring out '70s soulshine, we all felt that glow that summer can bring when the world – as crazy and fast as it is – gets sifted down to the good stuff: a weekend trip with a tire swing rope, clouds and dreams and a river rolling by and popcorn-crunching kids in sleeping bags watching a movie on a car hood under the Big Dipper.

If You Go: Lucasville

CALL ME THE BREEZE: The Scioto Breeze Twin Drive-In, 9959 U.S. 23, Lucasville, Ohio. Call (740) 259-2881. Open Friday, Saturday and Sunday during spring and fall and then nightly in summer. Movies run right at dusk. Box office open about an hour before the show. Tickets, $5.50; children 11 and under free.
GET THERE EARLY: On weekends, especially as the drive-in can fill up quickly and there's also playgrounds at some drive-ins, including the Scioto Breeze.
BRING IT IN: At the drive-ins you can bring lawn chairs, flashlights, a sweater or jacket, blankets, and coolers. No alcohol. The Scioto Breeze also has reasonably priced concessions.
GLANCE INTO THE SKY: Be sure to check the sky every once in a while and between movies since you might get to spy a shooting star or two.
ANOTHER DRIVE-IN: In addition to the Scioto Breeze, there is also a handful of drive-ins left in the region. The closest to Huntington is the Kanauga Drive-In, Ohio 7 North, Gallipolis (one hour from Huntington). Call (740) 446-1088. Movies show Fridays through Sunday in spring and fall and most nights during summer. Shows start at dark. Cost is about $5, $1 for children ages 6 to 11 and free for children under 6.
SWAPPING IT: You might want to go to the Scioto Breeze on a weekend when Swap Days are at the Scioto County Fairgrounds. Swap Days are the second weekend in April, June, and October.
A FAIR DEAL: Another good time to go to Lucasville is to hit one of the largest county fairs in Southern Ohio, The more than 100-year-old Scioto County Fair has national act music, demolition derbies and circus performers. The Fair runs the first full week of August.
SOPHIE'S CHOICE: A cool place to eat near the Drive-In is Sophie's Grill, located on U.S. 23 in a 1920s-era building. The restaurant smokes everything from ribs and chicken to brisket and salmon. Call (740) 259-3005.
OTHER COOL RESTAURANTS: Some other cool restaurant stops along the way to Lucasville include Fred's Restaurant in Wheelersburg (home to the region's largest pizza). Call (740) 574-2507; Hickie's Hamburger Inn in New Boston. Call (740) 456-9953; Ye Olde Lantern, on Second Street, in the Boneyfiddle area of Portsmouth. Call (740) 353-6638.

More Swappin' and Shoppin'

U.S.127 SALE: Held each August, this sale runs from Northern Kentucky all the way to Alabama. That's 630 miles and five states. Drive over to central or northern Kentucky and catch a few miles of this historic yard sale gone wild. Go online at www.127sale.com.

HIGHWAY 60 SALE: Running 45 miles across Carter County, Ky., and now into Rowan County as well, this is like a mini 127 Sale. The U.S. 60 Sale is held the first weekend in August. Go online at www.heartoftheparks.com.

MILTON FLEA MARKET: One of the largest flea markets in West Virginia, the Milton Flea Market is open year-round Friday through Sunday and outside as well (weather permitting). It's located along U.S. 60 just east of Milton. Be sure to check out the Halfway Market beside the Flea Market. Go online at www.miltonfleamarket.com

FIRST FRIDAY ART WALK: Starts at 5 p.m., the first Friday of each month, stop at any of the art galleries along Winchester Avenue in Ashland for some local arts of all stripes. Don't miss Pendleton Art Center, home to about 40 artists. Go online at www.firstfridaynews.com. Also, there are similar art walks in surrounding cities including Cincinnati, Columbus, Lexington, and Charleston.

LIL' LAMBS SALE: Held three times a year, the Lil' Lambs Closet Consignment Sale is held at Forrest Burdette Memorial United Methodist Church in Hurricane, W.Va. They've been holding these sales of gently used children's clothes, toys and maternity clothes for more than 10 years and give about $40,000 annually to charity. Call (304) 562-5903.

ROCK FOR TOTS: Since 1985, Rock For Tots has been hosting a charity concert and live auction in downtown Chillicothe now raising more than $34,000 a night for children's charities. Held at the Elks Hall, 42 W. Second St., Chillicothe, in early December, the event includes a dozen musical acts and live and silent auction of unique items. Go online at www.rockfortots.org.

ART IN THE PARK: The Tri-State Arts Association in Huntington takes over part of Ritter Park putting a wide array of artwork for sale under the majestic oak trees for two days each summer. Go online at www.tristateartsassociation.org.

MT. STERLING TRADE DAYS: Always held in mid-October, Court Days in Mt. Sterling Ky., swells the town's population from about 5,000 to an estimated 130,000 or more who come for this one-of-a-kind event. Call (859) 498-5343.

Mound City
Chillicothe, Ohio

During National Parks Week (in mid-April), the kid-laden Dave Trippin' wagon did its nomadic, patriotic duty and loaded up for a quick jaunt up to **Hopewell Culture National Historical Park** in Chillicothe, Ohio, home to the greatest concentration of the mysterious ancient burial mounds.

One of the closest of the 388 units of the National Park System, Hopewell sheds light on the ancient culture of the native Mound Builders whose complex, geometric Earthworks are prevalent in Southern Ohio, Kentucky and West Virginia.

Nearly 85 percent of the once more than 2,000 mounds and sites across the eastern United States have vanished – victims of time, farming, roads and assorted building projects. Some still remain.

And in some of the oddest places – since both Camden Park and downtown South Charleston still have highly visible burial mounds.

We headed up to the Scioto River Valley on a Monday to walk about the 120-acre Hopewell site to see what we could learn about this long-gone and forgotten culture that our highways roar past and/or over daily.

As is typical of the National Park sites, the price is right – $5 for the family.

Were we a little off in taking our 4-year-old to essentially a graveyard – albeit a pretty fancy one – for a fun day trip?

Miles:
95

Original Trip
April
2004

A trip back in time to Chillicothe and to this Mound City, filled with info and mounds built by the pre-historic Adena and Hopewell cultures that left such landmarks as Serpent Mound in Southern Ohio.

I wasn't sure, but I grew up in a constant day-tripping family that took me to Williamsburg, Va., and Appomattox Courthouse when I was about 5 and to Disney World when I was about 17.

Maybe the lesson is we're never too young to begin to learn some important things and never too old to revel in that sheer giddy kid-joy of wearing mouse-ears.

In Chillicothe, one of the first things we found out from the brochure was pure revelation – perhaps the Hopewell (who built mounds nearly 2,000 years ago) were the first Tri-Staters to go to Myrtle Beach.

Just a little humor there, archaeologists, but there is maybe a shred of truth in that statement. Found buried in the mounds were sharks' teeth from the Atlantic Ocean, conch shells from the Gulf of Mexico, copper from the Great Lakes, obsidian from Idaho and Wyoming, and mica from North Carolina.

The clincher would have been fossilized saltwater taffy, of course, but who would leave that behind?

Seriously, though, we were immediately impressed – both at the range of travel or the trade network established and at the exquisite art objects fashioned from some of these materials.

Although Hopewell Culture National Historic Park is made up of five separate and nearby earthwork complexes, this site (located three miles north of Chillicothe on Ohio 104) is the best site for visitation and interpretation.

A small, but very nice museum includes an award-winning 17-minute documentary (no, the kids didn't make it all the way through that one) "Legacy of the Moundbuilders" that richly detailed what is known about the Adena, the Hopewell and the later mound-building natives known as the Mississippian culture.

In general, the lifestyle seemed something to admire, or, looking through time's rear-view mirror, something more appealing than today's NASCAR-like societal pacecar.

The stable, farming communities had people who worked an average of three hours a day gathering the sustenance and spent the rest of the time with family and making arts and crafts.

They also honored their elders, and after they passed, honored their dead in such a special way that many compared the mounds to the Egyptian pyramids. These complex earthworks were built by people carrying dirt (not too many backhoes operating in 200 A.D.) and laid out in squares and circles.

Our 4-year-old son Jacob was fascinated by the touch-screen interactive film called "Earth Works," and he shifted through history's gears, helping us piece together some of the puzzle in our minds. We spent about an hour hiking the interpretative loop trail and wandering through the site (23 mounds rimmed by a square, low, earthen wall).

We spent the rest of the day being lazy, eating a picnic on blankets at **Yoctangee Park** in downtown Chillicothe.

On the drive home, we took what could be a day-trip in itself, a jaunt over to the 168-acre **Seip Earthworks**, just off of U.S. 50 east of Bainbridge, before swinging south on Ohio 41 to check out both **Fort Hill** and **Serpent Mound**, both fine examples of later mound-building. Serpent Mound, at a quarter of a mile long, is the largest serpent effigy mound in the United States.

Serpent Mound, and in particular Fort Hill, have good trail systems and have free programs that shine a light on these ancient, native cultures.

Any on the right day could make a good day-trip. Ohio 41, which winds through Adams County's Amish country, is always a joy to drive.

As the sun set, the radio played Rascal Flatts' "Mayberry," a song full of the desire to slow life down. We were glad we had gone this way back into time to have a National Historic Park practically to ourselves on a quiet Monday.

We were filled with a renewed respect of the rich, ancient culture that once was here and left with the lingering thought – what will our society be known for and what will it leave behind.

If You Go: Chillicothe

DIRECTIONS: Take U.S. 23 North out of Portsmouth, Ohio. Drive about an hour until you catch a whiff of "the smell of money" as the locals say. That's the Mead Paper Plant. If you're going to Hopewell Culture National Historical Park just follow the signs.

WHERE TO STAY: On the nice end, Christopher Inn, 30 N. Plaza Blvd., (off of Bridge Street), also four downtown B&B's. On the cheap, The Chillicothe Inn (740) 774-2512.

WHERE TO EAT: CrossKeys Tavern, 19 E. Main St., (740) 774-4157. Great pub lunch and live Dixieland Jazz music by the Goosetown Astonishers every Thursday at 8 p.m., a tradition that dates back 35 years.

SUMBURGER DRIVE-IN: 1487 N. Bridge St. A classic '50's drive-in. Call (740) 772-1055.

WHAT ELSE: 18.5 miles of bicycle trails including one that runs along the Scioto River in Yoctangee Park in downtown. Visit Adena Mansion and Gardens, home of Thomas Worthington, Ohio's sixth governor. Go online at www.ohiohistory.org. Hirsch Fruit Farm on Ohio 772 is a cool, pick-your-own site. Call (740) 775-7055.

PLAY BALL: Chillicothe's VA Memorial Stadium, located just north of town, is home to the Frontier League baseball team, The Chillicothe Paints. The team has drawn more than 70,000 fans for the past five years. Call (740) 773-8326.

SOME GOOD TIMES TO GO: Feast of the Flowering Moon (Memorial Day weekend), Tour of the Scioto River Valley in May, Gus Macker 3-on-3 tourney in June, Easy Rider Rodeo (not for kids) in late August, and the Southern Ohio Storytelling Festival in September.

JUST SLING IT: The Chillicothe area is flush with disc golf courses: At Great Seal State Park in Chillicothe, at Ohio University Chillicothe, at Pike Lake State Park near Bainbridge and at Rocky Fork Lake near Hillsboro. Go online at www.chillicothedisc-golf.com.

THE NATIONAL PARK: For more information about Hopewell Culture National Historical Park and the other 387 units in the National Park System, go online at www.nps.gov or www.seeamerica.org. To get a list of upcoming special events at each of such state memorial sites such as Serpent Mound and Fort Hill, go online at www.discoverohio.com and click onto special events.

More Native American Culture

SERPENT MOUND, 3850 State Route 73, Peebles, Ohio, (800) 752-2757, www.ohiohistory.org/places/serpent

ART OF THE ANCIENTS: An exhibit at the Southern Ohio Museum and Cultural Center, at 825 Gallia St., in Portsmouth. This exhibit features more than 10,000 artifacts from Ohio's pre-historic Indians. Go online at www.somacc.com.

FORT ANCIENT, 6123 State Route 350, Oregonia, Ohio, (800) 283-8904, www.ohiohistory.org/places/ftancien

HOPEWELL CULTURE NATIONAL HISTORICAL PARK, 16062 State Route 104, Chillicothe, Ohio, (740) 774-1126, www.nps.gov/hocu

LEO PETROGLYPH, Township Road 224, Jackson, Ohio, (800) 686-1535, www.ohiohistory.org/places/leopetro

SEIP MOUND, 7078 US Route 50, Bainbridge, Ohio, (800) 283-8905, www.ohiohistory.org/places/seip

STORY MOUND, Delano Road, Chillicothe, Ohio, (800) 319-7248, www.ohiohistory.org/places/story

FORT HILL STATE MEMORIAL, 13614 Fort Hill Road, Hillsboro, Ohio, (800) 283-8905, www.ohiohistory.org/places/fthill

MIAMISBURG MOUND, 101 North First St., Miamisburg, Ohio, (513) 866-4532, www.ohiohistory.org/places/miamisbg

SUNWATCH INDIAN VILLAGE/ARCHAEOLOGICAL PARK, 2301 West River Road, Dayton, Ohio, (937) 268-8199, www.sunwatch.org

BIG BOTTOM, State Route 266, Stockport, Ohio, (800) 686-1535, www.ohiohistory.org/places/bigbottom

TECUMSEH OUTDOOR DRAMA, 5968 Marietta Road, Chillicothe, Ohio, (866) 775-0700, www.tecumsehdrama.com.

BLUE JACKET OUTDOOR DRAMA, 520 South Stringtown Road, Xenia, Ohio, (937) 376-4358, www.bluejacketdrama.com

Cincinnati

Ohio

With another week of gray and rain on the menu, the Dave Trippin' wagon loaded up for Cincinnati to dive into a main course of museums in the Queen City.

Just for starters, there's the new **National Underground Railroad Freedom Center** and **Cincinnati Reds Hall of Fame** and **Museum** downtown as well as the super-sized **Cincinnati Museum Center at Union Terminal**, where there are 12 football fields' worth of museums.

No matter how you slice it, you'll run out of time before you run out of great museums in a weekend in Cincy.

We set out late on a Friday morning to make a Ohio River run for a little fun in a city known for – among other things – the world's largest Chicken Dance and as the northern-most nesting spot for many a Parrotthead (Jimmy Buffett's um, interestingly dressed fans).

With the lofty goal of completing a fun weekend to see some friends, perhaps learn a few things – while resisting the urge to flap our wings and dance in public – we set out westward with our two growing cookie monsters on board.

Hop onto the scenic byway of U.S. 52 in Lawrence County, Ohio, and it's a three-hour-or-so ride along the Ohio River to the impressive 158,000-square-foot, three-story **Freedom Center (513-333-7500)** that sits majestically between the new publicly funded playgrounds for the Cincinnati Reds and Bengals.

Miles: 155

Original Trip February 2005

Once a train stop, Union Terminal is the museum hot spot in Cincinnati. We check out that bevy of museums as well as the city's newest large museum, Freedom Center, the National museum dedicated to the Underground Railroad.

Since the past few Cincinnati trips have been to the southern side of the city (the Kentucky cities across the river of Covington and Newport), we were wowed by the sight of what lies over the **Purple People Bridge** – about $2 billion in riverfront investment on the Ohio side.

Opened in August 2004, the Freedom Center is visually stunning with three stories of glass overlooking the Ohio River. It is believed that about 40 percent of slaves fled north through the river to plug into more than 500 routes on the Underground Railroad, making Ohio one of the most well-traveled states.

With about 2 ½-hours before closing time (5 p.m.), we made whirlwind steps into the past, which churned back to life in living color in a powerful patchwork quilt of 12 exhibits, dozens of impressive and over-sized art pieces and more than 90 minutes of film.

The first thing you see is a "survivor" from another era – a two-story slave pen rescued and preserved from Raymond Evans' farm in Mason County.

Carl B. Westward's powerful poems are etched into the wood inside this hand-hewn memorial, a structure in which you best be ready to tell your ever-inquisitive child "the ugly truth," as Westward says.

Those words are hard to come by when talking to a Sesame Street-raised kid who says, "I love all the friends I meet."

Thank goodness for videos, eh?

To help tell the story when parents' feeble words fail, the Freedom Center is filled with short, powerful films, including on the second-floor a 10-minute animation that shifts from charcoals to oil paintings alive on screen, telling freedom's blues-swept song that brings tears.

Also on the second floor is a two-part film introduced by Oprah.

Called "Brothers of the Borderland," the film then moves into an interactive environmental theater filled with trees, stones, a river and crickets. You're immersed into the heart-pounding scene of slaves trying frantically to get out of Kentucky across the Ohio River at Ripley to the safe house of John Rankin high on the hill.

That is just a small slice of what's inside a museum that's powerful in singing the songs of freedom and its everyday heroes in surround sound.

After an evening of chilling with some friends, we set sights for a Saturday at the historic Union Terminal, Cincinnati's gorgeous art deco train station that now serves as grand central for the **Cincinnati Museum Center (800-733-2077)**, which has 12 football fields of museums under one roof.

Read that now and be tired out by it later.

We bought tickets for the **Cinergy Children's Museum** and found out that our membership to the **Highlands Museum and Discovery Center** in Ashland got us into the **Museum of Natural History and Science** for free (since those museums, as well as dozens of others around the country, have a reciprocal agreement).

Yahoo!

The Children's Museum has many interactive areas for play. We thought it was well worth a morning (and probably afternoon, too) when we stumbled into the Woods, a two-story Peter Pan-like playhouse filled with tunnels, trees, turns and decorations a la "Lost Boys" with found wood planks, a trunk of old clothes and other great surprises.

We didn't get to half the things in the children's museum (which really could take a whole day), but tummies rumbled and lunch at the food court called. It's located inside the Union Terminal lobby, whose ceilings are adorned with exquisite mosaic work of the city's characters from Native Americans to iron workers.

Fueled up and armed with our free tickets, we raced to the Museum of Natural History where mastodons, ice caves, a sand pit, health and body area and large collections of dinosaur bones awaited.

Like the joy of such engaging family films as "Finding Nemo," this museum offered that great space in time when parents and children are equally charged up by the experience.

After three hours – and countless trips – through the ice cave, we headed to our friends' house to chill before heading back out.

Since my wife Toril has re-kindled her pottery skills taking classes at the Huntington Museum of Art, I thought a nice treat might be a pre-Valentine's Day dinner at **Rookwood Pottery, 1077 Celestial St., (513-721-5456)**. The restaurant, in a former life, was the first large manufacturing operation founded and run by a woman, Maria Longworth Nichols Storer.

The Pottery biz, which once employed 225 workers and 114 artists, went cold in 1967, but the space perched with a bird's eye view overlooking downtown was fired back up in the 1970s as a restaurant in which patrons can dine from inside three of the giant brick kilns.

It was a great call and really nice evening walk through the funky, hilly neighborhood of Mt. Adams.

Filled up with food for the soul and thoughts for the road, we made our way out of Cincy on Sunday, warmed by a colorful weekend of art and awe and inspirational songs of freedom and already thinking about a return some spring day.

If You Go: Cincinnati

TRAVEL GUIDE: The official visitors guide to Cincinnati can be found at AAA offices and at Ohio roadside rests. It showcases about 40 signature events, 70 regional attractions and 165 places to eat, shop and play. Call (800) CINCY-USA to get a free copy.

ON THE WEB: Go online at www.cincyusa.com to order a copy of the travelguide. Also, you might want to check out www.cincinnati.com. The Freedom Center Web site is www.freedomcenter.org.

ALONG THE WAY: There's some great stops along U.S. 52 going to Cincinnati. Ripley is home to several important sites on the Underground Railroad, including two open to the public: the John Parker House and the John Rankin House, one of the most famous stops on the Underground Railroad. Call (937) 392-1627 or go online at www.ripleyohio.net.

GRANT'S BIRTHPLACE: Ohio birthed nine presidents, and the little town of Point Pleasant is where Ulysses S. Grant was born. Check out the tiny home and museum. There's a nice but simple picnic area overlooking the Ohio River, across U.S. 52 from the home. Open April 1 through Oct. 31. Call the caretakers at (513) 553-4911.

FOOD STOP: Moyer Winery and Restaurant, 3859 U.S. 52, in Manchester. Open since 1972, this restaurant is located 95 miles from Huntington and is a great scenic lunch stop with a panoramic view of the Ohio River. Enjoy Southern touches such as baked sweet potatoes and choose from nearly 20 styles of wine, most made from grapes grown down by the riverside. Moyer is open at 11:30 a.m. Monday through Saturday. Call (937) 549-2957.

Other Fun, Cool Dining

EAT ON A SCHOOL BUS: Located at 6591 Ohio River Road, Lesage, and a Huntington location of 1501 3rd Ave., come and see why Hillbilly Hotdog ,this quirky mom-and-pop (Sonny and Sharie Knight) owned shop, drew the attention of CNN Headline News and the Food Network in 2007. Eat on a school bus in Lesage. Call (304) 762-2458. And eat in a bath-tub in Huntington. Call (304) 522-0444. Go online at www.hillbillyhotdogs.com.

DOWN ON THE FARM: There may be 500 or so Bob Evans in the country, none are as cool as the restaurant at the 1,000-acre Bob Evans Farm. Eat at the restaurant, check out its adjacent shop, and then roam the grounds home to a Craft Barn, featuring locally made arts and crafts, the Homestead Museum, with art exhibits and museum to the restaurant; see the animals in the barns, and hike the many miles of trails as well. Go online at www.bobevans.com. Click on The Farm.

DOWN THE MOUNTAIN DINING: Located at Pipestem Resort State Park, the Mountain Creek Lodge is accessible by taking a six-minute tram down about 3,600 feet to the Lodge, located beside the Bluestone National Scenic River. Wonderful food in a spectacular location. Open May through Oct. 31. Call (800) CALL-WVA and ask for Pipestem.

SNACKING AT SNOWBALL: Mammoth Cave National Park has a unique dining hall in its underground Snowball Room that has been viewed by visitors since the 1840s. Food may be purchased from the park's concessionaire during the 45 minutes spent in this room, traditionally a 20th-century underground meal stop. Go online at www.nps.gov/maca.

A CAJUN FLOAT: For the past 20 years, June Robin and her son Darrin have operated The Cajun Kitchen, a floating restaurant in the Ohio River in Huntington's historic Guyandotte neighborhood. View the East End Bridge and enjoy homemade Cajun fare. Live music on weekends and Crawfish boil parties as well. Call (304) 529-3663.

SAY YOU WANT A REVOLUTION: The Riverview Revolving Restaurant, located on top of the hotel at 668 Fifth St., Covington, Ky., has a incredible view of downtown Cincinnati and good food to boot. Call (859) 491-5300.

SEE THE LIGHT: Located in a historic, turn of-the-century church, Cathedral Cafe, 134 S. Court St., Fayetteville, W.Va., is a cool stop for coffee or any meal and is vegetarian friendly. Check out the bookstore and the upstairs arts and crafts shop as well. Call (304) 572-0202.

Franklin Park Conservatory

Columbus, Ohio

In the city of Columbus, it's beginning to look a lot like Ch ... Chihuly.

While Christmas shopping trips to Ohio's capital city have long been tradition for many Tri-Staters, there's now another reason to hit Cowtown besides a half dozen shopping malls such as Easton Town Center, Polaris Fashion Place and Columbus City Center.

Miles: 140

Original Trip November 2003

The **Franklin Park Conservatory, 1777 East Broad St., (800-214-PARK)** is now home to glass artist Dale Chihuly's wild and colorful exhibit "Chihuly at the Conservatory."

With the same boundless spirit of Dr. Seuss' silly word sprays or Willy Wonka's wondrous world of chocolate, Chihuly creates his glass with a master's touch and a childlike exuberance.

While his spectacular creations can be found in more than 200 museums worldwide (including the Metropolitan Museum of Art, the Smithsonian American Art Museum and The Huntington Museum of Art), the Columbus show is the largest regional display of this playful pirate who has cranked out his crazy, twisted colorful pieces from his Tacoma, Washington, studio for the past 30 years.

A magical, must-see for glass lovers, Franklin Park Conservatory has the area's largest installation of the world's most popular glass artist, Dale Chihuly, who has created a whimsical glass curled world in natural settings.

Having fallen in love with glass with the Tri-State presence of such treasures as Blenko, Pilgrim and Gibson, and not ready to hop on a plane to Seattle with our two kids, my wife and I thought a holiday stop at the Conservatory would be fun.

Already a "chuly" fan, our 3 ½-year-old became smitten several weeks ago with Chihuly's curly-fry-esque work when he saw a postcard book of "Chihuly Over Venice," after which he made me draw really bad sidewalk chalk renditions.

Although we had to gator wrestle Jake into the station wagon to get to the conservatory (too many fun cousins and "SpongeBob" on TV at my sister's house in Clintonville), he popped back to life when I carried him into the museum.

With the Oscar-Award-winning tear flow miraculously dried, he jumped out of my arms. Yelling "Chuly," he ran toward a giant grouping of shells that might have been the kind that Timothy O'Leary would have seen on the beach.

Not recommended museum behavior I can tell you, but on the inside I felt a bit like that myself; hanging above my head was my first long look at Chihuly's work.

As Chihuly says, "Glass is the most mysterious of all materials. People look at glass and just wonder."

Like his first major glasshouse exhibition "Chihuly in the Park: A Garden of Glass" in Chicago, this exhibit (made specifically for the Franklin Park Conservatory) was a true treasure hunt for us and the rugrats. We found a wonderful world of glass that was floated in ponds, magically suspended in air bathed in the Conservatory's light and growing out of the soil among the Conservatory's vibrant plant collection in four climate zones (Himalayas, Rainforest, Desert and Pacific Islands).

Getting a kids' booklet called "Families Discover Chihuly," we set out to explore the 75,000-square-foot Conservatory.

In the booklet, we found out that Chihuly grew up with a deep love of nature and glass entranced by the flowers in his mother's garden and walking

the beach near his home to look for sea-worn glass washed up on shore.

That spirit remains.

Some of Chihuly's work hang grand. In the Tropical Rainforest, shiny colored glass balls like balloons are bunched from above like a clump of giant wild grapes.

Other creations are tucked away beside brooks and into the soil, like plants growing.

While most of the work is on the inside, some pieces are outside, including a collection of colorful balls in the Bonsai Garden.

In the Succulent Patio outside we found a garden railroad exhibition. It ran underneath Barry Gunderson's large-scale black and white sculpture "Understorms," through replica towns of Adams County's Serpent Mound, Ohio's first city of Marietta, an Amish farm and Marblehead up on Lake Erie.

Filled with such fun things as an "Ant Cam," some talking blue and gold macaws and thousands of plants including the giant fan palm and the corpse flower, the conservatory, which sits on 88 acres, is worth a visit any time.

And although here since 1892, it seems to have struck open a fountain of youth with "Chuly" in the building.

Who else would have thought to toss in 15 madly colored balls to float among the koi at such beautiful spots as Annie's Pond in the Pacific Islands zone?

Walking out into a world around us wet with winter rain and increasingly brown and gray, the tropical infusion of towering twisty plants like the South African tree aloe along side grand green and purple glass spears was like a splash of straight sunshine for the senses and soul.

If You Go: Columbus

DIRECTIONS: The Franklin Park Conservatory is located 1777 East Broad St. about two miles east of downtown Columbus. Take U.S. 23 north to downtown Columbus (it turns into High Street) and take a right on East Broad Street.

COST: $6.50; $5 seniors and students; $3.50 children 2-12. Members free.

CHIHULY RESOURCE CENTER:, The John F. Wolfe Chihuly Resource Center at the Conservatory has books and DVD's about the artist, a flat screen monitor and computer station, and glass artworks and drawings by Dale Chihuly. The Center is open 10 a.m. to 5 p.m. Saturdays and Sundays and 5 to 8 p.m.Wednesdays.

CONTACT: (614) 645-8733

WHERE TO EAT: Some old-school favorites include Schmidt's Sausage in German Village. Call (614) 444-6808. OSU Hall of Fame Cafe, 1421 Olentangy River Road, like MU HOF but all Bucks memorabilia including the 2002 National Championship Trophy. Call (614) 291-2233. Also, the reasonably-priced family-style joint Spaghetti Warehouse, 397 Broad St., is always a good choice. Call (614) 464-0143.

WHERE TO STAY: There are literally hundreds of choices in Columbus. Near downtown, Best Western Clarmont is reasonably-priced on the south edge of downtown. Call (614) 228-6511. But you might want to make an adventure of it and hit Fort Rapids, a new Columbus indoor water park and hotel with 278 guest rooms and 60 suites. Call (877) 33-SPLASH.

WHAT ELSE: Wexner Center for the Arts is free and on OSU's campus at North Broad and 15th Ave. Go online at www.wexarts.org. COSI, is a must-see hands-on science and fun center for kids, at 333 W. Broad St. Go online at www.cosi.org.

GOOD TIMES TO GO: Near downtown, check out the Comfest, The Ohio State Fair, Red, White and Boom, Columbus Rose Fest and Greek Fest.

ON THE WEB: www.fpconservatory.org.

More Glass

BLENKO GLASS: In Milton, W.Va. since 1921 this family-owned glass maker has made the Country Music Awards, has its stained glass in the White House and many other famous places, and has been the subject of several nationally-shown PBS documentaries by Witek and Novak. Factory tours weekday, and Visitor Center open seven days a week. Call (304) 743-9081. Go online at www.blenkoglass.com.

OSBURN MODERN GLASS: Dave Osburn put in 33 years at Blenko and was its production manager before buying glassmaker Charlie Gibson's studio and shop, just a couple miles from Blenko. Osburn started Osburn Modern Glass, 1000 Amos St., Milton., in 2006. Check out his unique colors and tableware and art glass works with designer Wayne Husted. Osburn also helps with the glass-blowing shop at Heritage Farm Museum and Village in Huntington. Call (304) 743-9280. Go online at www.osburnmodernglass.com.

HUNTINGTON MUSEUM OF ART: The Huntington Museum of Art glass collection contains more than 4,000 pieces of glass, ranging from ancient glass to sculpture from the modern studio glass movement. The Wilbur Myers Collection consists primarily of 19th and early 20th century European and American art glass including lots of examples of such regional companies as Pilgrim Glass. The Museum also is in partnership with artist Dwayne Wallace who continues to carve Pilgrim Legacy Glass. Call (304) 529-2701. Go online at www.hmoa.org.

MUSEUM OF ART CHIHULY TOWER: In 2006, the Polan Family dedicated a new, commissioned, site-specific glass sculpture by Dale Chihuly. The 10-foot-tall Huntington Museum of Art Tower (made up of 352 glass pieces) now stands in the C. Fred Edwards Conservatory. Call (304) 529-2701.

GLASSWORKS: Located in downtown Louisville, Glassworks has three working glass studios, two glass galleries, daily tours and much more. Call (502) 585-5421.

FENTON ART GLASS: The largest manufacturer of handmade colored glass in the United States, this family-run factory has been making glass since 1905 and operating in Williamstown, W.Va. since 1907. Check out such cool styles as carnival and iridescent from Fenton, which nearly closed its doors in 2007. Go online at www.fentonartglass.com.

RON HINKLE GLASS: WV glass artist Ron Hinkle has works in 33 states and you can see him make his creations at his studio and gallery in Buckhannon, W.Va. His shop is open Monday through Saturday. Call (304) 472-7963. Nearby is the new West Virginia Museum of American Glass in Weston. Call (304) 269-5006.

Athens
Ohio

Boy, nothing gets the kids fired up for a good road trip like telling them we're off to see a quilt show.

That's why one of the great prerogatives of a parent is knowing when to hold 'em and to just tell our two juice-box junkies that we're off again on another magical, mystery Dave Trippin' tour to somewhere cool in Appalachia.

Miles: 85

Original Trip June 2007

Since it had been way too long since the Lavender crew had bummed around the uneven brick streets of Athens, and since at least some of the 19,000 college students would be somewhere else, we decided to make the hour and a half drive to check out one of our region's coolest college towns.

A trip to see some of the world's best quilt art in a barn, a bicycle trip 'round the funky college town of Athens, a Meigs County, Ohio, river-side pitstop, a trip to the skate park and a whole lot of live music going on.

And, as increasingly rabid closet quilt fans, who could really miss the opening weekend of Quilt National '07, the mind-blowing contemporary art quilt exhibit at the **Dairy Barn Arts Center (740) 592-4981)**.

OK, let's shut the barn door right there, and say up front that even if they put the 15th biennial Quilt National '07 in, say an alley in Detroit, it would still be cooler than the deep end at Dreamland Pool.

It is that cool.

Made up of 83 quilts from nine countries and 27 states, QN (as us cool closet quilt fans like to call it) says collectively that modern-day contemporary quilt artists are gutsy enough to try about anything on a quilt and remarkably make it work.

While the four kids in our crew were playing hide-and-seek in the spacious 10,000 square-foot Dairy Barn show space, us adults were dropping jaws at some hard-core basting and fat quartering (Hey, man, you gotta drop the Quilt lingo when it's hot).

OK, so the toughest thing I ever stitched was a tiny cross-stitched race car, but even I, quilt-impaired man, was still knocked out by the artistry in these diverse quilts such as Kathy Weaver's "Robo Sapiens," Susan Shie's political punches on "The Pressure Cooker/Tower Card # 16," Martha Degen's presidential portrait in "The Yo Yo Quilt," and of course, the best of show quilt made by Noriko Endo of Chiba, Japan (outside of Toyko).

That Athens has been for the past 30 years home to such a cutting-edge display that pushes the art envelope not only in Appalachia but all over the globe is sort of a nice tapestry metaphor for the town.

Since OU was founded in 1804 (only a year after Ohio became a state) and decades before Huntington was even listed on a map, the hilly, little funky town of Athens has had its attitude molded by the school.

Armed with our motley collection of bicycles, and since we had eaten more lunch than should be legal at the **Wild Horse Cafe, 251 W. Main St.Pomeroy (740) 992-9115),** we wanted to get a good pedal tour of the town that *Mother Earth News* named last year as one of America's 12 best towns you've never heard of.

I guess *Mother Earth News* writers are too busy starting a worm farm to make it to Athens' wild and crazy and muchos famous Halloween party which annually helps get OU ranked as the top party school in these United States.

Supersized college parties aside, there's plenty of great fun to be had in Athens without donning a Dick Cheney mask and your skivvies and hitting the town hoping to frighten people.

We started our good times without costumes at mile 0 on the 19-mile and growing **Hockhocking Adena Bikeway**, which runs from Athens' east end to the also arts-filled town of Nelsonville, home to Rocky Boots and the Hocking Valley Scenic Railroad.

Before we channeled our inner Lance Armstrong, and since H-town and Kenova are getting skateparks put in, we checked out the well-known 18,000-square-foot **Athens Skatepark** that is just one of several features (including a pool, playgrounds and rec center) in the **East State Street Park (740) 592-3325**.

We could have made it the 16 miles to Nelsonville (probably by December) but we decided that the four-mile (one-way) portion around campus and hugging the slow-flowing Hocking River was just perfect for our crew since our offspring (he who shall remain nameless) Jake was about ready to pitch his Stingray in the river and stomp off mad forever.

Instead we (actually me) taxied the boys the four miles back in the wheeled carrier enjoying the vibe as college students waved as they floated down the Hocking in innertubes and on the other side, we saw more campus construction sprouting up just off the bike trail.

Although we would have liked to have said we planned this, we also found out later that our frugal mom-and-pop motel, **The Highlander,** was also located just across the street from the bike trail **(800) 878-9767)**.

For those wanting to make a weekend of the bike trail trip, there are also a couple cabins/B&B's located off of the trail as well.

After washing off the dirt from three counties, we walked up the hill to what has made Athens famous – a colorful, compacted collection of funky

shops, mom-pop and employee-owned restaurants such as **Casa Nueva**, live-music-drenched pubs such as **The Blue Gator** and **Union Grill**, galleries and an indie movie house (Athena Cinema) all steeped with their own homegrown flavor.

Since some of our 304 posse (Big Rock and the Candy @$$ Mountain Boys) was throwing down some of their eclectic string band blues at **Jackie O's Pub and Brewery (740)592-9686)**, we figured we should put on our best sandals and represent from the hills and alleys of H-town.

Armed with Athens' own top shelf sax man and clarinetist Ted Harris, the string band (last seen and heard in Huntington near The Spider at Camden Park) tore into its smoky old jugband blues.

With such tunes as "Homebrew Rag," and "Euphoria" bouncing off the bricks, kids, students with dogs, and tired folks in dire need of that long Memorial Day weekend stomped around like they just didn't care, dancing over the beer hose tossed out in front of the stage by brewmaster Brad Clark.

He was working on a 17-hour-day and showing why Jackie O's was sporting the Best of Show hardware on its wall, won from the 2006 Summer Sounds at the Huntington Museum of Art.

Enjoying the fruits, and the hops, of his labor it seemed right on Memorial Day weekend to be in a place that, through creative thought, hard work and community spirit, was OK with just being itself.

It kind of felt like freedom.

If You Go: Athens

DIRECTIONS: Lots of different ways to get there by hitting the country roads through Southern Ohio. From Huntington, take Ohio 7 to Pomeroy, Ohio and then catch Route 33 straight into Athens.
ALSO: From H-town you can also take WV 2 up to Point Pleasant, take US 35 west to Jackson and then take 32 and then 50 north to Athens.
ON THE WAY: Some cool stops along the way include such cities as Gallipolis, Ohio at such joints as Remo's Italian Hot Dogs that's been on Second Avenue in downtown for more than 50 years. Another cool stop is the Ohio River town of Pomeroy, Ohio, with such cool places as the Wild Horse Cafe, The Court Street Grill, and a host of downtown shops.
WHERE TO STAY: On the upscale, The OU Inn, 331 Richland Ave., is a good call. On a budget, The Highlander Motel, 42 W. Union St., is in walking distance of the clubs and shops and a block off the Athens bike path.
WHERE TO EAT: The employee-owned Casa Nueva, 4 W. State St., Athens is a long-time favorite with a great vibe, food and live music nightly. Go online at www.casanueva.com.
WHAT ELSE: Tons of cool college town shops including Athens Underground, 90 N. Court St., Athens. Call (740) 592-6286. Beads and Things, 8. N. Shaffer St. Call (740) 592-6453.

COMING AT YA LIVE: Athens is packed with good live music venues such as The Blue Gator, Casa Nueva, Jackie O's, Stuart's Opera House in Nelsonsville, Fur Peace Ranch in nearby Meigs County.
GOOD TIMES TO GO: Athens International Film and Video Fest held late April/early May; Ohio Brew Week held in mid July; Ohio Paw Paw Festival held in September and the Great Outdoor Adventure Fest held at nearby Hocking College in Nelsonville, Ohio the first weekend of October.
ON THE RADIO: Athens is home to the funky public radio station WOUB-FM, 91.3. Check out Rusty Smith/Mark Hellenberg's nightly show (7 to 10 p.m.) Crossing Boundaries as well as their Sunday show, Audiosyncrasies. Go online at www.woub.org.
ON THE WEB: Go online at www.athensohio.com. Call The Athens County Convention and Visitors Bureau at (800) 878-9767.

Other Quirky Museums

HARLEY-DAVIDSON MUSEUM: Located at Fourth Avenue and Fourth Street in downtown Huntington, this motorcycle museum is a love-in for Harleys from some of the earliest built by H-D to one of Evel Knievel's bikes as well. Call (304) 523-1340.

MUSEUM OF RADIO AND TECHNOLOGY: Located at 1640 Harvey Road, in Huntington, this 10,000-square-foot museum traces the history of radios, TVs and computers. Also, lots of local music memorabilia from such local native national country stars as Hawkshaw Hawkins and Molly O'Day. Museum open on Saturdays/Sundays. Call (304) 525-8890.

HUNTINGTON BEER MUSEUM: A Homer-Simpson-approved virtual museum that gives a toast to West Virginia and Huntington's brewing history. Site maintained by John Salvatore. Go online at www.huntingtonbeercans.com.

RANIER RACING MUSEUM: Located in Prestonburg, Ky., this museum pays tribute to Harry Ranier, who fielded cars in NASCAR for Davey Allison, Cale Yarborough and many others. Uniforms, trophies and other racing memorabilia. Go online at www.prestonsburgky.org.

WV FARM MUSEUM: Nothing so quirky about farming, but the West Virginia Farm Museum, located just north of Point Pleasant, is home to General, the world's largest stuffed horse. There's also 36 buildings on the 50 acres that also get lit up during Christmas. Call (304) 675-5737.

FIREARMS AT HUNTINGTON MUSEUM OF ART: Nothing weird about the Huntington Museum of Art, but this hilltop museum is packing serious heat with one of the coolest gun exhibits anywhere - The Herman P. Dean Firearms Collection. Go online at www.hmoa.org. Call (304) 529-2701.

WIZARD OF OZ COLLECTION: Only open by appointment to groups, the Wizard of Oz house in Barboursville is a life's love of Jane Craddock, a good friend of the Munchkins. E-mail jcraddock621@aol.com to see the museum-quality display of unique Wizard of Oz memorabilia.

BOB EVANS HOMESTEAD MUSEUM: Find out everything you ever wanted to know about sausage and its maker, Bob Evans, the late, great restaurant owner at the Homestead Museum at the 1,000-acre Bob Evans Farm in Rio Grande, Ohio. Go online at www.bobevans.com. Click onto the Bob Evans Farm site.

NATIONAL MUSEUM OF US AIR FORCE: A free museum at Wright Patterson Air Force Base in Dayton, Ohio. It's packed with more than 300 aircraft, President Kennedy's Air Force One, the only B-2 Stealth Bomber on display, an IMAX movie screen and much more. Call (937) 255-3286.

Portsmouth
Ohio

With a wobbly cassette tape of bluegrass legend Dave Evans' rolling out his Tri-State road classic, "Highway 52," we packed the station wagon, popped a top on some fruit juice, crossed the river to the Buckeye side and headed 60 miles west of Huntington snaking up the Ohio River to Portsmouth, the history-soaked seat of Scioto County, Ohio.

Miles: 47

Original Trip May 2003

Home to a bevy of famous folk from Branch Rickey and Roy Rogers to Kathleen Battle, Portsmouth has its history floating right on the surface like a beautiful piece of river-rounded driftwood.

While area river towns from Ashland and Maysville to Ironton have – and are – painting their floodwalls, Portsmouth, in the past 10 years, supersized it along Front Street.

Louisiana artist Robert Dafford began painting the murals in 1993. Dedicated in October 2002, the **Portsmouth Floodwall Murals** stand tall in living color on more than 2,200 feet of floodwall space that is considered one of the largest known art works by a single artist.

The 20-foot-tall paintings depict the good, the bad and the ugly – from the haunting, sweeping gray images of the 1937 Flood to glorious home-grown heroes like Rickey and Rogers and Jesse Stuart. Colorful murals paint Portsmouth's glory days of roaring steel mills, when Jim Thorpe was player/coach of the Portsmouth Shoe Steels in 1927 and when,

A colorful visit to the world's longest work of art by a single artist (the Portsmouth Floodwalls), the historic and funky shops of The Boneyfiddle area, and some backyard tire swinging along the Ohio River at a great place to land.

surreal as it may seem now, the Portsmouth Spartans put a 19-0 whipping on fellow NFL team the Green Bay Packers in the famous Iron Man game of 1932.

A neat way to see and to hear about the history of the 52 paintings is by taking a horse and carriage ride with John and Beth Colley on **Colley's Rent-A-Buggy (740-858-1291)**.

For the past four years, John Colley said the couple has been picking folks up in front of the **Ramada Inn, 711 2nd St**., for a 25-minute ride for $15 from 6:30 to 11 p.m. every Friday and Saturday night in the summer. Reservations are not needed.

At the mural's end, sits a great little picnic place, **Alexandria Park**, where you get a sweeping view of the Ohio River and the Scioto River as it pours into the Ohio.

And where you can see in the distance the river phoenix, **Portsmouth Raceway Park (740-354-FAST)**. Located just a mile west of Portsmouth, the park somehow rises each spring from being buried by acres of the Scioto River that fill the bottomland. Fittingly, in this last blast of May monsoons, the sign had a few letters missing and read, "Portsmouth Race . ark."

Just a block off of the floodwalls sits **The Portsmouth Brewery and Mault's Brew Pub, 224 2nd St. (740-354-6106)**.

With a foundation built with stone from the Ohio and Erie Canal, this restaurant, which features eight hand-crafted all-grain beers, is teeming with local history. Inside the Brewery, opened in 1843, is a brick arcade area. Inside the restaurant, the walls are lined with large black-and-white photos from the long-gone 308-mile canal.

Luckily, while we were there grabbing lunch (try the homemade bratwursts and potato pancakes), Steve Mault was out back grilling in the beer garden, which opened March 2002.

For the past 25 years, Mault operated one of Portsmouth's best-known eateries, **The Scioto Ribber (740-353-9329)**, which he passed to his son.

While out back gabbing with Mault, I got to meet lunch regulars Chip and Mary Maillet of Lucasville. The couple holds a neat place in Portsmouth's warm embrace of nostalgia, since Chip owns and operates WIOI 1010-AM, which has an adult, big band and swing format.

Those sweet strains of Glenn Miller and the like roll out of many of **The Boneyfiddle Historic District**'s cool, antique stores, such as **Gay 90's Antique Mall, 543 2nd St., Maynards Variety Store, 603 2nd St., and Remember When, 540 2nd St.**, which features a kitschy year-round retro Christmas shop area.

Containing about two dozen shops of all sorts, Boneyfiddle has a bakery, a knife store, a hardware store, a garden shop, cafés and includes such specialty shops as Journey Within, an au natural health shop at 513 2nd St.

At 5 p.m. each Thursday in May and June, the Boneyfiddle Events Committee presents Boneyfiddle Happy Hour next to **Market Street Hardware** and **Toy Town, 21 Market St.**, with live music.

Hitting a good show at the **Vern Riffe Center for the Arts** or the **Clark Planetarium** (both at **Shawnee State University**) is a good reason to boogie up to Portsmouth. We were in the area on a rare two days without a show, so we popped into the nearby **Southern Ohio Museum, 825 Gallia St. (740-354-5629)**. The museum is always worth the drive, since the upstairs holds

ANTIQUES

the largest concentration of works by Clarence Holbrook Carter, whose paintings are in the permanent collections of most major American museums.

His life quote was, "I have painted my world as I have seen it and felt it," and he did that extremely well. He loved the Ohio River and the steel mills and would go on painting sprees in Portsmouth in the summers – even getting a garden hose turned on him while he painted outside a home.

With Mother's Day waning and the need to feed the troops and frantically find flowers mounting, we ducked out of Portsmouth proper and headed back down east toward **Dick's Pizza, 6977 East Front St., Sciotoville (740-776-6231)**. Located next to Woolford's Landing campground, the restaurant (open Tuesday through Sunday) has a lofty motto of "The Perfect Place to Land," since its back yard opens to a beautiful panoramic view of the Ohio River.

But it lives up to the billing. Without asking, the waitress delivered animal crackers to our 3-year-old, and quickly delivered us plenty of sweet tea and one of Dick's wild pizza selections, this one a 13-inch BLT.

Top that off with a Mother's Day surprise of fresh flowers and plenty of swinging on one of the three tire swings out back, and Dick's quickly moves to the top as one of my favorite riverside restaurants.

If You Go: Portsmouth

GETTING THERE: Located at the junction of U.S. 52 and U.S. 23, if you're coming from Huntington, you may want to take both. U.S. 52 west to Franklin Furnace and then hop the bridge and swing down the Kentucky side on U.S. 23. You can also continue on U.S. 52 west.
WHERE TO STAY: The Portsmouth area has some cool B&B's including the Captain's Quarters, 529 Sixth St., where you can stay at the home of a riverboat captain. Call (740) 354-6609.
ANOTHER GOOD PLACE TO STAY: Ramada Inn, 771 Second St., is located in the heart of downtown (just a block or so off the floodwall) and has an indoor pool and Damon's Grill. Call (740) 354-7711.
SOME GOOD PLACES TO EAT: Scioto Ribber, Gallia St., (740) 353-9329; Ye Olde Lantern, Second Street, (740) 353-6638; Port City Cafe, Chillicothe St., (740) 355-9015.
COOL PLACE TO SHOP: The Emporium, 607 Chillicothe St. This antique mall in a building built in 1899, has 20 vendors including sellers of period furniture, fine art, vinyl records, TEAC phonographs and radios and much more. Call (740) 351-0842.
TIE ONE ON: Did you know that the world's largest shoestring manufacturer is in Portsmouth? Mitchellace makes 4 million pairs of shoelaces each week at its factory on Murray Street. It also makes the laces for NFL Footballs. Call for a tour at (740) 353-1116.
A GOOD TIME TO GO: The Roy Rogers Festival is the first weekend in June, Lobsterfest is in July, and River Days is each Labor Day. Also, there's a full schedule of national-act entertainment at the Vern C. Riffe Performing Arts Center on the campus of Shawnee State University. Call the Visitors Bureau at (740) 353-1116. Call the Vern Riffe Center at (740) 351-3622. Go online at www.vrcfa.org.
A STAR-STUDDED EVENT: Shawnee State University in downtown Portsmouth is home to The Clark Planetarium, one of only 50- Digistar Planetariums in the world. Call (740) 351-3125.
GET CULTURED: The Southern Ohio Museum and Cultural Center, 825 Gallia St., has some fascinating permanent collections including the paintings of Clarence Holbrook Carter and Art of the Ancients, a collection of 10,000 prehistoric Native American artifacts ranging from 1,500 to 8,000-years-old. Call (740) 354-5629. Go online at www.somacc.com.

More Cool Public Art

FESTIVALL CHARLESTON: Conceived in 2004 and first produced in 2005, FestivALL Charleston is a citywide arts festival with a theme of "A City Becomes A Work of Art." Enjoy high-quality artistic events including music, dance, theater, visual art and film. Art events include The Capitol Street Art Fair with more than 75 artists. Go online at www.festivallcharleston.com.

MARSHALL FOUNTAIN: The Memorial Student Center Fountain at Marshall University in Huntington was dedicated on Nov. 12, 1972 to honor those who died in the Nov. 14, 1970 MU football team plane crash. Standing more than 13 feet high and weighing 6,500 pounds, the fountain was created by sculptor Harry Bertoia. On Nov. 14 – a memorial service takes place and the water is turned off until next spring. The sculpture base was refurbished in 2008.

ORIGINAL QUILT BARNS TRAIL: Donna Sue Groves had a dream to honor her mom with a large painting on their barn of her mother's passion, quilting. That one led to more than the planned 21 quilt squares, throughout Adams County, Ohio, and now a national public art trend called the National Quilt Trail. Go online at www.adamscountytravel.org to find out how to see the original quilt blocks.

QUILT ALLEY: When the national Quilt Trail came to Ashland, it took a twist. Not only did quilt patterns or blocks get painted on barns but also on buildings and the extensive floodwalls at Ashland and Catlettsburg. Go online at www.abcquiltalley.com to find out where all the quilts can be seen.

EARL GRAY CARVINGS: Located along the 2 1/2-mile trail at the Huntington Museum of Art are about a dozen forest faces carved into the native sandstone by Glenwood, W.Va. folk artist Earl Gray whose works are shown around the United States. Go online at www.hmoa.org.

ART WORKS: Now numbering more than a dozen public art projects in Huntington, W.Va., you can see Building Blocks at the foot of the Robert C. Byrd Bridge at 6th Street, the Ritter Park tennis court Mosaic, Bridges on Main St in Guyandotte, Passages and Circle of Life on the exterior wall of the Huntington Museum or Art and Windows on the corner of 4th Avenue and 8th Street. Go online at www.hmoa.org.

VIA COLORI: Held in September in Goodale Park in Columbus, Via Colori gathers up more than 100 artists to produce a large-scale masterpiece on the pavement of their closed-off city streets. Go online at www.viacolori.com.

MOTHMAN STATUE: Local artist Robert Roach crafted one of the region's most famous (and most photographed) pieces of art. The imposing stainless steel Mothman Statue is the centerpiece of Gunn Park in downtown Point Pleasant. Go online at www.mothmanlives.com to see photos of the statue.

Conclusion

Since Toril and I are both life-long music fans, OK, music nuts pretty much, (Hey, anybody need a couple hundred bluegrass CDs), we thought we'd give you some Bonus Tracks.

Put down the torches Toril and I haven't hidden any Sonny and Cher duets sung by us in the back of the book.

What we have tossed into the pages is our own Dave Trippin' bonus tracks, "Exploring The Tri-State," which is three new and exciting ways that we've found to explore our own backyard.

Geocaching: a high-tech treasure hunt using a hand-held GPS unit to go and find boxes of treasure (usually small toys) that folks hide in the woods at your friendly neighborhood park, state forest or significant outdoors spot such as the Salt Rock Petroglyphs in Salt Rock, W.Va. It's a fantastic way to get kids active out and hiking in the woods.

Family Adventure Quest: a new program that we've tried out from the Kentucky State Parks system. There are 52 state parks in Kentucky, and this program, that runs February 1 to December 1 each year, is like your own "Amazing Race" of sorts. You go and fulfill all the requirements of the Quest at various state parks. It's part trivia, part adventure and part exercise getting out and about in the parks. It's also a lot of fun and a great way to explore the wealth of excellent Kentucky State Parks so close to us in Eastern Kentucky: Greenbo, Carter Caves, Yatesville Lake, Grayson Lake, Paintsville Lake, and Jenny Wiley.

We Are In the Movies: Our third story is about visiting the places in Ohio, Kentucky and West Virginia where major motion films have been made.

We've had a pretty nice run of luck in recent years with such films made here in the region as "We Are Marshall," "Seabiscuit," and Stephen Soderbergh's ground-breaking film, "Bubble," a quirky film made in Marietta, Parkersburg and at Lee Middleton Doll Factory in Belpre, Ohio, not with actors but with regular folks.

It was also the first movie in history to be released simultaneously to multiple formats (theaters, TV, and on DVD).

"We Are In the Movies," scouts out some cool places to day trip in the region that have some of that sparkle that drew Hollywood to that site and should draw you right in too.

Last but not least, there's a set of blank pages in the back of the book for you.

A journal writer since I was a kid, one of the things I do when a new year rolls in is set to dreaming. I always mark off a page called "Where These Feet Want to Be Walking" listing places I would love to get to in the New Year, Lord willin' and the Bookmobile doesn't run me over. Those places always run the gamut from Seattle to Sandy Hook, Ky.

It seems a year is never long enough to get where you want to go.

We thought that we would still share the fun of dreaming and exploring locally.

Go ahead write down somewhere crazy and hopefully like me you'll write down Cass Scenic Railroad, Fur Peace Ranch, Cranberry Glades, Greenbrier River Trail, Appalshop, in Whitesburg, Ky., and so many other great places we've got to get to since we've only just begun trippin'.

In the meantime, I hope you enjoyed our "Dave Trippin' Guide to the Appalachian Galaxy."

Keep on Trippin.'

Exploring the Tri-State

Geocaching

Thomas Wolfe said you can't go home again.

But he didn't have a hand-held G.P.S. to use for the adrenaline-pumping, modern-day treasure hunt called Geocaching and/or a Global Positioning Stash Hunt.

Started in Portland, Oregon, and Seattle, Washington, in 2000, Geocaching, the game "where you are the search engine" has grown to include nearly 500,000 caches (or small hidden boxes filled with various little treasures for the taking) in all 50 states and in more than 215 countries.

In the Tri-State, within a 50 mile radius of Huntington, there are more than 750 geocaches hiding out in parks, cemeteries and important spots such as the Marshall plane crash site, where few people go unless they have a reason.

Like many outdoors junkies here in the region, the Dave Trippin' crew has found more than a few of them from "Bigfoot Sightings # 4 Ohio River," in my hometown of Franklin Furnace, Ohio, to "The Moonville Tunnel" cache near the supposedly haunted old railroad tunnel in the backwoods near Lake Hope State Park.

A great family-friendly adventure that blends hiking with the thrill of a treasure hunt, geocaching works like this: Geocachers look up the coordinates on the Web site (www.geocaching.com), type the coordinates into a hand-held GPS (Global Positioning System) and then trek out to find the geocache, which is usually a waterproof container like a Tupperware container or ammo box filled with cool toys and trinkets and tucked under rocks or in a hollow log.

Think – McDonald's toys by using the hike-to and not the drive-through.

The idea is, once you find the cache, to take something from the cache, leave something in the cache and write about it in the logbook. Folks also log comments about the caches, rating it on how difficult it was to find and the difficulty of the terrain.

The cache can also be as simple and small as a pill bottle (with paper to log your visit) called a microcache and even a virtual cache (where you find an object and answer questions about it on the net) in busy parks.

Almost always though, the geocache is located somewhere cool that you would never go to otherwise like the old coke ovens forgotten and tucked away in our area forests.

Few folks in the Tri-State have taken to the adventure sport like forty-something, Mike Smith, of Burlington, Ohio.

Known by many for his rollicking comedy songs sung during those almost famous open mic nights at the now-gone (except on MySpace) Calamity Cafe in Huntington, he is known by the nickname "Pink Bison," in the geocaching world.

Smith has used his GPS and his nose for adventure on hillsides, fields and forests and out of the way places since he started on New Year's Day 2004.

In 2008, he went over the 700 geocache mark.

He has set out 21 caches himself, including a Christmas-themed cache in Huntington, some cemetery caches around Southern Ohio (including one near the airport in Chesapeake and one at the freed slaves cemetery in Burlington) and one at the almost-forgotten Fatima Shrine, a Catholic road-

side stop on old U.S. 52 near Haverhill, Ohio, that is graced with 16 gorgeous mosaics that depict the life of Christ.

"I love it," Smith said of Fatima Shrine. "That is one of my favorites because when people sign the log they're like, 'Wow, we didn't know this place was here and those mosaics are beautiful. Somebody put a lot of time into it. I don't know why it is neglected, but we'll go up and pick up the trash.'"

In addition to the thrill of the hunt, geocachers are also well known for CITO, that's Cache In and Trash Out, and usually at some important yet sadly dumped-on outdoors spot like the Salt Rock Petroglyphs.

Smith said it's been amazing to see the growth in the sport.

When he started there were only a handful of caches at Beech Fork, Harris Riverfront, Barboursville Park and Ironton.

In the past couple years alone the number has quadrupled, with well over 2,200 caches hidden within 100 miles of Huntington.

The Crawlathon at Carter Caves State Resort Park added geocaching as part of its annual caving weekend in 2006.

In West Virginia, the state has taken a lead. West Virginia offers one of the first state parks in the country, Canaan Valley, to rent out GPS units, one

of the country's first ski-in geocaches (at Snowshoe) as well as one of the first states to promote it through the Division of Tourism.

Justin Gaull, of the WV Division of Tourism, has been going around the state giving PowerPoint presentations on the new sport, showing folks in different areas of the state how it can boost tourism.

"We're exploring it and seeing what the potential of doing this is and seeing what is already in place," Gaull said. "I think we can do a lot from a state perspective for bringing in tourists to some of our out of the way places. I talked with the Coal Heritage Trail people about doing geocaching as a tourist attraction to see the sites."

Gaull said he thinks geocaching is a great addition to the already-large cache of West Virginia outdoor sports that includes whitewater rafting, skiing, rock climbing, hiking and mountain biking.

"They're now under park benches, they're down by the river, on top of buildings and they're just about in any zip code in the state," Gaull said. "I think that is the beauty of it. Geocaching draws people to those under-used areas. Can you imagine geocaches all along the Hatfield and McCoy trail? These are things we're going to explore and talk about in those communities."

*www.davetrippin.com/geocache

If You Go: Geocaching

A BRIEF HISTORY: When the GPS signal degradation called Select Availability (SA) was removed by the Clinton administration May 1, 2000, it opened up the possibility of games like this one. On May 3, a container of goodies was hidden outside of Portland, Ore., in celebration. By May 6, the cache was visited twice and logged in the logbook once. Mike Teague was the first to find the container and built his personal web page to document these containers and their locations that were posted on the web. In July 2000, Jeremy Irish found Teague's Web site and found his first cache outside of Seattle, Wash. Recognizing the potential of the game, Irish approached Teague with a new site design, used the name geocaching, and developed a new Web site. The site was alive for a while, but the official torch was passed to Irish on Sept. 6, 2000.
GEOCACHING NOW: Geocaching has grown to caches in all 50 states and more than 215 countries. There now are many variations of the game, including virtual caches, offset caches, puzzle caches and multi-stage caches. New ideas and new great games crop up every day. Go online at www.geocaching to check it out.
RULES OF THE ROAD: Here are some general rules when you are geocaching:

CACHE WITH FRIENDS: There can be dangers.

MARK YOUR START: Mark a waypoint where you parked so you can find your way back.

DO NOT DISTURB THE ENVIRONMENT: Leave nature the way nature designed it.

DEEP WOODS = BAD SIGNAL: Remember that your GPS signal will not work accurately in dense woods. Get close then check the obvious places (hollow logs, rock piles, downed trees).

KEEP IT COOL: Do not reveal a cache if there are non-cachers (muggles) around. This could result in the cache being vandalized or stolen.

PICK UP TRASH: Take trash around the cache with you. Leave the area looking nicer than you found it.

LEAVE SOMETHING: Take something from a cache only if you leave something. Try to leave something that someone (especially a youngster) would like.

SIGN THE LOG: Be sure to sign the log at the cache to let others know you were there. Check the log to see who has been there and where they are from.

NEVER RELOCATE THE CACHE: Put it exactly where you found it. Hide it well so it will not be accidentally discovered.

CATCH A TRAVEL BUG: If you are fortunate enough to find a travel bug and choose to take it, please place it in another cache within a week or two. Sign the log at the geocaching.com Web site and see prior visit logs. Be sure to log travel bug moves.

ON THE WEB: Go online at www.geocaching.com. Local sites include the West Virginia State Parks Web site at www.wvstateparks.com. Go to www.parks.ky.gov and click onto events to see annual geocaching weekends at Kentucky State Parks. Go online at www.crawlathon.com to learn about Geocaching during that caving weekend at Carter Caves.

Exploring the Tri-State

Kentucky Adventure Quest

Not wanting to contribute any more to the profits of our "refined" friends on the Kentucky side of the Big Sandy River, I had been traveling mostly by riding my rusty, beat-up bicycle over some of Huntington's bricked, maple-leaf-covered streets.

But after paging back through Jack Kerouac's "On The Road" (in which Sal and Dean roll through a life's worth of wine, women and jazz joints in about 200 pages), I could stand still no more.

The road was calling, and the combination of a beautiful fall weekend and the Kentucky Department of Parks' brand new Family Adventure Quest gave the Lavender posse more than enough reasons to burden the station wagon with outdoor gear and juice boxes and get going again.

The Family Adventure Quest is a scavenger hunt of sorts. Participants are asked to complete 25 quests, such as canoeing, archery, pottery making and fishing. They also have to answer some nature-based trivia about the Commonwealth.

Set up for teams of two to six people, the Family Adventure Quest gives families a year to complete the tasks and answer the questions and to send in the scrapbook, of sorts, with snapshots of the activities.

If you complete all 25 quests, you receive a $100 gift certificate to Kentucky State Parks.

To get started, you've got to go online or call and get the entry forms and send in $15. You get a Family Adventure Quest backpack, a disposable camera and a $10 parks gift certificate.

As a skeptic of just about every "great deal," I found this one is a good thing, if you like the outdoors. Huntington strategically sits within an hour and a half drive of six great Kentucky State Parks (Greenbo, Grayson Lake, Carter

Caves, Paintsville, Jenny Wiley, Yatesville and Blue Licks Battlefield).

We certainly had a splendid start to the Quest. The hills were covered in a quilt of color, revealed when morning's shroud of fog began to lift along the highway.

Since Greenbo State Resort Park was having some good Halloween activities, we rolled west down I-64 to the Grayson exit (172), where you can also access Grayson Lake and Carter Caves as well (through the back way).

I've always enjoyed driving north out of Grayson on Ky. 1 through the years. We stopped at Oldtown Covered Bridge, one of the area's few remaining covered bridges.

It spans the Little Sandy River on County 705 just north of the Carter/Greenup county line. It is one of two covered bridges in Greenup County, also home to the Bennett's Mill Covered Bridge on Ky. 7. That bridge is reported to be the oldest and longest single-span covered bridge in the world still open to traffic.

With the quest list and a Kentucky map in hand, we knocked out a few of the easier Adventure Quest questions that test your Commonwealth knowledge, then planned to rendezvous with another family team that was speeding up from Yatesville Lake.

Since Greenbo (and Carter Caves, too) happens to have an 18-hole miniature golf course at the campground, we decided that would be an easy quest to putt off the list, especially since the 18-hole course – we happily found out – is absolutely free to play.

And the setting was priceless. Kids were riding bicycles in small gangs, campfires were roaring, neighbors were chatting and playing music that was ringing off the colorful hills. It all got you to thinking that it's a shame the whole world ain't one big campground.

To me, that is one of the cool things about the quest: It gives you another good reason to get out with the family to good places and doing activities (like getting a snapshot with some free fishing gear at a Kentucky State Park).

While we did knock out one of the quests in Greenbo's almost-famous dining room (hey, it's hard to resist corn bread and beans on a cool fall afternoon), we had to hoof it out into these beautiful Kentucky hills that inspired the late Greenup County author Jesse Stuart to write.

The 3,300-acre park, which now has more than 25 miles of trails, did not disappoint our two teams' quest efforts to capture some good nature photos.

Armed with our G.P.S. unit (yeah, we're pretty much addicted to Geocaching), we enjoyed the Fern Valley Self-Guided Interpretative Trail and some of the Michael Tygart trail before off-roading it a bit.

We walked up upon a beautifully camouflaged box turtle sitting on yellow

and brown leaves, plenty of deer, the giant and majestic Pileated Woodpecker and a black snake, who, to quote the Crocodile Hunter, was "a bit grumpy."

After much hiking and leaf peeping, the teams went our separate ways.

Driving back to Huntington with dusk rolling in, we talked madly about it all, such a filled day, such a blessed time with family, such a beautiful country and – if we guessed right on the Kentucky state fossil and fish we would be only 15 questions and a lot more good times away from a $100 gift certificate.

If You Go: Start the quest

Here's a look at what you need to know to start the Kentucky State Parks' Family Adventure Quest:

WHAT IT IS: A year-long scavenger hunt-type program. It runs Feb. 1 through Dec. 1 of each year.
FIRST STEP: Go online at www.parks.ky.gov/adventure and find the entry forms for the Family Adventure Quest. You can also call (800) 255-PARK to order the packet. Once the forms are completed, send in $15 and the forms to Kentucky Dept. of Parks – F.A.Q., 500 Mero St., Frankfort, KY 40601.
WHAT YOU GET: The entry fee gets you a Family Adventure Quest backpack, a disposable camera (to take photos of your team doing the tasks), a $10 parks gift certificate and the list of the 25 tasks you must complete by December 1 of each year.
THE REWARD: The goal is to complete all of the 25 questions and challenges from Feb. 1 to Dec. 1. Teams that complete all 25 tasks in a year get a $100 Kentucky State Parks gift certificate, a $50 gift certificate (for 20 quests) and are entered into a prize drawing if you complete 15 quests correctly.
RULES OF THE ROAD: No more than three quests can be answered at the same park. Photos taken along the journey can be submitted in digital form on CD, as developed photos or as printouts on photo quality paper. Prints should be labeled, and digital files labeled with the question number, park name and subject.
WHEN YOU'RE DONE: Send the answers along with the photo prints or CD of photos to: Kentucky Department of Parks, Family Adventure Quest, 500 Mero St., 11th Floor, Frankfort, KY 40601.

We Are ... in The Movies

While "We Are" experiencing a little taste of the tourism and excitement after a major motion picture comes to town, the Dave Trippin' crew (which likes to drop in and check out cool places where flicks have been filmed) has compiled a few of our favorite such places.

While my boys and I try to shuck our fear of dolls that look like real children and work up the courage to visit the Lee Middleton Doll Factory in Belpre, Ohio (where Stephen Soderbergh shot his cool and quirky film "Bubble"), we offer these suggestions on visiting some sites where movies were filmed, all just a couple of hours away or less.

All points weird and pleasant

The 2001 film "The Mothman Prophecies" might have been filmed in Kittanning, Pa., but the great little river city where all the madness really went down, Point Pleasant, W.Va., has also been reaping the rewards of the film and its rippling tourism.

Jeff Wamsley, the author of two books on the Mothman, opened the Mothman Museum and Research Center in downtown Point Pleasant and has stocked it with some great props from the film starring Richard Gere and Laura Linney.

It's now open seven days a week. Admission is $3 and $1 for children under 10. Read more about the museum, the Mothman Festival (held each September) and about Mothman at www.mothmanlives.com.

We Are Marshall

The Warner Brothers film, "We Are Marshall" about the Marshall plane crash was

filmed all over Huntington and Marshall University.

And at some of the town's most powerful memories of the historic plane crash that is still the worse disaster in sports history.

Some prime spots are the Memorial Fountain at the Marshall Memorial Student Center, Spring Hill Cemetery, the Keith-Albee, as well as the Greyhound Bus Depot.

Go online at www.herald-dispatch.com. Click onto sports and then Marshall plane crash for a web site that includes a clickable map to every major spot where the film was made.

Visit 'Coal Miner's Daughter,' or at least her brother

One of my favorite movie spots anywhere is Butcher Hollow in Van Lear, Ky.

Located about 60 miles from Huntington (south on U.S. 23), turn off The Country Music Highway and take those curvy-as-a-copperhead roads back to Van Lear, Ky., home to beautiful Butcher Hollow, where country music star Loretta Lynn was born.

The subject of the 1980 biopic "Coal Miner's Daughter," Lynn, who moved away from this homeplace at age 13, was done up in style by Sissy Spacek, who won an Oscar for her troubles.

Make sure you stop by Webb's General Store (it's on the way and has awesome bologna sandwiches). The store is owned by Loretta's brother Herman, who can give you an unforgettable personal tour of the home place and give you some behind-the-scenes dish about his sis and about one of the greatest rags-to-riches stories in music.

Raining in toothpicks

One of my favorite place to eat when we roll down the AA to Northern Kentucky is Pompilios, the family-run Italian restaurant at Sixth and Washington in Newport, Ky., that began in 1933.

It's got good, cheap homemade eats (entrees are $7 to $9), and it's also got a pretty cool tie to Huntington and the movies. The "Rain Man" scene, in which Dustin Hoffman's character instantly counts a mass of dropped toothpicks, was filmed there.

Hoffman, who won an Oscar for his performance, modeled his character after autistic Huntington resident Joe Sullivan.

You can see "Rain Man" memorabilia at the restaurant and score a great kid-friendly meal. For more info about Pompilios, call (859) 581-3065.

Dreaming of a 'Seabiscuit'

If you're shooting a movie about horse racing, there's no place better for rolling some film than at Keeneland Race Course, a national historic landmark on the west side of Lexington, Ky., at 4201 Versailles Road.

Only two hours west of Huntington down I-64, Keeneland has been seen in the recent movie "Dreamer," starring Kurt Russell and Dakota Fanning, and it also served as Baltimore's Pimlico race track in the movie "Seabiscuit."

If you want to see in person one of the world's most beautiful racetracks (and lose plenty of cash in the process), then you are in luck. Keenland hosts a spring meet in April and a fall meet in October. Races are not held on Mondays and Tuesdays. Call (800) 581-3065.

Rolling film on the river

You can see two of West Virginia's movie landmarks in one great day trip down the wild and wonderful whitewater rafting trip on the Lower New River.

John Sayles' wonderful 1986 film "Matewan," which starred Chris Cooper, James Earl Jones and David Strathairn, was shot in the little town (and we do mean little) of Thurmond.

If you do a full day Lower New River trip, you will put in just above the Thurmond, and you will take out just past the New River Gorge Bridge at Fayetteville, which is seen in the 2003 Dreamworks film "Win a Date with Tad Hamilton."

You can find out more cool West Virginia film places at www.wvfilm.com.

For whitewater rafting, the wildest ride is in spring when the New River is a giant beast frothing with as much whitewater as the Colorado River through the Grand Canyon.

Get the hookup on a whitewater rafting trip by going on the West Virginia Division of Tourism Web site and clicking on whitewater rafting or call (800) CALL-WVA.

Ghost Busters

The Buckeye State has certainly got its burger's worth of attention out of the Ohio State Reformatory.

Built in 1886, the Reformatory served as a prison for 94 years, housing more than 154,000 prisoners.

Then its Hollywood-star-studded afterlife began. The site has been used as the setting for major motion pictures including "Shawshank Redemption," "Air Force One," and "Tango and Cash."

Listed on the National Register of Historic Places, the prison has the world's largest free-standing steel cell block, and you can visit it if you dare.

The Reformatory is now open for overnight ghost hunts that have been featured on the Sci-Fi Channel. You must be 21 years or older to enjoy the overnight experience that runs each Sunday May through late November.

Go online at www.mansfieldtourism.com.

If you go: "We Are Marshall" filming sites

Above is a map of some of the "We Are Marshall" filming locations

1: Downtown along 4th Ave. was a key filming location outside the Frederick Building and the Keith Albee Theatre. The Keith Albee also served as the location for the movie's premiere.

2: Steel of West Virginia was the location for numerous scenes where Ian McShane's character Paul Griffin worked as a steel executive.

3: A home along Merill Ave. near St. Mary's was used as the home of Coach Jack Lengyel.

4: Spring Hill Cemetery has a memorial honoring the plane crash victims and was the filming location of a pivotal scene in the movie

5: Marshall Campus has numerous locations where filming took place including; Buskirk Field, Morrow Library, The Memorial Fountain, The Lawn on Old Main, Memorial Student Center, the basketball courts near Twin Towers and the exterior of Joan C. Edwards Stadium

Where These Feet Want to Be Walking

Where These Feet Want to Be Walking

Trips	*Date Tripped*

Trips	*Date Tripped*

Index

C

G

H

I

J

K

L

M

N

O

P

Q

R

S

T

U

V

W

X

Y

Z

Connect With Us

Do you know a great little town, good place to canoe, great festival or place here in these hills that we didn't get to?

Then please shoot us an e-mail and we'll get it on our list of places to go.

Also, if you see any info in Dave Trippin' that has changed, please e-mail us as well so we can update that.

E-mail us at

lavenderpublishing@gmail.com

lavender@herald-dispatch.com.

Dave Trippin' continues to be a Sunday travel series published one trip at a time in *The Herald-Dispatch*.

If you live in the Tri-State area be sure to pick up the H-D published *Tri-State Visitor's Guide* that is printed twice a year and that includes events, festivals, attractions, recreation, shopping and dining in the Tri-State area.

Thanks for purchasing Dave Trippin.'

For fresh weekly travel tips, go online at www.herald-dispatch.com; www.davetrippin.com, www.myspace.com/davetrippin and www.wtcr.com and www.wkee.com for Dave's weekly road-trip and entertainment picks called Dave's Drive-Through Weekend.

Acknowledgments

The Dave Trippin' travel series would never have been possible without the wonderful kindness and trail magic of so many good family members and friends who housed the Lavender crew during their journeys.

'Round here we always say "come see us sometime" and the Lavender crew did, and we usually called first.

We thank them and apologize for any mess left behind: Cindy and Ian Pruitt, Jill and Jamie Jones, Joe Stevens, Kris and Charlie Preston, Fred Herz, Chris and Pete Knapp, Len Hanger, Amy Weirick, Jennifer "Aunt Jenny" and Charles Lear.

A big thanks to *The Herald-Dispatch* Executive Editor Ed Dawson and Publisher Pat Frantz for the freedom and support to do the project.

Editing thanks goes to a long list of features editors whom I have worked with in our five years of writing the Dave Trippin' travel series for *The Herald-Dispatch*. Those fine editors have been: Amy Baker, Andrea Copley-Smith, Jill Nevels-Haun, Maureen Johnson and Robyn Rison.

Thanks to all of our region's state and national park personnel and outdoors-tourism-related companies who are hard-working stewards of our wild and wonderful places.

Thanks to all of the mom-and-pop shop owners for showing such pride in our hand-made arts and crafts heritage and keeping it alive.

Thanks to Linda Giles and the Starmers for help editing, and Kathleen Kneafsey for picking the cover photo.

Thanks to you for purchasing a home-grown, family-made product.

No animals or children were hurt in the making of this book.

A portion of the proceeds from the sale of Dave Trippin' goes to feed two wild, red-headed, juice-box junkies in West Virginia.

About the Author

Dave Lavender is a life-long Tri-Stater, born and raised in Franklin Furnace in Southern Ohio.

Educated at Shawnee State University and the University of Kentucky, Dave has been a working journalist for more than a decade and has been writing and living for the past eight years in Huntington, W.Va.

An entertainment, outdoors and travel writer for *The Herald-Dispatch* in Huntington, W.Va., Dave likes to whistle while bicycling to work.

He also does a weekly entertainment report, Your Weekend Ahead, for WSAZ-Newschannel 3 (NBC) as well as Dave's Drive-Through Weekend, a weekly radio report heard on Clear Channel Radio stations in the region.

Dave was last seen on national television cutting the burger he proudly named "The Doublewide," Hillbilly Hotdog's nearly 15-pound hamburger.

About the Photographer

Toril Lavender was born in Tucson, Arizona, and raised in Fayetteville, New York. A graduate of Syracuse University's Newhouse School of Communications, Toril was a national award-winning photographer for Gannett and a freelance photographer with such publications as *The Washington Post.*

Now a recovering journalist, Toril is a stay-at-home mom. When not putting together Legos with sons Jacob and Will, she currently works as a freelance graphic designer and photographer in Huntington, W.Va. In 2007, her photos were featured in Susan Hom's book, "Life's Big Little Moments: Grandmothers and Grandchildren."